"If an institution is the lengthened shadow of a single man, then the history of modern naval aviation might well be described as the lengthened shadow of Dan Pedersen. Here, in direct, vivid, and unvarnished prose, is the high-flying, supersonic tale of the Topgun program and its extraordinary founder. Through it all, Pedersen's innovative spirit, as well as his essential modesty, shines through."

—Hampton Sides, *New York Times* bestselling author
Ghost Soldiers and *On Desperate Ground*

"Pedersen's soaring new memoir details the roots of America's aerial combat crisis in Vietnam and the stunning response that resurrected American primacy in the skies...[Pedersen] often writes with the precision and artistry of a skywriter, especially when he describes his love of flight....[A] spellbinding memoir."

—*The Charleston Post and Courier*

"Goose and Maverick, move over—this is the true heart of Topgun, told with energy, style, humor, and tactical brilliance...a masterpiece that captures the essence of naval aviation in all its complexity and beauty. Dan Pedersen takes us on a high-speed jet ride through the fast times of Topgun, the Navy, and the need to fight our enemies from a position of superiority."

—Admiral James Stavridis, USN (Ret.), Supreme Allied
Commander of NATO (2009-2013), chairman of the
U.S. Naval Institute, and author of *Sea Power:
The History and Geopolitics of the World's Oceans*

"Capt. Dan Pederson became one of a handful of aviators who convinced Navy brass that a change in tactics was essential....The lives he saved though Topgun training earn him the title of American Hero."
—*Washington Times*

"A superb read... Dan Pedersen's *Topgun* is a riveting, seat-of-the-pants flight into the lethal world of the fighter pilot told by the man who started it all!"

—Dan Hampton, New York Times bestselling author of Viper Pilot and Lords of the Sky

"With the hot-seat velocity and cockpit realism of a military combat thriller, the author delivers exacting details and emotional acuity.... A noble, thrillingly realized combat aviation memoir from one of America's finest." **—Kirkus Reviews**

"Teeming with white-knuckled action and the dynamic personalities who would come to define a generation of combat pilots, *Topgun* brings the deadly dance of air warfare alive."

—Dick Couch, New York Times bestselling author of The Warrior Elite and Chosen Soldier

"[A] fast-paced memoir... This remembrance of aerial derring-do is sure to appeal to military aviators and fans of the world of fighter pilots, past and present." **—Publishers Weekly**

"For those who will never experience the thrilling privilege of soaring at Mach 2 in the back seat of a Navy F-4 Phantom fighter, Dan Pedersen's superb memoir is the next best thing... Many aviators-turned-authors lose readers in jargon and procedures, but Pedersen's full-hearted personal narrative engages them with maverick charm, showing how he and his innovative team reinvented the art of air-to-air combat in the jet age. *Topgun: An American Story* is as revelatory as a freshly declassified briefing, written with the flair and insight of Tom Clancy."

—Michael Fabey, author of Crashback: The Power Clash Between the U.S. and China in the Pacific

"A powerful insider's account of an important and uniquely American institution." **—The Naval Historical Foundation**

TOPGUN

An American Story

DAN PEDERSEN

hachette
BOOKS

NEW YORK BOSTON

Hachette Books
Hachette Book Group
1290 Avenue of the Americas
New York, NY 10104
HachetteBooks.com
Twitter.com/HachetteBooks
Instagram.com/HachetteBooks

First Trade Paperback Edition: March 2020

The photo credits on page 305 constitute an extension of this copyright page.

Hachette Books is a division of Hachette Book Group, Inc. The Hachette Books name and logo are trademarks of Hachette Book Group, Inc.

The publisher is not responsible for websites (or their content) that are not owned by the publisher.

The Hachette Speakers Bureau provides a wide range of authors for speaking events. To find out more, go to www.hachettespeakersbureau.com or call (866) 376-6591.

Library of Congress Cataloging-in-Publication Data

Names: Pedersen, Dan, 1935– author.
Title: Topgun : an American story / Dan Pedersen.
Description: First edition. | New York : Hachette Books, [2019] | Includes index.
Identifiers: LCCN 2018042059
ISBNs: 9780316416269 (hardcover) | 9780316416283 (trade paperback) | 9780316416276 (ebook)
Subjects: LCSH: Pedersen, Dan, 1935– | Fighter pilots—United States—Biography. | Navy Fighter Weapons School (U.S.)—Biography. | Navy Fighter Weapons School (U.S.)—History. | Fighter plane combat—United States—History. | United States Navy—Officers—Biography. | Vietnam War, 1961-1975—Aerial operations, American. | Vietnam War, 1961-1975—Personal narratives, American.
Classification: LCC UG626.2.P43 A3 2019 | DDC 358.4/35—dc23
LC record available at https://lccn.loc.gov/2018042059

ISBN: 978-0-316-41628-3 (trade paperback)

Printed in the United States of America

LSC-C

10 9 8 7 6 5 4 3 2 1

For Mary Beth

God bless all naval aviators, past, present, and future.

CONTENTS

FOREWORD

We who served at the Navy Fighter Weapons School are bound together as brothers. It is a fifty-year-old culture of excellence, and an extraordinary aviation legacy. The pilots call it Topgun. Where did it come from? How did I get to be a part of it? How did they?

Our journey is brilliantly portrayed in this book, seen through the eyes of the man whose innovative leadership was based on the enduring principles of our tradition. Dan Pedersen risked his career to accomplish a seemingly impossible task. His success has endured for more than fifty years now.

I first met "Yank" in 1968, when I was assigned as an instructor in Fighter Squadron 121 (VF-121) at Naval Air Station Miramar, California, also known as Fightertown USA. Our job was to transition pilots and naval flight officers into a new fighter aircraft, the F-4 Phantom. Over the course of six months we trained them to fly the Phantom day or night, in any weather, anywhere in the world, from the pitching decks of aircraft carriers.

As a twenty-four-year-old lieutenant with two combat tours to Vietnam, I was in awe of the Navy's fighter community, and the people with whom I served. Dan cut an imposing figure at six feet three inches, with penetrating hazel eyes and a John Wayne swagger that exuded self-confidence, with the ability and experience upon which reputations are built within our tight-knit community. He was the Hollywood image of a fighter pilot, seldom appearing without his Ray-Ban sunglasses.

As the head of the tactics phase of VF-121's curriculum, Dan was disciplined, focused, and demanding of himself and others. He established high standards of performance, constantly reinforcing the mantra that "In combat second best is dead last." Yet he also possessed a good sense of humor, insisted upon leading by personal example, and seldom phrased anything as a question. One exception: Sometimes he would stride up to a student and ask, "Hey there, tiger. Are you ready for this hop?" When Dan was named to start the new fighter aviation schoolhouse, we all knew it was in good hands. General George Patton said it best: "Wars are fought with weapons, but they are won by men." Even in today's environment of geopolitical complexity and the sophistication of the fifth-generation jets and weapon systems, it is still the man in the machine who will bring victory. That human resource is the work product of Topgun.

Topgun's mission was to challenge the status quo. To do that, Dan selected eight young, very junior officers with unique experience, ability, and passion. His vision and leadership gave us direction. His words gave us inspiration: "There is an urgency here beyond anything we have ever done." We were using "Yankee ingenuity," hard work, combat experience, and imagination to fix a problem. Too many of our brothers were dying over Vietnam, and we could make a difference.

Topgun became a culture of excellence that over the past five decades has consistently produced the Navy's most accomplished, innovative, and adaptive warriors as well as the most compassionate and inspirational leaders. The course has expanded from four weeks to twelve and a half. The school is responsible for providing training in air combat maneuvering and weapon systems deployment for Navy and Marine Corps squadrons, advanced predeployment training for fleet units, and the development of new tactics to confront emerging threats. Its founding principles have been carefully guarded and preserved. The extraordinary qualities of leadership demonstrated by each generation have ensured its survival in the face of resource constraints, professional envy, and PC careerists.

When I have the opportunity to meet the young instructors today, I recognize that while we are from different eras with different equipment, the mission remains unchanged: to control the skies over the battlefield and do whatever is necessary to support our forces on the ground or at sea and ensure their survival.

As I reflect on the humble beginnings of this storied institution, I am struck by several facts. None of us among the original nine officers who established Topgun imagined that we would be a part of an aviation legacy that would span five decades, change the course of tactical aviation in the United States and around the world, and influence aircraft and weapon systems design and pilot training.

The current sophistication and capability of the Navy's aircraft and weapons is beyond anything the original nine could have imagined at the time. Today, the complexity of the battlefield and volume of information available to the pilot are nearly overwhelming. What has not changed are the human elements that make Topgun relevant. The school is still run by junior officers. Then, as now, the focus was upon finding individuals who possessed the following traits:

- A passion for the mission, necessary to sustain the individual in an extreme environment.
- Leadership by personal example—a compassionate, inspirational person willing to take responsibility.
- Extraordinary airmanship required to operate in so unforgiving an environment.
- Humility derived from a sense of being part of something much greater than oneself.
- Subject matter expertise that is beyond reproach.

- A work ethic that will drive that person to do whatever it takes for however long it takes to ensure success.
- Personal discipline to endure the rigorous training and attention to detail required to constantly perform at an optimum level.
- Integrity, adaptability, innovation, and a willingness to challenge the status quo.
- Credibility established through demonstrated performance sustained over time.

All of this is refined in the furnace of uncompromising peer review. The extreme selection process and the rigorous training ensure that Topgun's culture of excellence and its legacy will endure.

As I meet the young officers serving on the staff today, it is strongly affirming to see that our legacy and the future of this nation are in such good hands. The brotherhood of Topgun today remains strong.

For the first time, in this book, the story of Topgun's creation and evolution is told by the man who made it happen at the start. Dan is rightly regarded as the "Godfather of Topgun." His book will take its place among the finest combat aviation memoirs of his generation. It deserves the interest of anyone who appreciates high performance and how it is handed down through generations.

—*Darrell "Condor" Gary*
Topgun's junior Original Bro

PROLOGUE

Palm Desert, California
2018

Though I'm eighty-three years old, I still look up like a kid whenever I hear an airplane passing overhead. Sometimes it'll be a pair of Super Hornets smoking over the desert. Watching them thunder past just under the Mach, I'll get the same electrified thrill I got the first time I lit the afterburner on an F4D Skyray and blasted off North Island's runway to find myself two minutes later at fifty thousand feet.

There is no other rush like it. It is visceral. It fills you with a sense of rapture that only exists out there on the razor's edge.

We flew almost whenever we wanted, and often whatever we wanted. It was all about who you knew. If you wanted a new flying experience after duty hours, there were certain guys, like the Navy chief in maintenance control—the keeper of the keys—who'd give you a wink and send you up for the sheer fun of it. After all, you were a naval aviator.

Sometimes, a World War II F6F Hellcat from the local Palm Springs Air Museum will fly over our house. I'll look up and think, *Yeah. Flew one at North Island*. Beautiful ride, that old tail dragger. The museum also owns a P-51 Mustang that sometimes buzzes by on weekends. Seeing it takes me back to a poker game in Monterey one night. We'd taken a dentist for his last dime, but he wanted to keep playing. He asked for credit. Having heard that he owned a hangar with two P-51s in there, I asked him for a ride. He agreed, and I beat him. Twice. And that's how many times I got to fly that sleek Luftwaffe killer.

When my dad died and I moved my mom up to Port Angeles, Washington, I'd take an F-4 Phantom and cruise north through the Sierra Nevadas and the Cascades, seldom getting above five hundred feet. With nobody in sight, just pristine wilderness, lakes, and rivers, I wound around those mountain peaks, feeling freer and more alive than I ever did on the ground. I'd land at Whidbey Island and spend the weekend with my mom before returning to my command on Sunday afternoon.

We have some helicopters in our area, Jet Rangers and such. Their choppy, eggbeater sound puts me in the cockpit of a Sea King I once flew all the way up the West Coast, tracing the beach, just above the whitecaps, from San Diego to Washington State. Beachcombers, swimmers, kayakers, surfers—they all looked up toward the *thup-thup-thup* of our rotors. Sometimes I waved back, feeling blessed for such moments, doing something so few ever get to do.

Where else could you do such things but in the Navy?

I don't fly anymore. It's a function of age, not of desire or heart. One of my "Original Bros" at Topgun, seventy-four-year-old Darrell Gary, still straps himself into his own Russian Yak and stunts about the sky. It was the same plane our enemies learned to fly before tangling with us over Vietnam. Darrell formed his own precision aerobatics team with a group of former U.S. pilots and one Brit. "I hate taking time out of my day to eat, sleep, and excrete," Darrell likes to say. "We can sleep when we're dead."

How can you not love that man? We nine Original Bros were cut from that same cloth. Darrell and Mel, Steve, Smash, Ski, Ruff, J. C., and Jimmy Laing. In civilian life, you rarely encounter people of similar temperament, focus, ability, and passion. Maybe it's because only rarely are people thrown together to fight for a failing cause on guts and pride, while surrounded by hostility that pushes you ever closer together.

In the 1960s, America fought in Vietnam with the wrong planes, unreliable weapons, bad tactics, and the wrong senior civilian leadership. A lot of important things were broken. But we loved what we did, and treasured the relationships built in aircraft carrier–ready rooms and bars from North Island to the Philippines. The Navy had given us a home filled with committed, driven men who shared the same passion. When the air war started in earnest, we were tested by months of exhaustion that showed the deeper meaning of our connections.

Operation Rolling Thunder began in 1968. As we flew combat missions, striking Secretary of Defense Robert McNamara's hand-selected targets, we lost planes and men almost every day. Flying from Yankee Station, the area in the Gulf of Tonkin where the aircraft carriers operated, we learned what it was like to sit at a wardroom table surrounded by empty chairs. Half the time we never knew what happened to them. Maybe another pilot noticed an enemy surface-to-air missile launch or caught a fleeting glimpse of a burning American plane heading toward the jungle below. Sometimes we'd hear the aircrew requesting help on the ground, dodging enemy patrols and calling for rescue. When the helicopters went in, the North Vietnamese were often waiting. They shot up the helicopters and their escorting planes. We sometimes got our man and lost three more in the process.

We were flying not just for each other. We were flying for each other's families. The man on your wing usually had a wife, maybe some children. You took care of him to take care of them. We all faced moments where we risked our lives for each other to ensure the contact teams did not knock on our brother's door back in San Diego, Lemoore, or Whidbey Island.

When the enemy scored, the families were devastated. You seldom see that written about. But we've all come home to tell widows and fatherless kids how sorry we were. We gave them what peace we could. The truth is, that loss never goes away. It warps the rest of their lives as they wrestle with the pain. That old adage "Time heals all wounds"? Bull. Fifty years on, I've seen those families still break down in tears as they talk of their fallen aviator.

You don't get over that kind of pain. You just learn to live around it. It becomes part of who you are, and for us out on Yankee Station, that grief motivated us to sacrifice for each other.

Not everyone could hack it. There were days on Yankee Station when I watched aircrews lose their nerve. All of a sudden, some mysterious mechanical issue came up and a flight had to be scrubbed. Sometimes it happened when the plane was on the catapult and ready to launch. They just couldn't bring themselves to face—again—the most fearsome air defense network in the world, erected by the North Vietnamese, with Russian help, around Hanoi. On rare occasions, some men turned in their wings and went home rather than face that crucible again. It was easier to fly for an airline.

Twenty-one different aircraft carriers operated for more than 9,100 total days in the Gulf of Tonkin. In three years, the Navy lost 532 aircraft in combat. Including other operational losses associated with that war, the Navy had 644 aviators killed, missing, or taken prisoner of war. The total fixed-wing aircraft losses of the Navy, Marine Corps, and Air Force together exceeded 2,400. Of course, it was intensely personal. Darrell Gary lived with nine guys in two houses on the beach in La Jolla when he went through training. After their first trip to Yankee Station, six came home.

Worse, we were losing the larger war. Destroying the targets given to us by the Pentagon seemed to make no difference in the war to the south. The losses mounted, and the MiGs started seeking us out. The North Vietnamese possessed a small but well-trained air force, proxied by their Chinese and Soviet allies. As good as it was, they were not in the same league as the Soviet Air Force, so it sent shock waves through the Navy when North Vietnamese pilots started shooting us down. During the Korean War, the North Korean Air Force was virtually wiped out in the opening months. A decade later, the Vietnamese MiGs gave us a real fight. They shot down one of ours for every two MiGs that we claimed. We considered the loss rate intolerable, given our long history of deeply one-sided kill ratios. In World War II, U.S. naval aviators crushed the Japanese in the central Pacific on the way to Tokyo, with Hellcat pilots, who scored three-fourths of the Navy's air-to-air victories, posting a kill ratio on the order of nineteen to one. In Vietnam, we simply were not allowed to win, so the Navy bureaucracy did what bureaucracies do best: It continued on course. Micromanaged from Washington, D.C., we made the same mistakes month after month. It nearly crippled U.S. naval aviation.

In January 1969, a plain-spoken carrier skipper named Frank Ault wrote a report to the chief of naval operations detailing deadly flaws in our fighter tactics and weapons systems. His list of complaints was a long one, and the Navy decided to act. Unfortunately, many in senior commands worried more about their careers than about fixing the problem. By approving the creation of an air combat postgraduate school—which we quickly named Topgun—they gave the appearance of doing something to change things. Under President Johnson's and Secretary McNamara's leadership, the Navy bureaucracy seemed more interested in appearing to solve problems than risking failure by actually trying to solve them. They gave the leadership of Topgun to a relatively junior officer—me.

The eight men who joined me in a condemned trailer at Naval Air Station Miramar in late 1968 had gone into the war thinking we were the best pilots in the world flying the best aircraft armed with the best weapons. The North Vietnamese showed us otherwise. We were ready to do whatever it took to find a way to win.

The community we loved was in crisis, and for whatever reason it fell to us to help find a way forward. As we got started, not a man among us was willing to put his career over doing the right thing. We went to war against conventional thought. We asked questions, sought out answers, chopped red tape. We broke rules. We borrowed, stole, or horse-traded for everything we needed. Ultimately, the Bros created a revolution from nothing but pride and devotion.

I want to tell you about the Bros. I want to tell you about our community, how it was in the years before Vietnam when we frittered away the birthright of victory that our forebears had handed and chose to stake our future on untested technology. I want to tell you about a few of us who kept the legacy alive, flying off the books, in ways that were never discussed in professional spaces, lest the wrong ears hear. Most of all, I want to tell you about the founding days of Topgun and its enduring legacy. It stands as proof that a small group of driven individuals can change the world. We live today in times of great uncertainty with problems that seem unsolvable. The Bros faced that in 1968. Topgun is a reminder that things can be changed.

Along the way, I hope to leave you with an appreciation of the cost. Naval aviation back then wasn't just a job or career; it was a monastic calling. You had to love it more than anything else in your life to stick with it when things went so wrong. That primacy of position in our lives wrought havoc with everything else not connected to our ready rooms. We became outsiders in our own nation, unable to relate even to the people we grew up with back home. Darrell learned this when he attended his high school reunion in Oakland. He had nothing in common with even his oldest friends. Alienated by the experience, he turned around and flew straight back to the brotherhood that had become his home. He never attended another reunion.

It wasn't just old friends we left behind. Our families took a backseat to our flying and our responsibilities as officers. The glamour of marrying a handsome, fit fighter pilot with a bright career ahead soon wore thin as we served at sea and our spouses remained behind. How many women stand for another love in their husband's life? Each night when we were on Yankee Station, the unknown gnawed at them. They feared for their pilots. Our wives never knew when a contact team might appear on the porch. Every time the doorbell rang, they cringed with dread. Late-night phone calls produced a panic. So it had to be. For us, flying always came first.

One night I was aboard ship, ready to take my first ship command, when I got a phone call. Somehow my eight-year-old son had found my direct number. I answered. He was crying. He begged me not to leave.

"Please, Dad. Come back...everyone else has a dad home with them. I don't."

Those words linger. Neither of us ever forgot them.

Every naval aviator had moments like these. It was our reality on the ground. I have one regret in my twenty-nine-year career: It was brutal on my family.

That's the deeper story, beyond the Hollywood portrayal of us. All too often, we are painted with the Val Kilmer "Iceman" stereotype—cool, capable speed addicts who live on the edge for the sheer thrill. We live harder, party harder, womanize harder, and are somehow larger than life.

This book will challenge the stereotype. We are flesh and blood. We live in a dangerous world that whipsaws us from elation to fear in a heartbeat. This brotherhood conceals its emotions to outsiders, so perhaps some of it is our fault. Yet to me, what I saw my brothers achieve out in the fleet is even more remarkable because we are only human and as fallible as everyone else. The difference is the consequences of those fallibilities. When you are dodging missiles over Haiphong or landing aboard a flattop in the middle of a tropical storm, mistakes are often fatal.

I can't fly anymore, but my heart is still up there. Lying in my yard and watching these jets stream past, I try to figure their speed and altitude. I've been doing it so long I know their schedules. When an aircraft is late, I wonder if the crew got hung up at the gate, or if the taxiway was jammed. It's one of many ways I keep myself in the game. Pushing a jet through the sky will always be my abiding love.

CHAPTER ONE

ADMISSION PRICE

Over Southern California
December 1956

Sixty-five and sunny; blue skies all the way home. God, how I loved December in California. No snow, no shoveling the walk to the driveway. Just plans for Christmas dinner in the backyard as the last rays of sunlight bathed the L.A. basin in golden hues.

From the matte gray cockpit of my Lockheed T-33 jet trainer, I looked down at the suburban sprawl born of the postwar housing boom. The orange groves were vanishing, replaced by blocks of little pink houses and picket fences that looked like Legos from my twenty-thousand-foot vantage point.

I used to shine shoes down there. Lee's Barbershop in Whittier.

I shifted my eyes from the scene below to scan the instrument panel of my "T-bird." Altimeter, heading, airspeed indicator, turn and bank indicator, vertical velocity gauge. I swept them all in a heartbeat, trained to do so by the best pilots in the world until each scan of the dials and gauges was an act of unconscious muscle memory.

My path to Pensacola began right down there. At Los Alamitos, I enlisted in the U.S. Navy as a seaman recruit. The naval air station was full of World War II vintage aircraft. As an apprentice engine mechanic in a reserve squadron, I worked on the F4U Corsair. When that legendary gull-winged beauty became a relic in the jet age, the unit I was attached to became the first in the reserves to get jets. A young lieutenant helped me to make the transition. He took me flying in his two-seater. Inspired, I applied to the Naval Aviation Cadet program, which sent enlisted men to flight training in Pensacola. With the help of that generous lieutenant, I passed the exams and made the cut. In 1955, I decamped to the famous naval aviation training center on the Florida panhandle.

Now the long-sought reward was close enough to touch. As long as I kept my grades up, I'd stand an excellent chance of flying jet fighters with gold Navy wings on my chest.

That morning over the L.A. basin, we whistled through the wild blue in technology that would have dazzled those who flocked to California looking for work two decades before. The age of the Joads and Okies was long gone. The jet age was upon us, and I embraced it with all my heart.

To the people down below, this may not have meant a thing. They were going about their peaceful lives, caring for family, stressed out over work and the growing traffic. Some would open the *Los Angeles Times* as they sipped their morning coffee for a keyhole view to the outside world. Eight hundred and ninety-six drunk driving arrests in the county this Christmas season was a headline in the *Times* that morning. Beside that story, a tiny blurb described how the Japanese were detecting radiation in the atmosphere. That could only mean the Russians had detonated yet another nuclear bomb.

Vice President Richard Nixon talked of the ten thousand Hungarian refugees the Air Force was flying to the United States for a new lease on life. Victims of Soviet oppression, they'd fought and lost in the Budapest uprising. When Russian armor rolled through their streets, they were lucky to have survived.

The people below me could not imagine such a life. Living in their orderly tract houses, they enjoyed well-kept lawns, sidewalks full of playing kids, and a sense of peace underwritten by men such as I had come to know in the past year. Home for the holiday, I would soon join them guarding our ramparts in the Cold War. The morning was simply gorgeous. The engine's whine was like music to me, the soundtrack to my new life. I was entering a profession unlike any I'd ever dreamed of.

My dad, a veteran of World War II, had served in Europe in the Army Signal Corps, keeping communications flowing between the front lines and headquarters. He came home to Illinois in 1945 to find his job had been filled. Victory in Europe cost him his career, and he found himself forced to start over in middle age with a family depending on him. Never showing us the fear he surely felt, he moved us to California, believing that every problem can be overcome by hard work. He got a job laying pipelines in Palm Springs. After a shift in the sun, which baked his Scandinavian skin to leather, he would come home with twelve-hour days in his eyes. He never complained; he worked and lived for us. His example of resilience instilled in me that same devotion. I was blessed and knew it.

There was a difference, though. I loved every second in the cockpit. This wasn't work; it was freedom. Every flight pushed our personal boundaries and revealed that we were capable of more. With each test, we grew as aviators and young men. Along the way, achievement became a drug. I couldn't wait for the next jump forward toward a fleet assignment. From the tie-cutting ceremony after

I soloed to the first time I landed aboard an aircraft carrier, it was a journey marked with memorable moments. A year at Pensacola gave me a sense of identity and purpose that I never felt back home. I wanted Mary Beth Peck to pin my aviator's wings on me at graduation. We had met in high school at a church function; I was seventeen, she was fourteen. Even in Southern California, with probably the highest concentration of beautiful girls anywhere, she made everyone else look ordinary. Blonde hair, eyes like the sky at twenty thousand feet. It took only one conversation to realize she wasn't just a beautiful face. Mary Beth possessed a soft-spoken eloquence and powerful intellect.

We courted properly, and our families grew close as we fell in love. She had written me every day since I'd left home to seek this new path through life. No matter how tough it got at Pensacola, I never let my head hit the pillow until I'd filled a page for her in return.

We had not seen each other since I left Los Alamitos for Pensacola. I'd left home a boy, working my way through junior college. That morning, I returned at the controls of a modern jet trainer, the double solo bars of an advanced naval aviation cadet on my chest. Christmas break was my chance to show her and our families the man I was becoming.

Wings banked now, the T-bird's polished aluminum skin reflected the sun as Bill and I began our approach to Marine Corps Air Station El Toro in Irvine. The base's distinctive double-cross runways stuck out among the tract homes and orange groves. El Toro served as home to some of the greatest combat aviators America ever produced: Joe Foss, Marion Carl, John L. Smith—the men who had stopped the Japanese advance in the Pacific during World War II. Most of the people in Orange County knew little of that legacy, but from the moment I started training, we naval aviation cadets were immersed in the heritage that was ours if we proved ourselves worthy.

At Pensacola, we flew the SNJ Texan and the T-28. On my first morning there, our drill sergeant woke us in the barracks with the rattle of his nightstick along the steel frames of our bunks, then double-timed us out to an aging hangar beside the seaplane ramp. In the very same building where some of naval aviation's pioneers established our tradition, the drill sergeant smoked us with forty minutes of PT. Each morning started with the same ritual. We worked out in the hangar among the ghosts of those who had paved the way for us. Thanks to them, naval aviation became the rebel branch of the service, always striving to develop new ideas, new technology, and new ways of fighting that would send the age of the battleship into history. From the battles of the Coral Sea and Midway to the Great Marianas Turkey Shoot, they transformed the U.S. Navy into the most effective naval fighting force on the planet.

Everywhere we went at Pensacola, we felt that tradition and it was an honor to be invited to be part of it. Would my generation contribute to perpetuate it in the years ahead? One thing for sure, I was not going to be the one who washed out and went home to be just another college kid with ducktail hair, working odd jobs to cover tuition.

Where other cadets bought cars and spent time in town, drinking at Trader John's and other local aviator watering holes, I made a point of staying on base. My dad's ethic became mine. I studied and worked hard. I was determined to be among the top cadets who upon graduation would be handed the keys to the latest and greatest fighter jets our country produced.

After Basic School at Pensacola, we were required to take a cross-country instrument flight to California, the final stage before we finished Advanced School in Beeville, Texas. The fringe benefit of this last evolution was a chance to visit home.

As we started our descent toward El Toro, Bill Pierson, my instructor in the rear seat, coached me over the intercom. I eased the throttle back and entered the landing pattern. Gear and flaps down, nose flared, I set the T-bird onto the runway. I taxied to the ramp by base operations, shut down the engine, and opened the canopy. Bill jumped out to grab a cup of coffee while our airplane got refueled. I pulled my helmet off and slid on the pair of Ray-Bans that I'd purchased at the Pensacola PX. They were a little over-the-top Hollywood for a cadet. In Florida and Texas I usually only wore them to the beach. What the heck. It was California.

Mary Beth stood on the tarmac, looking up at me with my parents at her side. She was a vision in an angora sweater and below-the-knee skirt. Wearing flat-heeled shoes and with her hair down, she had a smile on her face. Maybe just a hint of awe as well. I could hope.

I unstrapped and climbed out, dressed in a khaki flight suit, a matching jacket, and Navy-issue chukka boots. I'd barely made it down the ladder when she wrapped her arms around me. In an instant, the year of separation seemed like an eyeblink. I knew beyond a doubt, this was the woman I wanted to marry.

Bill watched from the doorway to base ops, a paper cup of coffee in hand. He was a veteran of Korea and countless days at sea. He had shared moments like this one and knew their power. He also knew to stay clear and let me have it; for that I was grateful. The holiday break passed quickly.

I was born in Moline, Illinois, in 1935, and my father served in the army during World War II. My parents were immigrants and

I was a first-generation American. Dad, named Orla or Ole, was born in Denmark in 1912 and his parents, Olaf and Mary Pedersen, immigrated the next year. My mother, Henrietta, was one of three beautiful sisters from the Isle of Man. She met Dad at a high school basketball game.

I remember the smell of potato sausage in Mom's kitchen on the evening we ate Christmas dinner on the back porch. That was a Danish tradition passed down from my paternal grandfather. When I was a kid in Moline, I'd rush from school to his little Scandinavian specialty store, passing barrels of pickled fish. A pot of that potato sausage would be simmering on the stove, filling the place with the scent of home and warmth.

My first flying experience had been in 1946, not long after dad returned from Europe. My father was intrigued with aircraft, as he had some experience with B-25 bombers near the end of the war. One evening, at Moline Airport, he said we were going flying. What a surprise for a ten-year-old boy. The flight was in darkness, early in the evening in a prewar Ford Trimotor, distinctive with its three clattering Wright engines and corrugated aluminum skin. I marveled even then at the beauty of being aloft at night.

Before I went to Beeville, Mary Beth gave me a Christmas gift. I unwrapped it to discover a gold signet ring with a tiny diamond inset on its flat face. She had my initials inscribed on it along with 1956 and Love, Beth on the inside. She was a freshman at Whittier College working in the student union cafeteria. She must have gone into debt to pull this off.

All too soon, this beautiful interlude ended. My instructor met me at El Toro a few days after Christmas. I wore the ring on my right hand as I kissed Mary Beth goodbye on the ramp. Soon I would be an officer and a gentleman. I'd ask her father for permission to propose. We'd start a life in the Navy together. A final hug, no tears, and I scrambled up the ladder and into the cockpit. As Bill Pierson and I taxied out to the runway, I saw her waving goodbye to her naval aviation cadet.

When I landed at Beeville, my first jet fighter awaited me on the flight line. She was a Grumman F9F Panther, a well-traveled aircraft whose dark blue aluminum skin was dotted with patched-over bullet holes. Like my instructor, she was a veteran of Korea, her paint dulled by years of service. With her straight wing and her sub–Mach 1 top speed, the Panther had been relegated to stateside pastures, where she helped train the next generation of naval aviators.

I stood under my bird and shared a *Bridges at Toko-Ri* moment. How many times had I seen that movie? A dozen? The flying scenes were spectacular. The poignancy of the love story and the fact that pretty much everyone dies in the end was lost to my visions of glory. That first morning with that Panther, I climbed into the cockpit and fell in love.

She was a delight to fly, balanced on the controls and fast for a first-generation, single-engine jet. Alone in the cockpit, I tried aerobatics with her and shot up towed sleeves with her four 20mm cannons. The thrill of it left me craving more.

As we closed in on the final lap of our training, a few boxes remained to be checked. One included a cross-country formation flight to Dallas and back. Three of us cadets took off with a storm closing in on us. The cloud ceiling was under a thousand feet. Speeding over the Texas countryside, we hugged the earth in an arrowhead formation at about five hundred feet, each of us taking turns in the lead. Two miles behind, our instructor trailed along in another F9F observing us at the edge of visibility. The weather worsened. Visibility diminished. We reached Dallas, landed safely. After resting and refueling, we flew back in the afternoon.

At four hundred miles an hour, a Panther travels almost two football fields a second. You have to think a step or two ahead at all times, or the speed simply overwhelms your ability to respond. Get behind the aircraft, and the struggle to catch up will make you mistake-prone. The best pilots ride the wave and are always thinking a move or two ahead of the aircraft. You have very little time to react to something. So when something suddenly flashed *between* our three Panthers, I was stunned. Looking in my rearview mirror, I saw a red-lit radio relay tower stretching skyward into the overcast. We were at five hundred feet. Those radio towers were fifteen hundred feet tall. It was only an act of God that kept one of us from careening into it with fatal results.

We landed back at Beeville shaken but intact. Our instructor taxied to the ramp several minutes later, and I felt a swell of anger rise in me. *Where were you? Miles behind us out of sight when we almost flew into that tower?*

After I calmed down, the lesson came into focus. When you're a fighter pilot, alone in that cockpit, your fate is in your hands. Blaming others is just a dodge. It's no way to grow or improve. It was up to me to see that radio tower. No one else.

Near misses aside, I ranked near the top of my class in the final stage of advanced training. I felt myself developing into a confident young pilot. Inevitably, such self-realizations will lead the universe to knock you down a peg. Mine was a brutal humbling with lifelong implications.

That day I was supposed to fly a graded check flight in a T-bird with an instructor named Tony Biamonte. We planned and briefed a flight to Foster Air Force Base near Victoria on a day when a solid wall of clouds marched over the Lone Star State to twenty-five thousand feet. Visibility was at a minimum, even down on the deck. In the days before ground control radar, pilots navigated by low-frequency radio signals called LFR. It was still in use as a redundant backup system in the 1950s, and every cadet needed to know how to use it in a pinch. This weather called for it.

We took off into the soup, spiraling upward until we broke into blue skies above twenty-five thousand. Tony sat in the rear seat; I was in the front. Victoria was only about fifty miles away, so this was a quick flight. After checking in with Foster control, I started our descent. We went from blue skies to a world of swirling grays so thick I could barely see our wingtip fuel tanks.

Being inside a cloud is a disorienting experience. Look outside the cockpit too long at the dark heart of a cloud, and you'll lose all sense of up or down, inverted or upright. Mesmerized, you won't be able to tell if your wings are level, if you're in a bank, or if you're dropping out of the sky. With no frame of reference, your senses go haywire. The same thing can happen while flying at night. In moments like these, you bet your life on your instruments. You have to trust them, not what your body is telling you. It can be hard to believe the gauges over the wisdom in your own gut.

I was wrestling with that phenomenon while trying to carefully listen to the LFR signals telling me where I was in relation to the runway. I could feel myself starting to stretch to keep hold of the situation and stay ahead of the aircraft.

As we began our descent, I tried to keep a mental picture of where I thought we were. That mental picture was crucial. You have to see your bird in the air in your mind's eye, erasing the clouds and overcast until the landscape below comes into focus. You build the picture with the radio signals. Each Morse code letter, either an A, an N, or a Null, gave you a sense of your position. As I dropped into the pattern, I listened as the letters changed. With each new Morse code signal, I updated my mental picture.

At about two thousand feet, I had us on our downwind leg of the pattern. This meant we were running parallel to the runway a few thousand feet to the side. As we passed ninety degrees to the edge of the runway, I heard the Morse code letter change. That was the cue to make a turn onto the final approach. One more turn and I'd have this box checked.

We were still in heavy overcast, the T-bird buffeted by turbulence. Between studying my instruments, prepping the aircraft for landing, and trying to listen to the radio signals, I grew confused and uncertain.

Is my mental picture wrong?

The signal changed. New letter.

Wait, which end of the runway have I reached? Which way to turn?

I thought I knew where we were, but my confusion destroyed my confidence.

I turned the wrong way, sending the T-bird directly away from the end of the runway. I realized my mistake within seconds. Stopping our descent, I called the tower, fessed up, and asked to return to a holding pattern.

I could feel Tony's presence behind me right then. I had screwed up. Naval aviation is an unforgiving calling. One error and people— including yourself—die. In training, even a few seconds' worth of a wrong turn will count against you.

It certainly did here. Tony scrubbed the exercise, telling me to return to Beeville instead. I flew back, tense and upset with myself, seething at the mistake. When we got back on the ground, he asked, "You know what you did wrong?"

"Yeah." I explained what had happened, mentioning that I corrected the mistake very quickly.

He nodded agreement on that last point. Still, he did not let me off the hook. "I want you to fly this check ride again."

I'd failed a flight, the only one in eighteen months of training. He saw the expression on my face and tried to reassure me. "Listen. Dan, everybody gets one down check. Don't worry about it. It is a good lesson in humility."

I hit the books harder than ever. I studied LFR approaches. I flew the mission profile in the base simulators every day. I went back to the basics and studied Morse code again. There was no way I was going to fail again. In my obsession to succeed, I jettisoned every routine aspect of my life and used the extra minutes to study. That first night, my head hit the pillow, and as I fell off into an exhausted near-coma, a part of my brain felt like I'd forgotten to do something.

I haven't written Mary Beth.

For the first time since I'd left home for cadets, I'd failed to finish a letter to her.

The next night, the same thing happened. I was falling behind. Her letters arrived like clockwork. Now I'd missed two days and I foolishly let my responsiveness slide even further.

All week, I remained singularly focused. Life distilled down to one thing: Learn LFR approaches and do it right the second time. Mary Beth and every other aspect of my life took a temporary backseat as I worked to overcome my error. No cell phones or long-distance to explain; besides, I was too embarrassed. Big mistake.

This was my initiation into the constant battle all naval aviators face: the demands of the job versus the need for a personal life. The job is so demanding that it almost always wins. In a civilian career, balancing professional and personal lives requires careful attention, but it can be done. In naval aviation, there is no balance. The job always has to come first.

At home, she checked her mailbox every day to find it empty. She went from puzzled to alarmed to deeply hurt as each afternoon brought the same empty box. My grandkids would call this "ghosting." Imagine you and your love have been texting on your phones day after day while separated for some reason. Suddenly, one of you stops. A few hours might not seem significant, but the communication becomes one-way. The stress level rises. A day passes. Then two. Wondering becomes an agony. No explanation—the person simply vanished, became a ghost.

The word *ghosting* hadn't made it to Webster's English Dictionary yet, but that week in 1957, it's exactly what I did to Mary Beth as I focused on passing the check ride. When I climbed back into the T-bird for the do-over, the hard work paid off: I aced the flight, landed the aircraft without issue, and returned to Beeville with my confidence restored.

Tony died two months later during a similar LFR check ride with another naval aviator. Life in aviation, even in training, was deadly serious. It required everything you have. Living an intensely focused, out-of-balance life wasn't just an expression of our passion for flying. It was required in order to survive.

That was one of my last check rides. I finished advanced training and didn't slip in the class rankings. With the ordeal behind me, I wrote Mary Beth for the first time in several weeks. I couldn't bring myself to tell her about my brush with failure. How could I explain my poor judgment in a letter? I decided to wait until I returned home to explain it to her in person. I needed her to see me as infallible, the confident pilot who'd climbed out of the T-bird at

Christmas, rocking those Ray-Bans and beige chukka boots. So I took the path of least resistance: I wrote as if nothing had happened. I didn't even acknowledge vanishing for all those days. I just picked up where I'd left off.

On March 1, 1957, I got my wings. The graduation ceremony in Corpus Christi was almost anticlimactic. I wanted Mary Beth to pin my wings on me, but flying to Texas was not financially feasible for her or my folks. Instead, my flight training roommate and friend from home, Al Clayes, pinned my wings on my chest that day. I did the same honor for this newly commissioned U.S. Marine aviator.

The Navy commissioned us all ensigns and made Big Al a Marine second lieutenant. We were officers and gentlemen at last, waiting for our first assignments with increasing trepidation. Through the grapevine, I'd heard that there were very few jet fighter pilot slots available on the West Coast that spring. I wanted to be back in California, close to home and Mary Beth, so I'd asked for duty on my side of the country.

When my orders arrived, I tore open the envelope, running through my worst-case scenarios, the first of which was blimps. Yes, the 1950s Navy still flew airships. We called them "poopy bags." Nobody wanted to go from flying Panthers and T-birds to puttering around at seventy knots with a gigantic bag of gas over your head. No thank you. Then there was ASW. Antisubmarine warfare. This meant multiengine flying and interminably long patrols over open ocean, where everyone aboard tried not to fall asleep.

I took a breath, looked down at my orders, and read the official verbiage directing me to report in thirty days to San Diego.

I read it twice. Then a third time just to be sure I wasn't dreaming.

I was going to a squadron known as VF(AW)-3.

V stood for heavier than air. No blimps for me.

F stood for fighters.

AW stood for all-weather.

I'd done it. I was going to be a jet fighter pilot.

I was on the road to Topgun.

CHAPTER TWO

FIRST TRIBE

Texas to Naval Air Station North Island, San Diego
Spring 1957

It's 2300 here in the California desert, eleven o'clock in the civilian world. I come out every night and sit by the pool at the same time with my wife's two little white-poofball Maltese pups. They curl up under my lounge chair, which I'll adjust to be flat. Then I'll lay here and look up into the night and wait.

The stars are old friends, of course. We all did our share of night flying. At sea aboard an aircraft carrier, the air wings assigned the rookie pilots night flights based on the phase of the moon. A first-timer would need to land by the light of a full moon. If he hit that forty-foot zone in which the tailhook can catch a wire—as it will have to on a carrier or heaven help you—the next time he flies, the moon will be a crescent. Less light, more challenging. The biggest test came on nights with no moon—and bad weather. Nothing gives a naval aviator more gut-check moments than a night carrier landing in a heavy sea. It takes a special breed of cat to do it consistently, that's for sure.

Whenever the moon looks like the base of a thumbnail, I remember when I commanded the carrier USS *Ranger*. Somewhere in the

Pacific, under a sliver moon, our air wing conducted night ops. One of our young pilots had trouble getting get his F-14 Tomcat back down on the deck. As he made his approach and the landing signal officer (LSO) talked him toward that number-three wire, I watched from my bridge chair. I could tell he was "killing snakes in the cockpit." That means he was overcontrolling the aircraft. He was feeling overwhelmed and his heart rate was spiked. We'd all been there. The LSO told him to go around and try again. We call that a wave-off.

He did, and the same thing happened. His bucket was full. He was battling fear, the darkness, his instruments, the procedures needed to bring the bird back aboard. It got away from him again.

All night, he tried to land on the *Ranger*. Twice he had to climb above the clouds to refuel from an airborne tanker. I finally had to call him on the radio, something ship captains almost never do. We leave talking to the pilots to the air boss or their squadron commanders.

"Look, son, we're into the wind and we're not going anywhere. We're here for you, and we've got all night. Just relax a bit and smooth it out."

Those are the moments I loved the most—the kind of mentoring and loyalty to each other I never found anywhere else but inside the brotherhood of naval aviation.

That nugget took twelve passes before he was safely on the flight deck. Now think about that. Each approach is a gut-check moment. The deck may be moving with the swells and you can't see the horizon in the darkness. You're utterly reliant on the LSO and your instruments. A mistake can kill you. Worse, if you make that mistake as you touch down, you'll probably kill others, too. Even when we weren't in combat, the stakes were high.

Twelve tries in, he made a perfect landing. Maybe in the civilian world, some manager would give a young employee twelve chances, but I doubt it. In our world, we knew what to do. We sent him right back up the very next night. And when the time came to land, he rolled into his approach like a fleet veteran and caught the number-three wire like a seasoned tail hooker. Later in his career he flew with the Navy's famous demonstration team, the Blue Angels.

Love of aviation led us to our careers, but we all stayed in the service because of the people. Men like the ones who had gotten us through nights like that.

My first unofficial act as an ensign in the U.S. Navy was to buy a car. My gang of new officers, at lunch for the first time at the officers' club in Corpus Christi, Texas, decided that at least one of us needed to have a set of wheels. We rolled dice to see who would go down to the dealership, and I lost.

I picked out a brand-new 1957 Ford Fairlane. Raven black with black and colonial white matching interior. Sidewalls straight out of *American Graffiti*. I drove home from Texas in my new ride, eager to see Mary Beth, make amends, and take her for a spin. I had thirty days of leave before I needed to report to VF(AW)-3, and I intended to use every minute of it courting my girl.

The morning after I got home, I drove the Fairlane over to Whittier College. I found Mary Beth working at the cafeteria in the student union. She seemed unusually quiet. As I showed her the new car, I knew something was wrong.

"Beth, is something on your mind?"

She hesitated, searching for words.

"You didn't write," she said. "I didn't get any letters for a while."

I was about to explain, when she said, "Dan, I'm seeing someone. When you didn't write. Well, he was persistent. I gave in." I didn't know what to say. He was a football player at the college. They'd been seeing each other for only a few weeks.

I went home to regroup. My folks' house was a sad place that evening. I stayed around town for two more weeks, marking time and feeling increasingly like an outsider in my own home. It was the first taste of alienation most of us naval aviators experienced as we began our journey into the brotherhood. The layers of our old lives would fall away like leaves in the months to come. Nuggets—rookie naval aviators—still had some connections to the outside civilian world, but already we were seeing them strained to the limits by the demands of flying high-performance aircraft. Increasingly, our lives were whittled down to the job, the people working with us, and a few problematical connections on the ground.

It was a brutal process for all of us. Hollywood often portrays us as skirt-chasing, hard-drinking types without delving deeper into the situation. The truth was, by the time you reached your first squadron, those superficial nights with beautiful girls were all that naval aviators had room for in their lives. The problem arose when we tried to form deeper connections. The love of my life was the first sacrifice I made for those wings of gold.

When sticking around town became intolerable, I decided to report early to my new squadron. While I was packing, my mom came to me and watched me fill my suitcase.

"Dan," she said gently, "Mary Beth has made her choice. You've got to respect that."

I wanted to win her back. My mom could see right through me.

"Don't do it. Don't interfere. That isn't your place. It wasn't meant to be." One thing we did not do in the Pedersen household was defy our mother. Her words followed me all the way to San Diego.

Joining your first squadron is a life event for naval aviators. You make lifelong friends and the lessons in the air come at you like a firehose. Your mind needs to be clear; you've got to be ready for the challenges ahead. If you're not, you're going to have an accident. No matter what area of naval aviation you're in, it is deeply unforgiving of mistakes.

In downtown San Diego, I found the Coronado Ferry at the end of Broadway and drove the Fairlane aboard. My mind was anything but clear. I wasn't joining the squadron two weeks early that day, I was running from home and the life I'd wanted but could not have.

At North Island, the guard at the front gate gave me directions to VF(AW)-3. I barely noticed the planes coming and going off the runways as I drove past long lines of attack jets, patrol planes, and fighters. The squadron had its own high-security compound. Fenced off, patrolled by guards with leashed attack dogs, it stood in stark contrast to the relatively relaxed security at the main entrance. It was my first indication that my new squadron was a distinctive one.

I parked by the hangar after showing my orders a second time at the guard station. I reached across the bench seat, grabbed my fore-and-aft cap along with the manila envelope containing my orders, and went to check in at the admin office.

The officer of the day greeted me warmly with a "Welcome aboard" and a handshake. He took me to meet the squadron's executive officer, Commander Eugene Valencia.

Meeting the exec was a formal call, part of the ritual when a new guy came aboard. I was led to his office, stepped inside, and introduced myself.

Round-faced, solidly built, with slightly thinning hair, my new XO happened to be the third-highest U.S. Navy ace of World War II, one of the great legends of our community. In one engagement over the Japanese home islands in April 1945, he shot down six enemy planes. He finished the war with twenty-three flags on the side of his F6F Hellcat.

I was a raw ensign fighting to hide a broken heart. The man introducing himself to me held the Navy Cross and six Distinguished Flying Crosses. I was in awe. Yet Commander Valencia was anything but arrogant. He greeted me and set me at ease with his relaxed, unassuming nature. It was hard to believe that a man with so many accomplishments could be so grounded and approachable.

From the XO's office, the officer of the day led me to the hangar. He explained that the squadron stood on twenty-four-hour alert as a component of the North American Air Defense Command. VF(AW)-3 was the only U.S. Navy fighter squadron assigned to protect America's shores. We were the anomalies—naval aviators under direct U.S. Air Force control. At any moment of the day or night, two crews stood ready to scramble and be airborne within five minutes. More crews waited in the ready room on ten-minute alert. Should the order be given, they would run to the aircraft waiting in front of the hangar and launch down Runway 18 in a mad dash.

It was the height of the Cold War. The great threat to the American homeland wasn't intercontinental ballistic missiles; it was Soviet nuclear-armed bombers. In case of World War III, our job was to get to the incoming Red Air Force bombers before they could hit Southern California.

The Navy gave us the best equipment, the most advanced electronics—and the best crews. Every year there was a competition to see which outfit was the best squadron protecting American airspace. Every year, a two-star Air Force general came to North Island to bestow that award—it always went to the lone Navy unit in the mix. It was a tremendous point of pride for the Navy, and for VF(AW)-3.

I was allowed to poke my head into the ready room for just a short minute that afternoon. The crews were lounging there in their flight suits, waiting for the Klaxon to sound. The officer of the day said, "Why don't you go get your flight gear and put it in your new locker." He pointed out a bank of them in the main hangar. When I found my assigned locker, I opened it up to find that it was full of somebody else's stuff.

"I think there's been a mistake," I said.

The officer of the day looked stricken. "Sorry about that. We forgot to clear it out."

Clear it out?

"That locker belonged to the lieutenant j.g. you're replacing. He was killed a little while back. Accident. Go ahead and throw everything away. The rest of his effects already went to his family."

I walked back to the locker and stared at the items inside with a new perspective. A ratty old T-shirt hung on one hook. A few other knickknacks and toiletries sat on the shelf. Then I noticed something unusual. A pair of eyes were staring back at me. I reached in and pulled off the top shelf a tiny stuffed mouse. It was about two inches tall, with big eyes, soft gray fur, and a tail. The toy seemed out of place in a fighter pilot's locker.

Was it a gift to his child, never delivered because of that last, fatal flight? Was it a gift from his child to him? If it was a lucky talisman that served as a reminder of who waited for him back home, I hated to think it had failed him.

Suddenly, I didn't want to know. Talk about an attitude adjustment. My problems seemed trivial, selfish, compared to the death of the mouse's owner.

I trashed the shirt and toiletries. But as the mouse hovered over the can, I held it there and regarded it again. *Who am I to throw away another man's mouse?*

I took the little guy back to my flight bag and made him a nest deep inside. As I stowed my gear in the reclaimed locker, his cartoon eyes stared up at me from beside my helmet. I set my Ray-Bans on the shelf, closed the locker, and headed off to get a room assignment in the bachelor officers' quarters. After I unpacked, I went to the ready room to meet the squadron.

Ties off. Formality forgotten, one of my new squadron mates greeted me with a grin and said, "Welcome to the best squadron in the United States Air Force!" Mom had told me to go make the best life I could. Carry on. Move forward. Easy things to say. Yet here I was, surrounded by men driven by the same passion for flight that burned in me. They were achievers, hard chargers, type A. The kind of men whose respect, once earned, offered meaning never found anywhere else. These men were among the best pilots in the Navy, and here they were opening a place for me in their circle. That night, I found my tribe, the men who would teach me to be a fighter pilot.

CHAPTER THREE

THE NAVY WAY

North Island
June 1958

The buzz of the Klaxon sent us scrambling. Unidentified aircraft inbound. Pilots drinking coffee and playing acey deucey in the ready room were always waiting for this moment. I was on "alert five" status, ready to be airborne, in case of a contingency, within five minutes. The Klaxon started us sprinting to the flight line. We climbed into our cockpits, taxied to Runway 18, and did a rolling takeoff with an unrestricted climb.

The aircraft we called the Ford was officially known as the Douglas F4D Skyray. It was a tailless aerodynamic marvel created by legendary designer Ed Heinemann. It looked like something straight out of a sci-fi movie with its missile-shaped nose and rakish bat wing. It was so hot that to earn cockpit time in this beast, each pilot in VF(AW)-3 first had to fly three hundred hours in the older F3D Skyknight interceptor. The trick in that single-seater was to learn to handle the radar and speed procedures by yourself.

I could feel the Pratt & Whitney J57 engine surging as I checked the instruments. At 140 knots, I rotated to climb attitude about thirty degrees, while sucking up the landing gear and turning to the assigned vector to find my target. Everything in the green. The Skyray streaked for the heavens like a homesick angel.

Continuing to pull back on the stick, I reclined until my nose had moved from thirty degrees to sixty. Almost straight up now, I accelerated with the afterburner pushing the aircraft to the perfect climb speed. I passed ten thousand feet in fifty-five seconds. The stars lay dead ahead.

Two minutes and thirty-six seconds later, I was at fifty thousand feet. On a clear day, from this vantage point nine miles above the Pacific, I could see the Sierra Nevada to the north, far past Los Angeles. To the east the Colorado River snaked around Yuma, Arizona.

The target was somewhere out there in the night, ahead and below me. The Mount Laguna radar station and the Manual Air Direction Center at Norton Air Force Base coached me toward it until I detected the target with my own sensors. The Skyray had a secret airborne radar installed in the nose. It was a circular cathode ray tube screen with a hood attached to it. To see it in daylight, the pilot leaned forward and put his eyes into the hood to watch the radar beam sweep left to right. If that seems like a dangerous way to fly, you get used to it. Westinghouse built a turn and bank indicator, an attitude gyro, into the screen. We could fly the aircraft with our eyes on the radar scope. The radar controls were just aft of the throttle, so we'd fly with our right hand on the stick and run the radar with our left.

Thanks to our burner, we could reach a target in mere minutes. Our powerful radar could spot the enemy long before we could see them visually. The target pulsed onto my radar screen and I started the lock-on procedure. The screen displayed a small circle. Our job was to ease it over the target dot. That done, we were ready to fire when the target was in range. We could fire dozens of unguided 2.7-inch rockets to hit our target.

The Skyray rolled out of the Douglas Aircraft factory at El Segundo with four cannons and sixty-five shells per gun. With the advent of unguided rockets and heat-seeking air-to-air missiles, the Navy deemed the guns so much needless weight. They were removed, and their ports faired over. Welcome to the dawn of Push Button Warfare.

In these peacetime intercepts, we always needed to establish visual sight of the target to figure out what it was. I dropped down on the target to discover on this night, like almost every other intercept, that our bogey was a wayward airliner. I flew along with it for a few minutes, wondering if the passengers inside could see me out there off their wing. My nav lights were switched off, so I would have just been a ghostly outline to anyone who happened to be peering out their porthole window.

No threat to the country on this night. Mission accomplished; time to return to North Island. That afterburner sucked almost three thousand pounds of fuel—461 gallons—just to get to fifty thousand feet. We were fast, could scale the stars at Buck Rogers rates, but the Skyray did not have a lot of endurance, even with two external fuel tanks slung under the wings. She was a sprinter, built to counter a threat we hoped we would never face.

I headed back for North Island and eased into the pattern, passing over the Hotel del Coronado, always checking out the pool as I paralleled the beach. On final approach, the Skyray demanded full attention. Unlike the T-bird, which was a beautifully balanced and stable bird, the Ford was twitchy, nervous, and laterally unstable. That instability gave it tremendous maneuverability and roll rate, but it was not for a novice pilot. They were tricky to land on carriers. Nuggets had to fly in an older interceptor before getting the keys to the Ford.

You couldn't see very well when you were coming in hot, thirty degrees nose up. The Skyray landed so nose-high that Ed Heinemann designed a retractable tail skid with a small wheel embedded in it. When we extended the landing gear, the skid lowered and locked into place. If you landed properly, the skid would be the first part of the aircraft to contact the runway, followed by the main wheels, then the nose wheel.

I spotted the approach lights near the end of the runway. They stood on tall wooden poles like streetlights on steroids. I was wary of them. They could disorient you, especially on foggy nights. I put the nose on the centerline, scanned the instrument panel, and eased off the throttle. The Ford descended toward the runway on a ground-controlled radar approach on glide path, on centerline, until touchdown.

Two months into my time with VF(AW)-3, I received a call at home in the middle of the night ordering me back to North Island. I was living with several of the other pilots in a rental house on Coronado, so I was close by. At the compound I discovered that a lieutenant j.g. friend had flown into one of those approach lights in dense fog, after getting disoriented on final. His F4D exploded and killed him instantly. The skipper made me the assistant accident investigating officer; it fell to me to go with the squadron commander and a chaplain to break the news to his wife.

After that terrible doorway moment on her front porch, I returned to the field to spend the morning helping to clear the wreckage off the runway. That was the worst and hardest duty I ever had in my twenty-nine-year career. Part of the task required finding my friends' remains. We spent hours collecting pieces, and I thought about his newly widowed wife and their children.

His death left me ultra-careful as I made those night approaches, especially in bad weather. After dark, thick fog usually moved in from the bay and North Island. It made for very difficult, near-zero-visibility landings. Sometimes the fog proved so thick that we diverted to the naval air station at El Centro or another local strip. The fog is what got my friend. In his final seconds, it disoriented him and he clipped one of those stanchions. It was both a tragedy and cautionary tale.

These Skyrays were the wave of the future. If we did our jobs right, we'd never even see the Soviet bomber we blew out of the sky. In the months to come, beyond-visual-range attacks would become the order of the day, thanks to the advent of two key pieces of technology: the Sidewinder and Sparrow air-to-air missiles. These were the first generation of guided weapons. The Sidewinder, officially known as the AIM-9, used infrared sensors to track and destroy a target. The longer-ranged Sparrow relied on radar guidance.

In September 1958, our allies in the Taiwanese Air Force took the Sidewinder to war. They mounted them on their vintage F-86 Sabres. Through the end of that summer, the Taiwanese had been fighting a bitter air war against the Red Chinese Air Force, which was equipped with the newer Soviet-built MiG-17 Fresco.

The Taiwanese pilots scored history's first guided missile kill on September 24. The Sidewinder came as a complete shock to the Communists. Before the fight ended, the new missile helped them knock down about ten MiG-17s. The fight validated the enormous investment in missile technology we were making all through the 1950s. Of course, combat creates totally unanticipated moments. On that day, one of the Sidewinders failed to explode after spearing a MiG-17's wing. The Chinese pilot returned to base with his prize stuck in his aircraft, and within weeks the Russians were reverse-engineering our ultra-secret technological marvel. A few years later, in Vietnam, we would face those Russian-made Sidewinder knockoffs—we called them AA-2 Atolls.

After the Sidewinder's inaugural success in combat, the Department of Defense, Air Force, and Navy moved quickly toward long-range guided missile technology. The day of the Red Baron's swirling dogfights over the Western Front in World War I seemed a thing of the past. No longer did you have to close within a few hundred feet to score a kill. Pilots could shoot an enemy plane out of the sky long before getting into dogfight range. The Navy and Air Force agreed with the DoD whiz kids, who decided the day of close-range air combat was over. The new fighters would have multiple pylons for missiles, but no internal gun. Why waste space and weight for such an anachronism?

In my squadron, the senior leadership came of age in the World War II and Korean War era. Their combat experience looked a lot more like the Red Baron's day than our Buck Rogers dot wars on a radar screen. Nobody influenced me more than our executive officer, ace Eugene "Geno" Valencia, who took several of us young pilots under his wing and mentored us. In after-hours bull sessions at the famous air station I Bar, or the base officers' club, he would sometimes open up and talk about fighting the Japanese in the skies over the Pacific. As a young nugget, I relished the stories. In 1957, Geno had taken me to a big gathering of naval aviators in Rosarito Beach, Baja California, Mexico. It was known as the Tailhook Convention. As Geno's aide-de-camp, I carried the briefcase full of scotch. I heard sea stories and hangar tales that set my hair on end from some of the Navy's greatest aviation legends. Another time, Geno took some of us junior officers to an American Fighter Aces convention. I had devoured the memoirs of the World War II aces, looking for lessons I could apply to my career. We met some of America's best fighter pilots, and we absorbed everything they told us. All of them had fought Zeroes and MiGs. We wanted to be them!

They told us how, during the Pacific War, they learned to avoid getting into a turning dogfight with more-maneuverable Japanese fighters. Trying to turn with the more agile Japanese planes would get your tail shot off. So they took their shot and flew away—"One pass, haul ass" was the axiom. They learned to work together in pairs, cooperating to make sure that an enemy couldn't latch on to a pilot's tail. The other American pilot was always ready to turn toward his partner and stick his guns in the enemy's face.

My flight leader, Bill Armstrong, explained to me that in Korea, the opposite was the case. The tactics of World War II would get a pilot killed going up against a Communist MiG-15. Those jets were faster and flew higher than anything the Navy had, including the hot F9F Panther I had flown in training. Given the MiG's speed advantage, the horizontal plane became the Panther's playground. It could out-turn the MiG-15. So in just six years, we changed tactics altogether. "One pass, haul ass" went away and U.S. fighter pilots found their advantage in the sharp-turning dogfight.

In the missile age, it was all changing again. At least that's what the Navy believed. We would simply be directed by ground control to a point in the sky, lock our little circle on the dot, and let loose with a missile. No more seat-of-the-pants maneuvering in sharply turning fights. Technology promised a revolution.

Classically, the fighter jocks flew in many roles. We flew close to bomber formations, covering them en route to a target. We intercepted enemy bombers, tangling with their own fighter escort. We carried out sweeps in search of anything in the air to shoot down. We even carried out bombing missions ourselves, supporting troops by dropping napalm along the front lines. Fighters were jacks-of-all-trades, with the primary job of driving the enemy from the skies so our own planes could operate without interference. Each of these missions involved close-in dogfighting. The Navy concluded that long-distance radar interception would make all of these tactics obsolete. A flight of missile-armed fighters would stand off and destroy targets without ever needing to engage at close range. Just watch that cathode ray tube, secure the lock, and release the missiles. The bombing mission would be handed over to dedicated attack squadrons.

In our tight-knit group, some of us didn't like where the Navy was heading. The old ways had developed for a reason. Had air warfare really changed? It turned out, there was another factor at play here. It had everything to do with budgets. Through the mid-1950s, training for the kind of Korean War dogfighting we'd experienced proved both expensive and dangerous. Blasting off the runway and going climbing to fifty thousand feet at the edge of the sound barrier put a great deal of stress on an airframe. So, for reasons of safety, every plane came with a designated service life. The defense contractor guaranteed the airframe could withstand a certain number of flight hours before needing to be replaced. Somewhere in the Pentagon, some bean counter concluded that the heavy G loads of dogfight training wore out aircraft at least five times faster than simple intercept flights did. And dogfight training cost lives. Men made mistakes in those twisting, turning mock duels. They exceeded the limits, and died in unrecoverable spins or midair collisions. The loss of expensive aircraft could be (painfully) overcome, but the loss of well-trained pilots who took years to learn the ropes was a double blow.

So during my time at VF(AW)-3, the old ways were outlawed. Dogfighting—officially known as air combat maneuvering (ACM)— was forbidden. In 1960, the year before I left for my next assignment, the Navy shuttered the last of the old schools that trained fighter pilots to dogfight, the Fleet Air Gunnery Unit at El Centro. From then on, air combat maneuvering was banned. If you were caught "hassling," as we called dogfighting, your career could end.

The edict against dogfighting divided our squadron into three factions. Our senior leadership, whose experience ran counter to everything the Navy was now doing, had fought in two wars and had seen friends die. Having spent years away from their families on fleet deployments, they focused on being dads and husbands. At the end of their careers, they were content to mentor us nuggets on the ground, share their experiences, and teach us how to be leaders. They left the bulk of the flying to the younger guys.

In the second camp were the junior officers who bought into the new way. They never hassled, never pushed their Skyrays to the edge of the flight envelope.

The third group, a quiet group of young tigers, thought otherwise. I was one of them. And we decided to do something about it.

CHAPTER FOUR

FIGHT CLUB

Off San Clemente Island, California
1959

Do you remember the day when you first got the keys to your folks' car? Or maybe you salvaged some wreck off a lot, put in some wrench time, and took it out to see what it could do? In the 1950s, car-crazy high school kids always seemed to know where the street races were happening. Southern California had plenty of abandoned military airfields. And runways make great drag strips. Kids would take their beloved rides out there on Friday nights and tear around the old runways. Decades after those racing strips had disappeared, an underground racing scene developed. It was portrayed very well in the film *The Fast and the Furious*. The underground races were never formally organized. Just a few whispers at lunch and we made a deal to meet at a certain time and place. The network spread the word, one kid at a time.

Well, we developed a similar sort of underground subculture with supersonic fighters. Off the California coast, about eighty miles west of San Diego, there's a sector of restricted airspace that encompasses San Clemente Island. It's a military reservation. Air controllers call it Whiskey 291. The U.S. Navy squadrons in Southern California use it for training exercises. That was our playground.

I first heard about the West Coast's illicit dogfighting scene one night after hours in a San Diego bar. It might have been the Hotel del Coronado, or a Mexican restaurant where we knocked back tequila. It was certainly not at the North Island Officers' Club, or in the ready room. Too many "ears" could make things difficult.

We were free to fly almost whenever we wanted. Our squadron had plenty of aircraft and our chain of command encouraged us to get stick time. Almost always we could find a valid reason to fly. Sometimes we'd check out a bird for a weekend to practice cross-country navigation. I'd go to Texas, or Oklahoma, or Arizona. Once, when one of my fellow nuggets, Don Hall, was getting married in Phoenix, I flew a Ford to be part of the wedding. I can't imagine doing that in today's Navy.

Here's the thing: You learn by *doing.* Those of us who lived to fly learned our craft by flying a lot. We intercepted wayward airliners, and did our own troubleshooting when things went wrong with our birds. The men I most admired in the Navy were old-school fighter pilots. I wanted to be a throwback, ready to face adversity on my own wits. One look at the Eastern Bloc order of battle and it was clear that if World War III broke out, we were going to be heavily outnumbered. I imagined a zombie apocalypse with airplanes. We would pick off the first ones with our sniper rifles, our missiles. But behind them there would be more rushing at us. And a sniper rifle is the wrong weapon to have when they're grabbing for your shirttails.

What would happen to us when our missiles were gone? Our Fords we flew had no gun. And we were no longer being taught how to win a dogfight. It felt like a big gap in our combat aviator toolbox.

One Friday afternoon after a long week standing on alert, I went to the maintenance shop and signed out a Ford. I had heard at the bar that Friday afternoons before cocktail hour was the best time to find our version of a street race.

I took off from North Island and headed west for Whiskey 291, the unwritten rules in mind. One of them established a "hard deck" at five thousand feet. This meant that the fight was over the moment you dipped below that altitude. It was a nod to safety. If you ran into trouble and entered a spin, you'd need that altitude to recover. Aside from that, it was the Wild West. You'd find somebody who was willing to fight, give each other a hand signal, and get it on. What happened in Whiskey 291 stayed in Whiskey 291, unless you met your opponent later and had the chance to talk over drinks. There were no debriefs. No reports. No paper trail at all.

By joining this "fight club," we were keeping the flame alive for a certain way of being a fighter pilot. Three of the five junior officers from VF(AW)-3 whom I lived with on North Island loved this business, and in the months to come we would spend a lot of unofficial time hassling with other aircraft out over the Pacific. It was a whole lot of fun. It was also serious. We were preserving our birthright as naval aviators.

The first time I went out there, south of San Clemente, I was amazed at what I found. Marine A-4 Skyhawks, Air National Guard F-86L interceptors, Air Force F-100 Super Sabres, and lots of Navy guys flying F-8 Crusaders. There were even a few other Fords from North Island. The word had spread far beyond the Navy community, and the services mixed it up with fierce relish because they all were going through the same institutional evolution away from air combat that we in naval aviation were experiencing.

Mel Holmes, who later became one of my Original Bros at Topgun, served at North Island in a utility squadron just a few hangars down from my compound at the same time I was there. Mel loved to hassle out at Whiskey 291. Though I didn't know him at the time, I'd like to think we went head-to-head out there.

I learned the ropes that first time out. Pick your opponent, roll up alongside, and give the signal—the signal being the "bird." A smile and wave, and a forty-five-degree break in opposite directions. A break means we rolled the wings and turned one way. The guy to the left broke forty-five degrees left. The guy on the right broke forty-five degrees right. We'd extend out away from each other for several seconds until we were a few miles distant, then we began the fight.

We turned into each other, pushing throttles forward in what to the uninitiated looked like an aerial game of chicken in Mach 1 fighters. Approaching head-to-head or close to it, two fighters inevitably passed each other close aboard. We called this the Merge. Closing somewhere north of a combined thousand miles an hour meant the Merge is over in mere seconds. Before a collision, we'd break away, showing our first, best move. That was when the hassle began.

There was no script for what happened after the Merge. We reacted to each other, flying our aircraft as best we could. We learned that power is king. Power gives you the ability to climb above a fight to reenter it with even more energy in a diving attack. Power means you can push your bird in a tighter and tighter turn and maintain your airspeed longer.

The Ford had tons of power. It was nimble, quick, and a hard target. It was an adrenaline rush to push to the edge of its performance envelope. Usually just a full turn or two was enough to determine who was going to win. The hassles rarely lasted more than five minutes. But that's an eternity in aerial combat, a world where split seconds make the difference between victory and defeat.

When we had enough and were ready to admit defeat—maybe our opponent gained position at six o'clock and never let go—we waggled our wings, pulled up alongside our opponent, and flew wing to wing. Sometimes we smiled unseen behind our oxygen masks and waved. *Nice fight, brother.* Sometimes we just eyeballed each other, pissed off that somebody had gotten the better of us. Invariably somebody out there was a little better than I was, but each time I went out, win or lose, I improved.

These fights required real physical endurance. The hard maneuvering threw you around inside the cockpit and put heavy G forces on your body. That first day left me almost intoxicated with exhaustion. I felt more alive in that world than anywhere else. The rush is that powerful.

Afterward, I decided I'd go out and hassle at Whiskey 291 every chance I could. I wanted to learn, and the best way to learn was by running up against a pilot with more experience than you. If you lost, you lived to learn again. But some of our guys would rather die than lose. They were the ones I looked for. We'd push our birds to the absolute utmost, and sometimes beyond.

If the planes were different models, it sometimes came down to what airframe had more power and agility. Both pilots would pull the stick into their stomachs, draining power to tighten their turns as they tried to gain an edge on their opponent. The most aggressive pilots would "pull well into the buffet," as we said. A fighter on the verge of a stall falls out of controlled flight for a moment, then recovers. You can feel it in the seat of your pants and in the stick. Then the entire aircraft shakes. If you keep pulling and don't ease up, the fighter will stall, snap-roll inverted, and begin falling. It's easy for your opponent to whip around and eat your lunch. The best pilots know exactly how far to pull into the buffet and keep the plane from stalling. In the air, tiny advantages make a difference.

More than once, I watched two planes battling it out in the vertical, going straight up after each other like rockets, burners lit. They'd reach the edge of their respective flight envelope and enter an inverted spin. You could tell it had happened when the engine's smoke trail started streaming over the plane's belly and beyond the nose as the plane sank earthward, tail first, wings no longer gripping the sky. Those were dangerous moments, but with enough altitude for seven or eight revolutions, you could pull out of it.

I learned the basics of air combat in those hassles. Never lose sight of your opponent: "Lose sight, lose the fight." Never go vertical unless you can own it, meaning you have enough pure engine power to blast skyward and leave your opponent unable to follow you and hammer you from behind. Turning fights are like back-alley brawls. When similar aircraft engage like that, the difference is pilot skill and aggressiveness. The winner usually is the one with the most guts to push his aircraft to its aerodynamic limit.

To win, you had to feel the aircraft, know exactly where you were based on visual cues with the horizon or the ground. Maybe you take a quick look at your fuel gauge, or glance at the altimeter once or twice. But that was it. This kind of flying requires your eyeballs out of the cockpit as much as possible. If you glance down in the middle of a scrap at a pivotal moment, you're liable to lose your target in the split second it takes your brain to process and your eyes to refocus on the switch from instruments to blue sky.

Every pilot had his own bag of tricks. We learned by watching other guys beat us with them. Others we picked up in late-night shop talk in the Coronado bars. Unusual maneuvers, little ways to extract just a bit more performance from your aircraft and other jewels, were shared and discussed. The knowledge—and liquor—flowed with equal speed in those sessions.

Sometimes we ignored the hard deck. That's when it truly became a game played on guts, the two of us twisting and turning in a roller-coaster maneuver we called the "rolling scissors." I'd see my opponent coming in behind me, looking to make a high-speed pass. To counter, I'd pull up and roll inverted. The attacker would pass right below my canopy, and so I'd lower the nose and roll back toward him in a dive. This made my pursuer my target—though a fleeting one. I would have a tiny window to take a high-deflection shot at him as he pulled hard into me, then he had the chance to barrel roll and pursue me as I went past. Each time we crossed paths—that was the scissors. Picture the flight paths intersecting like the X of a pair of scissors, chopping away at the sky. Two evenly matched pilots could do this over and over. Often we dropped below five thousand feet and stayed after each other until we were on top of the whitecaps. Real combat has no hard deck.

In this way we preserved our perishable skill sets and kept alive the fading art of the dogfight. The rest of the Navy was letting it slip away in the early 1960s. I flew whenever I could. Holidays were great times to hassle, because the married guys were home with their families and the pace of activity on base relaxed. I was still trying to get over Mary Beth, so I'd climb in a Ford and go look for a good fight.

Some of the best pilots flew the Navy's Vought F-8 Crusader. In later years, the F-8 would be called "the last of the gunfighters" because it carried four 20mm cannon and five hundred shells. The F-8 community had learned to dogfight in the Fleet Air Gunnery Unit, which disbanded in 1960. They were indeed the last of their breed. And boy, were they good.

We could outclimb the F-8, but they could reach 1,200 mph in burner, while we could only get to just above Mach 1—740 mph. The Crusader, in the hands of a good pilot, was a world-beater. With a Skyray, we needed a turning contest. That big bat wing gave us the edge here, and we could turn inside the heavier F-8. Drag 'em down to the hard deck (or below) and turn and fight. That was our win. The best F-8 guys knew better, and they stayed in the Crusader's envelope, using their speed and power, where they could dictate the terms of the fight.

Fighting against different types of planes was useful. It taught me more than fighting against the same type of plane I was piloting. In later years at Topgun we would call it "dissimilar air combat training." But back in the late 1950s, we didn't have a name for it. We just intuited it based on experience. Each fight with a different type of aircraft, each with its own advantages and weaknesses, taught us how to exploit our edge and minimize theirs. How did we learn? By losing. Failure is a teacher. Be honest with yourself, extract the lessons, and you'll never make that error again. I spent many long flights back to North Island replaying what I did wrong, so that on my next bout in the interservice fight club, I'd bring the heat and win. When we founded Topgun, this part of the experience in Whiskey 291 became a very important component of our culture.

A few days before Christmas in 1958, it was a quiet time at the squadron. Most everyone had gone home. I had been going home on weekends. I was eager to have news about Mary Beth. On one visit I saw her after a Whittier College football game. She was with her new beau. I waved at her, trying to hide my sadness. As she offered a furtive wave, I noticed tears in her eyes. After that, I went home less frequently and spent my weekends flying.

One day down at maintenance control, I checked out a Ford and took off out over the ocean. It was a crisp winter morning, without a cloud in the sky. Once I got to altitude, I could see for almost two hundred miles. The view was simply breathtaking.

Instead of heading out to San Clemente, I turned north toward Los Angeles and my folks' home. I hadn't gone far when a pair of contrails caught my attention off to my right. They were *vertical* contrails, in the restricted airspace around Edwards Air Force Base. *Somebody is getting it on.*

I couldn't resist. I banked my Skyray east to see who was hassling. I came upon an F-8 locked in a wild duel with an Air National Guard F-86. As I closed, I could see from the markings that the Crusader belonged to a squadron based at Miramar. Those guys were damn good. To my surprise, though, the F-86 pilot was eating the F-8's lunch. As I closed in, the Crusader quit. The two planes linked up, and the F-8 waggled his wings and broke for home.

I slid alongside the Sabre. *I'm your Huckleberry.*

The National Guard pilot studied me and my Ford. He nodded. I nodded. He flipped me the bird—the magic signal—and I flipped it back.

Game on.

We broke forty-five degrees and separated to a distance of about seven miles. Before turning back for the Merge, I checked my altitude. Twenty-seven thousand feet. Part of me wondered if this was too risky. On such a clear day, surely people below could see what we were doing. What if someone called Edwards, reporting us?

No time to worry. I checked those concerns as I wheeled around and barreled straight for the F-86 with the pride of my service on the line. It was time to avenge my Crusader brother.

The Sabre and I hit the Merge at more than a thousand miles an hour, and I broke hard to start the fight that suited the F4D best: a horizontal turning battle.

I made a one-eighty and saw him already in the horizontal, turning for me. Wings vertical, we watched each other from out of the tops of our canopies. A full three-sixty later, he had gained a good angle on me, closing on my tail. I started to sweat. I turned as sharply as I could, and the plane began to buffet, losing speed. By the second revolution, the Air National Guard pilot was pinned to my six.

In a real combat situation, tracer rounds would have been streaking past my windscreen. I had to do something fast, so I lit the afterburner and went vertical. No way could a Korean War–vintage aircraft hang with me there.

I rocketed straight up, trading energy for altitude. When I got up above him, I could trade it back. I came down on him in a subsonic dive and made a pass. He juked out of the way and rolled into a dive after me.

As my Skyray pushed toward Mach 1, the F-86 stayed on me. I pulled back up into the vertical, but found I couldn't shake him. I had the superior aircraft; he was the superior pilot. In two and a half minutes, with the Sabre on my six, I had to admit defeat. I rocked my wings. He joined up on me as we made a slow turn toward the L.A. basin. He nodded and saluted me. I returned it, then headed for North Island.

Not long after I landed, somebody told me I had a phone call from the Air National Guard's 146th Fighter Wing at Van Nuys. A lump formed in my throat. Had I been reported? On the other line was a major, probably one of the wing's squadron leaders. He asked me if I'd been up in an F4D over Edwards airspace. I said yes.

"You're not bad, son," he said, "but you've got a lot to learn."

We talked the fight over. I learned his F-86 had an afterburner too. Earlier versions didn't. I wondered if that's how he beat me. At length, I finally said, "Hey, no other phone calls, okay, sir?"

"Oh, no calls. I wouldn't do that to you, son." He knew the rules of the game.

We hung up, and I never spoke to him again. But boy, the lesson he gave me that holiday's eve lingered for the rest of my career. When you pick a fight, you better know the capabilities of the aircraft you are facing. And it's a dangerous mistake to assume you're better than your opponent. When you start a fight, you should always assume you're facing the very best. Otherwise, chances are you're going to have a really bad day.

The road to my longest season of bad days began almost as soon as I got my orders to leave VF(AW)-3. I reported to VF-121 at Miramar to transition to a brand-new McDonnell Douglas bird, the F3H Demon. In late 1962, I joined the Black Lions of Fighter Squadron 213 (VF-213). In February 1963, we deployed on board the carrier USS *Hancock* and spent the next eight months in the western Pacific.

Naval aviation is the tip of the American spear. Wherever trouble brews, the aircraft carriers go. When the *Hancock* went into the South China Sea our purpose was to send a message to the Red Chinese: Lay off Taiwan.

It was not a pleasant experience.

CHAPTER FIVE

WHERE ARE THE CARRIERS?

Off the Saigon River, South Vietnam
November 3, 1963

Black night. No moonlight for the nuggets. Not even a star visible thanks to the storm clouds stacked from a thousand feet on up to heaven. USS *Hancock*'s wooden flight deck was slick from intermittent tropical downpours. The old girl was almost twenty years old now, a carrier built in wartime with funds raised by the John Hancock life insurance company. This wooden deck had seen everything from fires inflicted by exploding Japanese kamikazes to raging typhoons off Southeast Asia. She sat in mothballs during Korea, but as the Cold War intensified, the need for more flight decks grew urgent. The Navy pulled her from the fleet reserve in Bremerton, Washington, and updated her with an angled flight deck and four steam catapults for jet operations.

Two decades after joining the fight against Imperial Japan, the *Hanna* found itself in the middle of a new crisis in the western Pacific.

Aboard this storied flattop, I sat in the cockpit of my McDonnell F3H Demon interceptor on the alert five catapult, watching the deck crew hustle around me. Lacking inspiration? Watch a deck crew in action, especially at night. It was one of the most tightly choreographed performances you'll ever see. Every member of that team worked in complete harmony in one of the most dangerous work environments you can imagine. Their margin for error is so slight—one wrong move and the sailor can get sucked into an engine or blown overboard by the exhaust blast. Yet they work in this danger zone of roaring afterburners and high-tension cables with fearlessness and focus. It is an awesome sight to see.

That night, I couldn't see much. Just flashlights moving around and glowing yellow wands giving me signals from the deck on the left side of the cockpit. I could just make out the dim outlines of the flight-deck crew by the glow of their lights.

The conductor of this little symphony was called the shooter. An experienced commissioned officer, he wore a yellow shirt and carried a pair of those yellow glowing wands. He gave the order to fire the catapult when the time came to send me on my way.

Getting ready to go, another yellow shirt, the flight-deck director, waved me forward to the catapult track. I eased off the brakes. As the nose wheel reached the catapult shuttle and nestled in, I set the brakes again and made sure the foldable wings were locked in place. Sailors swarmed under the Demon. Red-shirted ordnancemen pulled the arming pins out of my four AIM-7 Sparrow missiles, our radar-guided air-to-air weapons. Another team slung a bridle behind my nose wheel and attached it to the shuttle in the catapult track. I felt a bump as the Demon went into tension, the catapult locked and loaded, ready to sling me off the bow.

I wasn't supposed to be on the catapult that night. I was due for shore leave in Hong Kong, one of the best of all possible ports of call. Great food and nightlife, and deals on Rolex watches. Before we could enjoy any of it, the *Hancock* received an emergency sail order. We weighed anchor at 0830 and sped southwest with a pair of destroyers. We had no idea what was happening, other than that some kind of crisis was afoot and a carrier was needed off Vietnam.

My very first cruise gave me a front-row seat to U.S. naval power projection in action. Deployed to WestPac, we guarded the sea lanes, trained off the coast of Japan, and flew the flag at various ports of call. Our F3H Demons intercepted Soviet bombers that periodically dropped down to snoop on us. We'd chase them as soon as our radars caught them coming down from Vladivostok. When the Tupolev Tu-95 Bears took their photos of us, we wanted a Demon in the frame. Proving up our ability to destroy them at will was a game we played with the Russians for the entire Cold War. More than once, I watched a Russian gunner wave at me as I snapped pictures through the canopy. Such moments were rare and fleeting, just two aircrew at the tip of the spear, making momentary personal contact at altitude over the world's largest ocean.

Truth was, my transfer to VF-213 and the two ensuing deployments were like the sophomore blues. On my first deployment, the Black Lions were led by a skipper who pushed the young guys hard. Too hard, occasionally. As the squadron safety officer, I watched him make several bad decisions and finally couldn't stand idly by. After one of our pilots, apparently exhausted, died in a preventable deck accident—after landing and getting free of the arresting cable, he just slid to the edge of the flight deck and fell over to his death—I urged the skipper to dial it down or other guys were going to die. He ignored me, and later wrote up an unsatisfactory fitness report that described me as "disloyal." This second deployment went more smoothly without him.

When it was conceived in the early 1950s, the Demon was powered by a Westinghouse J40, supposedly a world-beater. It proved to be a dog. It failed constantly, killed pilots, and never produced the thrust the Demon needed to be an effective interceptor. The Navy canceled the Westinghouse contract and equipped the F3H with an Allison engine designed for the B-66 bomber. Even with the upgrade, transitioning from the Skyray to the Demon was like trading in a Porsche for a Dodge.

In cold, wet weather, the engines tended to fail when the metal housing around the Allison shrank, causing the turbine blades to scrape the inside of the enclosure. Though this merited a full redesign of the engine, there was no money in the Navy budget for it. Instead, the manufacturer shaved a small amount off the turbine blades. Problem solved, right? Yes. But the solution detuned the engine, leaving the Demon underpowered and slow to accelerate. Once up to flying speed, it handled nicely enough, though it was no bat-winged Ford.

I do miss my days flying that plane. You never forget taking off from a carrier. At night and ready to launch, the deck crew raises the jet blast deflector, a sheet of hardened steel that protects everyone aft of my Demon from the engine's exhaust. Scanning the instruments, I see that everything is in the green. A quick glance forward reveals nothing but blackness. I can't even see the end of the flight deck.

The red shirts back out from beneath my wings, having armed my missiles. A final check by other crewmen and I'm clear to go. Advancing the throttles, I hear the engine spool up.

I look over at the shooter's yellow wands. He signals me to light the afterburner. A whoosh and bright reddish glow erupt behind me as a long tongue of flame shoots out the Demon's exhaust pipe. Seconds away now.

I lean my head back, pressing against the ejection seat. If you don't, you'll have a sore neck as the catapult slings you forward. Simultaneously, I use the catapult grip that holds my throttle in place, so my hand doesn't reflexively pull it backward as I accelerate. Lastly, I jam my right elbow into my hip, so I don't accidentally pull the control stick back, overrotate the nose, and stall out. You can easily do that on a pitch-black night with absolutely no horizon. What a way to go.

The shooter leans forward and brings his wand down to the deck—the launch order.

The catapult fires, and the shuttle rushes in its track toward the bow. I go from zero to a 150 miles an hour in two seconds flat.

God, I miss it.

Halfway toward the bow of the deck and I am already flying the aircraft. In such moments, you don't look out at the darkness ahead. Rather, you're entirely focused on the instruments once your eyeballs are uncaged and your vision returns. A moment later, I feel the wheels leave the deck. The bridle drops free, and I raise the landing gear.

Nothing to it, really. That night, I sped to altitude and to my assigned patrol station off the Saigon River, never breaking clear of the weather. What a terrible night to be flying, but the situation in South Vietnam was briefed to be critical. Of course, they didn't give us any details. If we'd been able to watch the evening news broadcast back home, we'd have learned that an Army-led coup was underway in Saigon against Ngo Dinh Diem, the despot who had run the country into the ground over the past eight years. Regime loyalists and rebels battled in the streets as chaos engulfed the nation. Diem and his brother had been captured by rebels the day before and rumors abounded that they had either committed suicide or had been executed.

The Navy wanted the *Hancock* on scene should the situation spin out of control. If an evacuation of the American military advisers in the country was necessary, we would provide air cover. That night, though, exactly what I could do with my air-to-air missiles, in storm clouds above twenty thousand feet, was anyone's guess.

I patrolled in complete darkness. Somewhere behind me was my wingman, but we never had visual on each other from the moment we left the *Hancock*'s deck. It was that kind of night.

I don't remember who was up with me that night, but if it was Lieutenant John Nash, I know I wouldn't have needed to worry about him. Nash joined the Black Lions not long after I arrived. He was serious, intense, and utterly driven. What he lacked in humor aboard ship he more than made up for in the air. He was a relentless, aggressive pilot who backed up his self-confidence with simply incredible flying. He was one of the rarest: a man seemingly born to fly, as if it were coded into his DNA. In later years, I counted him among the ten best fighter pilots I've ever known. He coined the phrase "I'd rather die than lose." That was his mission statement. He lived it fully, in training and in combat. I would later use his enormous talent when I chose him as an Original Bro at Topgun.

The Demon was equipped with an excellent airborne radar system. As I bored holes in the cave-dark night, I kept my eyes on the radar. Could those Russian Bears drop down for a visit this far from Vladivostok? Did the North Vietnamese have an air force? I had no idea. But somebody wanted us up there that night for a reason.

I peered out into the darkness for a moment. It was easy to get vertigo in such black conditions. Try standing in a closet with the lights off for ten or twenty minutes, and you'll start to lose your balance. Your inner ear gets confused. Your senses send confusing messages to your brain. Now imagine that closet moving at 450 knots, without any point of reference in sight. Again, you embrace your instrument training and trust the gauges and dials on the panel in front of you.

This is all well and good until the power fails and your panel lights go out. A Demon did that to me on our first cruise the year before, and I never quite trusted the bird afterward.

That night was very similar to this one, except we broke out above the cloud layer at fifteen thousand feet. No moon, no visible horizon. My Demon suffered electrical failure and the lights went out in the cockpit. A wind-powered auxiliary unit was supposed to deploy in such a situation, but that failed as well. There I was, surrounded by absolute darkness, using a ninety-degree-angled flashlight to periodically check my instruments. I was flying that mission with our squadron executive officer, Lieutenant Commander Joe Paulk, who realized my predicament and came to my rescue.

Joe signaled to me with his flashlight, *Follow me*, and pointed back to *Hancock's* latest position.

It was an eerie sensation flying on his wing in the dark en route to the *Hancock's* waiting deck. I forced myself to keep my wings level relative to his wing and belly navigation lights. I used small, precise control inputs, made easier by Joe's smooth flying.

We broke out of the cloud layer about a mile and a half astern of the ship. We could see the white strobes beckoning us. I continued flying Joe's wing until his lights went out and he turned away to give me a clear shot at the deck.

The electrical failure had knocked out my radio, which meant I could not talk to the landing signal officer. All I could do was watch his lights: A green one meant to keep coming. Flashing reds would be the dreaded wave-off—go around and try again. I didn't have enough fuel for that, so if I missed I'd have to eject, trusting that somebody would find me in the stormy sea.

I made it down and felt the tail hook catch one of the deck wires. The Demon lurched to a halt. A close call for sure, but it wasn't over.

The next night, while flying the same Demon, the same thing happened again. I was on Joe's wing, and he brought me back to the *Hancock* in an encore performance. I landed safely after another gut-check approach. Perhaps we joked about him saving me twice.

Fighter pilots never like to reveal weakness or fear to each other. The fact is, I went belowdecks and sat alone for a while, trying to drink a cup of coffee as I tried to figure the odds of *two* electrical failures on consecutive moonless nights. That same aircraft had flown perfectly twice during the daylight between my events.

I said a prayer in the wardroom, coffee cup in hand. *Thank you, God, for making sure Joe was there to help me get back to my family.*

Over the South Vietnamese coast, a year later, my radar swept the sky ahead of me and found nothing. The panel lights glowed reassuringly as my eyes scanned across the instruments. Nothing out of the ordinary. Just another night in heavy weather on the ocean frontier. Still, those two electrical failures remained in the back of my mind. Should the worst happen, I had triple checked my ninety-degree flashlight to make sure it worked and remained in easy reach in a flight suit pocket. Little pieces of gear can make all the difference in a critical moment.

My radio crackled. The controller on the ship below gave me a vector. Something was up offshore and he wanted us to drop down to investigate. Into the heart of the scud layer we went, navigation lights burning orange holes in the milky soup around us.

At fifteen hundred feet, we still had not found the bottom of the cloud layer. Suddenly, a muzzle flash lit the blackness below. Another flash strobed the sky, revealing holes in the cloud layer. A warship was down there on the water, firing its main batteries. I began to get vertigo.

Get a hold of yourself, Dan. Trust the instruments.

Dizzy and lightheaded, I felt like I was floating. My body told me we were heading one way while my instruments told a completely different story. I might have been descending but did not know how to move the stick. Finally, returning to my instruments, I was able to recover from the vertigo.

A final salvo of naval gunfire, like yellow-red lightning, flared underneath me. I forced myself to focus on the instrument panel while my world tilted crazily. When the sensation passed, I leveled off and reported the gunfire to our controller on the *Hancock*. "What do you want me to do?" I asked.

What could we do? We didn't have bombs or unguided rockets. The Demon was configured for an air-to-air fight. It had a pair of cannon, but the Black Lions rarely flew with loaded guns—the shells were extra weight that the already underpowered bird didn't need. The *Hancock* ordered us to return to the ship. We banked away from whatever fighting raged on the wavetops and fought our way through the overcast for another white-knuckle carrier landing.

When I was three miles astern, they gave me corrections to stay on the centerline of the glide path all the way to the deck. The ship appeared ahead of me. I held my approach and listened as the LSO coached me down. I dropped on the deck and felt the hook catch the three wire. Good landing. The aircraft functioned beautifully, and I lived to record another night landing in my logbook.

After my wingman got down safely, we went below for the debrief. Who had been shooting at whom? We never learned. Maybe it was one of our destroyers offshore, supporting some of our advisers in some battle right off the beach. Maybe it was a South Vietnamese warship shooting at rebel units involved in the coup. It was a foretaste of what was to come in the years ahead. We'd just witnessed a naval action almost a year before the Gulf of Tonkin incident pulled America into Vietnam's civil war.

Somewhere after midnight, my head hit the pillow. Sleep did not come. I couldn't help dwelling on the narrow margin we lived in on these night missions. Bad weather. Vertigo. System failures. Landing in total darkness. The risks never gave me pause. Well, unless we lost somebody. I just never thought it might be me. But things were different for me now, and in that moment, I felt mortal.

Mary Beth had gotten married to her football player. I never tried to win her back. Her marriage was the final nail in the coffin of my wishful thinking. I had to let her go. Eventually, I met a wonderful young woman in Coronado, Maddi, and married her in 1959. A year later, our daughter, Dana, arrived. My wife and I began a seventeen-year journey in Navy life, with far too much time apart.

Flying is a dangerous game of risk versus reward. Push too far and you pay the price. Before I joined the Black Lions, I only had to look out for myself and my squadron mates. Different game now. I lived for two others who depended on me. Becoming a family man coincided with my first fleet assignment aboard the *Hancock*. My 1962 deployment lasted from February to November. We got back to the West Coast and started training for the next one, running simulated intercepts in our Demons three or four nights a week. On that schedule, even when we were at home we were not really home. I've already explained what that did to families. Our 1963 deployment began in the spring after being home for less than six months. Hugs, goodbyes, tears on cheeks. Dana's little hand pressed into mine. Then back to the ship to manage a long-distance relationship through handwritten letters, voice messages on cassette tapes, and an occasional phone call.

The second parting for my family was worse than the first. I didn't want to be a stranger to my own daughter, but what choice did I have? The Navy needed me on the other side of the Pacific; it was my sworn duty to go.

We did not stay long off South Vietnam. The new military junta restored order surprisingly quickly in the wake of Diem's death even as the war against the Communist insurgency continued. Three weeks later, after John F. Kennedy was shot to death in Dallas, Lyndon Johnson was sworn in as president. The *Hancock* sailed for home port a few days after the assassination. We reached San Diego on December 15, 1963, to a joyous reunion. It was our last peacetime holiday season for a decade, and the only "home by Christmas" moment that many of us ever shared.

CHAPTER SIX

THE PATH TO DISILLUSIONMENT

Pearl Harbor, Hawaii
January 1967

I stood at attention on the flight deck of the *Enterprise* as the world's first nuclear-powered aircraft carrier steamed slowly in the channel past Hospital Point. A couple of tugs hove to, but were not needed. Every skipper in the Navy knew this channel like his own hometown.

Ahead and off to port, USS *Arizona* lay in her grave. Above the national memorial, her flag flew proudly, the Stars and Stripes full in the wind. Beneath it lay the remains of more than a thousand sailors, killed on the first day of war on December 7, 1941, a full generation earlier. The USS *Arizona* Memorial is the closest thing to a shrine that the Navy has, this side of John Paul Jones's crypt at the Naval Academy. Ever since that day of infamy, it has been tradition to render honors to those sailors whenever a warship arrives in Pearl Harbor. A flight-deck parade was the order of the day. A voice came over the ship's loudspeaker, "Attention on deck, hand salute!" As one, the crew of the *Enterprise* touched our foreheads with our right hands and held position.

I'd done this before aboard the *Hancock*, but it was different now, and everyone could feel it. Some of my shipmates held back tears in their eyes. After three years of war, we knew the cost. All those men, entombed in that shattered hull. Airpower did this.

After this short stop at Pearl, my unit, Fighter Squadron 92, would be on its way to Yankee Station, the patch of water in the Gulf of Tonkin where our carriers operated against the North Vietnamese. VF-92, known as the Silver Kings, would join President Johnson's three-year-long air campaign against North Vietnam, Operation Rolling Thunder.

I held the salute as we steamed past the *Arizona*, oil still rising to the surface from her rusted fuel bunkers after all these years. The white memorial was filled with people, civilian tourists mainly, who looked away from the names of the dead to behold the Big E sliding through the channel with a thousand men at rigid attention in their tropical whites.

I'd returned from sea duty aboard *Hancock* just as the last hopes to avert war in Vietnam were dashed. As the Gulf of Tonkin incident drew the United States into an open-ended, overt commitment, I received orders sending me to the fleet antiair warfare training center at Point Loma in San Diego. While other aviators went to war, I was on the beach, helping the Navy evolve from analog technology to digital battle management, developing computer systems for our shipboard combat information centers. After two cruises on *Hancock* it was a welcome rest. I enjoyed two good years ashore with my wife and daughter.

In August 1964, the president authorized airstrikes against Communist targets. On August 5, Everett Alvarez, the son of Mexican immigrants who settled in Salinas, California, was shot down while piloting an A-4 Skyhawk bomber. The first U.S. naval aviator to be taken by the North Vietnamese, he endured more than eight years of torture in captivity.

I thought of the friends I'd lost since that first accident a few months after joining VF(AW)-3. Since then, the roster of the killed, missing, or wounded had grown long. Vietnam was chewing us up just as the Navy was trying to maintain America's global commitments elsewhere, from the Atlantic to the Indian Ocean. A lot of guys started getting out. When Rolling Thunder started, I was home. I was tempted to get out too. The airlines were hiring, offering salaries double or triple what we made as naval aviators. But I wasn't wired to be an airline pilot.

Whenever I was in San Diego, I went to North Island to see an old neighbor from my VF(AW)-3 days, Roger Crim. He was in charge of test flying the aircraft that had been patched up at the maintenance and overhaul facility. He usually let me check out a repaired bird. Thanks to him and one of his chiefs, I was able to fly everything from an F6F Hellcat to the aircraft that replaced the Demon, its larger, twin-engine cousin, the McDonnell F-4 Phantom II.

The first time I flew the Phantom, feeling the rush of reaching Mach 2, convinced me to stay in the Navy. When my tour of duty ashore came to an end, I arranged to receive orders to train to fly the new fighter, before joining a squadron on the *Enterprise*.

After ten years of flying fighters, I felt ready and confident. I'd aced the F-4 training at VF-121, the West Coast's replacement air group (RAG) for the Phantom community. This squadron prepared all new F-4 crews for their Vietnam deployments. We flew constantly, training hard at our beyond-visual-range missile intercepts. We even got to shoot a drone down with a Sparrow, one of the only times I'd actually fired one of these new high-tech weapons. On the ground, our instructors gave us intelligence briefs and taught us about our weapons and sensor systems. Then came survival training. We had to escape and evade the enemy force (our instructors) as if we had ejected into hostile territory. After a few days, I was captured—everyone was—and thrown into a thirty-six-by-twenty-four-inch wooden box with just a couple of breathing holes. When I made the mistake of revealing to the "enemy" guards my fear of spiders, they made sure to let me live with one for a while in that box. One cold night it crawled right across my face. This, of course, was nothing next to what the North Vietnamese were doing to our downed aviators.

After a few days in Pearl, we were on our way west to Sasebo, Japan. Our arrival was met by massive protests. Students and radicals opposed the Vietnam War. Others protested the first-ever appearance of a nuclear-powered ship not far from Nagasaki, which had been devastated by an atomic bomb on August 9, 1945. Armed with clubs and throwing rocks, the protesters tried to storm the base. The police, wielding truncheons, water cannon, and bare knuckles, needed two days to return the Japanese city to its natural state: quiet law and order. Things were raw then. When the carrier *Oriskany* called at Sasebo around the same time we did, we learned that its air wing had lost half its aircraft over North Vietnam, and had suffered a third of its aircrews either killed, wounded, or missing in action. Their casualty list eventually included Lieutenant j.g. John McCain, the future senator from Arizona who was captured in October 1967.

Only a few weeks before our ships crossed paths, one of *Oriskany*'s F-8 pilots, Lieutenant Commander Dick Schaffert, fought an epic duel against six North Vietnamese MiG-17s and MiG-21s. He had been escorting an A-4 Skyhawk strike when they were attacked. Schaffert fired all three of his Sidewinder missiles, but each malfunctioned or missed. When he switched to his 20mm cannon, the high-G maneuvering jammed the pneumatic feed system, leaving him defenseless. Nevertheless, he stalemated the MiGs with an exceptional display of flying before slipping away on the dregs of his remaining fuel. Other *Oriskany* fighters showed up a moment later and downed one of the MiGs. They fired seven missiles in that fight. Only one hit.

Aboard the *Enterprise*, we didn't know any of this at the time, but there was enough scuttlebutt to give us a sense that the intel briefings back in California had been anything but thorough. We didn't know what we didn't know. The enemy was a mystery to us. We didn't know their current capabilities; we didn't know anything about their tactics. The intelligence officers who briefed us talked a lot about the antiaircraft weapons we would face, as well as the surface-to-air missiles the North Vietnamese received from the Soviet Union. We heard that MiG interceptors were based near Hanoi, but learned little of those airfields, or the geography and weather of North Vietnam. I assumed that as we got closer to Yankee Station, we would receive more thorough briefings and get an accurate air order of battle—basically a list of North Vietnamese forces arrayed against us. That never happened. The reports that could have helped us turned out to be highly classified.

Though we were supposed to be heading to Yankee Station, a crisis developed off North Korea. En route to Subic Bay in the Philippines, we received orders to reverse course and speed to the Korean Peninsula. The North Koreans had sent a commando team to assassinate the president of South Korea, then captured a U.S. Navy vessel, USS *Pueblo,* in international waters. Four torpedo boats, MiG-21 fighters, and two submarine chasers pursued the little intelligence-gathering ship. Their gunfire killed a sailor from Oregon. The North Koreans then boarded the ship, captured the crew, and began torturing them. They also scooped up enough classified material and encryption gear to allow the Soviets to read certain types of U.S. Navy communications for the next twenty years.

It was humiliating. We were locked in a war seemingly without end, and now another one seemed to be flaring. The Big E steamed off Korea as a show of force.

We arrived on station to face terrible winter weather. We sailed through blizzards and snow squalls that left us unable even to see the end of the flight deck from the ship's island. Then Washington told us we would be flying patrols in these storms. Of the almost hundred pilots aboard, only six were selected to fly in that horrible weather. I was tapped to fly wing on our squadron commander, Commander T. Schenck Remsen.

Nicknamed "Skank," Remsen was one of the rarest of leaders. A talented pilot, he led from the front and always took the toughest assignments. He had a natural energy about him that inspired the junior officers, and his concern for their well-being engendered absolute loyalty to him. Naturally, when word arrived that we needed to fly a patrol along the Korean coast in a snowstorm at night, Skank took the mission.

The flight deck turned out to be covered in ice. The crew had to assist us to our F-4 Phantoms so we didn't slip and fall. Once in the cockpits, we were towed to the catapults, so we didn't slide around on the ice. A night cat shot is always an experience. Add snow flurries and heavy seas and you've got a real adventure.

We climbed above twenty thousand feet but never broke free of the storm. It was so thick that Skank and I couldn't even see each other. My back-seater, Dennis Duffy, tracked him on radar and we followed a few miles behind. Snow and ice lashed our Phantoms. The windscreen was a kaleidoscope of snowflakes. It was like flying through a snow globe.

The *Enterprise* finally vectored us to a holding pattern before we returned to the ship. As our approach time drew near, I thought it strange that they never gave us a weather report. We started our descents individually through the heart of the blizzard. Visibility was almost nil. Skank went in to land first, guided by radar from the ship. He saw nothing on that first approach. No lights, no carrier. Just blizzard and blackness. The landing signal officer said, "You sounded good when you went by us!"

When he finally landed, Skank and the landing signal officer talked to me as I swung around the ship again. Stay low. Follow the ship's wake. I got down as close to the water as I dared. Forty feet, maybe. The flight deck sits sixty-five feet off the swells. A red light began flashing in my cockpit. Low fuel. This was it. Either land or eject into the frigid seas and see how good our survival suits really were. Our life expectancy in the freezing water was five minutes. No thanks.

In the darkness, I found the carrier's white wake and followed it until I spotted the drop lights on the ship's stern ahead. They were *above* me. The landing signal officer told me to climb. I pulled the nose up. As the Phantom's nose topped the ramp, I pushed the stick forward, and an instant later, pulled back up. This was an old trick a World War II ace named Zeke Cormier taught me. It saved my and Dennis's lives that night. The Phantom touched the deck, the tail hook caught an arresting wire, and we jerked to a stop.

As we waited for the deck crew to clear us, my knees trembled and my feet shook on the brake pedals. Of all the flying I'd done to date, this was the most demanding. Why somebody in Washington wanted us in the air that night is anyone's guess. I can't think of what we accomplished in our ninety-minute sortie, other than perhaps impress the North Korean radar operators, who undoubtedly tracked our progress through the weather. We had risked our lives for nothing. Who were these politicians to play games with our lives? I'd never questioned our chain of command before, at least not above the squadron level. We trusted that our leadership would not saddle us with needless risk. But that flight was the first step down a path of disillusionment we all experienced in the western Pacific. I sat in the squadron ready room with a mug of hot coffee and a bag of popcorn. *You're all right, man. You can enjoy life again.* But our problems only got worse from there.

Not long after our *Pueblo* diversion, the *Enterprise's* air wing went into battle over North Vietnam. I flew my first combat missions filled with assumptions and expectations based on the stories I'd been told by the combat veterans I'd known. They had ripped a swath through our enemies in a way that has rarely been equaled in history. I expected to do the same over North Vietnam. But that was not how Operation Rolling Thunder rolled.

Conceived in Washington by Secretary of Defense Robert McNamara and approved by President Johnson, our bombing campaign was meant not to destroy the enemy's ability to wage war. It wasn't designed to demolish their air defense network, so we could operate over North Vietnam with impunity. It had nothing to do with tangible results or victory. It had everything to do with sending gradual messages to Hanoi. Where I had expected to be the tip of the spear, we were instead the thumb and forefinger of Lyndon Johnson's gradual escalation of pressure on the North Vietnamese. We weren't allowed to apply pressure anywhere that it might hurt. We were allowed just to pinch their metaphorical shoulder as a warning that if they didn't behave, we would pinch harder.

Gradual escalation of pressure on an enemy was a strategy conceived by people who probably had never even been in a schoolyard fight against a bully. Imagine the school bell's ringing at the end of the day. You head out to walk home, and along the way you see a bully beating up on a younger kid. You go over to help, but instead of knocking down the bully, you tap him lightly on the back of the head and say, "Keep that up, and I'll get serious!"

What's the bully going to do?

The Rolling Thunder campaign was LBJ's personal billy club. He would send us to smack the North Vietnamese for sending supplies and troops to the insurgents, then order unilateral stand-downs— known as bombing pauses—to give the North Vietnamese time to internalize the punishment and heed its lesson. But the pauses just gave them time to rearm. The American response seemed only to embolden Hanoi and convince its leadership that we were more worried about widening the war and possibly fighting China or the Soviet Union than we were about defeating them. They used the bombing pauses to resupply and prepare for the next onslaught. A lot of Americans died as a result. Some were friends of mine.

On Yankee Station, the *Enterprise* air wing learned what this meant to individual aircrews. Johnson and McNamara microman-aged the losing air war from Washington, D.C., going so far as to pick our targets. There were perhaps 150 worthwhile things to bomb in North Vietnam. Airfields, military bases, supply facilities, power plants, bridges, rail centers, oil and lubricant facilities, a few steel mills, and of course Haiphong's port facilities. As both China and Russia wanted to be Hanoi's primary ally, they tried to one-up each other with military support. Large convoys of weapons and war matériel flowed across the Chinese border into Vietnam, while the Russians heavy-hauled tanks and surface-to-air missile systems via cargo ships to Haiphong Harbor. The enemy thus had sanctuary to bring in whatever was needed, and for years.

Afraid of escalating the war, the Johnson administration refused to sanction attacks on Haiphong Harbor or the shipping there. As we started flying missions up north, we would pass near those cargo ships as they waited their turn to offload at the docks. We could see their decks crammed with weaponized MiGs and surface-to-air missiles that would shortly be used against us.

But we couldn't hit them. And we couldn't mine the harbor, either. What a tragedy. The simple execution of an off-the-shelf aerial mining plan, long before perfected during World War II and carried out in three days, could have shut down that big port—the only one of its kind in North Vietnam. But the word from the White House was no.

Those big surface-to-air missiles, as large as telephone poles, would spear up into the sky after our aircraft, homing on their radar signatures. They took a heavy toll. We could seldom bomb the missile sites for fear we might kill their Russian advisers.

When the North Vietnamese began flying Russian- and Chinese-built MiG fighters, the Navy and Air Force asked Washington for permission to bomb their airfields. The request was denied. Categories of targets that could not be struck under any circumstances included dams, hydroelectric plants, fishing boats, sampans, and houseboats. They also included, significantly, populated areas. Seeing the military value of these restrictions, the North Vietnamese placed most of their SAM support facilities and other valuable cargo near Hanoi and Haiphong—places we were forbidden to strike. The airfields around Hanoi became sanctuaries for the MiGs; the commander in chief of U.S. Pacific Command, Admiral Ulysses S. Grant Sharp, who had overall responsibility for the air war, urged the Joint Chiefs of Staff to lift the crippling restrictions. Meanwhile, the enemy fighter pilots could sit on their runways in their planes without fear of attack, waiting to scramble when our bombers showed up.

Eventually, Johnson and McNamara caved to pressure and agreed to allow strikes on the airfields. Yet they micromanaged even this, picking specific airfields and leaving others out of bounds. "It was always necessary virtually to beg target authorization out of Washington bit by piece," Admiral Sharp wrote. Instead of letting the Navy launch a blitz that might break the back of the North Vietnamese Air Force, we hit a few air bases at a time while leaving the rest unscathed.

Postwar research suggests that Hanoi occasionally received updated target lists about the same time we did on Yankee Station. Our own State Department passed the list to North Vietnamese via the Swiss government in hopes that Hanoi would evacuate civilians from the target areas. Of course they cared little about that. They simply used the valuable intel to duck the next onslaught, moving MiGs out of harm's way and bolstering antiaircraft artillery and surface-to-air missile batteries in the target areas for good measure. Destroying the MiGs on the ground proved difficult enough, but we were also ordered not to attack them in the air unless they could be visually identified and posed a direct threat.

This was a setup for failure. And it got a lot worse.

Those rules of engagement negated the way we had trained to fight in the air. The value of our F-4 Phantoms was their ability to destroy enemy planes from beyond visual range. The AIM-7 Sparrow was the ultimate expression of that new way of fighting. Track and lock with the radar system, loose the missile from ten miles out, and say goodbye to a MiG. This is how the Navy trained us to fight. We abandoned dogfight training because of the Navy's faith in missile technology. Most of our aircrews didn't know how to fight any other way. Yet our own rules of engagement kept us from using what we were taught.

The rules of engagement specifically prohibited firing from beyond visual range. To shoot a missile at an aircraft, a fighter pilot first needed to visually confirm it was a MiG and not a friendly plane. The thought of inadvertent or accidental shootdown of our brothers was of course intolerable. It did happen, sadly, in the heat of combat. Yet three years along, the training squadron in California was still teaching long-range intercept tactics to the exclusion of everything else. Our training was not applicable to the air war in Vietnam.

This played directly into the kind of fight the MiG pilots wanted.

The MiG-17 was a nimble fighter armed with cannons, but no missiles. It was old school, derived from the lessons the Soviets learned in the Korean War. With such a plane, the North Vietnamese needed to get in close and track our planes with their gunsights. They would sometimes wait to open fire on us until they were within six hundred feet. Here we were, trained to knock planes down at ten miles. The F-4 carried only missiles; it did not have an internal gun because contractors and the Pentagon believed the age of the dogfight was over.

We brought our expensive high tech into this knife fight in a phone booth. The result? The MiG pilots scored a lot more heavily than they should have.

That one-versus-six fight that the Oriskany's Dick Schaffert survived illustrated another problem. He started the day with four AIM-9 Sidewinders. On deck, just before launch, one of the missiles was found to be nonfunctional and was pulled off his aircraft. That left him three. He fired all of those at the MiGs, but none hit. His gun failed him, too.

Our weapons didn't work as advertised. I'd like to say this was an anomaly, but the exact same thing happened before Pearl Harbor with our torpedoes. Those weapons were the high-tech wizardry of the 1930s, which meant they were expensive. The Navy couldn't afford to go blow up their torpedoes in training shoots. Instead, they used a dummy warhead that would cause the torpedo to float after its run. Very few live warheads were ever detonated prior to 1941.

So imagine the surprise when the torpedoes proved to be unreliable. They ran in circles. They didn't explode. The Navy bureaucracy resisted any suggestion that the torpedoes were malfunctioning, blaming instead the frontline sailors who were supposedly using the weapons improperly. It wasn't until 1943 that the problem was finally identified and solved. It was a purely technical issue.

Over Vietnam, our Sparrow missiles usually malfunctioned or missed. So did the AIM-9 Sidewinders. How could we not have known this prior to 1965? Well, history repeats: The weapons were so expensive that the Navy could not afford to use them in training. Live-fire shooting was done against drones flying straight and level, like an unsuspecting bomber might be caught doing. We didn't know we had a problem until the weapons had to be deployed against fighters.

While we never lost air superiority over North Vietnam, the MiGs and their pilots remained a significant threat. Their success against us pointed to a larger and more ominous problem: If the 170-odd MiGs of the North Vietnamese Air Force could inflict so many casualties on us, what would happen in a war with the Warsaw Pact and the Soviets, where they would outnumber us in the air maybe five to one? If Vietnam was a preview of our performance, we would be chewed up and overwhelmed.

We had to find a way to win in spite of these technical problems and political interference. Robert McNamara was a numbers guy. Under him, the Pentagon measured success in the ground war by the body count. In the air, the metric was the number of sorties flown over North Vietnam. One sortie equals one plane flying one mission. A ten-plane raid resulted in ten sorties. This became a delusional world. A sortie counted in the total even if our bombers were forced to dump their payloads short of the target, which often happened when MiGs appeared.

Facing pressure to generate sorties, the carriers were worn ragged. Aircraft handling crews worked twelve hours on, twelve off, spotting and respotting the decks, launching strikes, recovering aircraft, arming and refueling the birds, racing to meet the sortie rate required of them. Each pilot often flew twice a day, with each mission taking several hours to brief and debrief. We flew to the edge of fatigue and beyond. Aviators who were shot down and recovered were back in action in a short few days. During the *Oriskany's* December 1967 MiG battle, Commander Schaffert flew with an undiagnosed broken back because no other pilots were available. The injury prevented him from turning his neck to check his tail. To compensate, he unstrapped his shoulder harness and swiveled his whole upper torso. If he had to eject, he probably would have died. The Bear, as he was called, is a combat legend in naval aviation. He survived Vietnam to become a respected author on the war's history.

While the tempo took a heavy toll, it also led to needless tragedies, including major fires aboard our carriers that were the result of exhausted crews making mistakes. Scores of sailors and aviators died in those accidents, and the fires on two carriers were serious enough to risk the loss of the ship.

We were losing good men needlessly in the push to maintain the sortie rate. Why? Competition between the services. With the Air Force and Navy battling furiously for appropriations, both were determined to outdo the other in sorties flown.

In 1967, just before the *Enterprise* arrived in the Gulf of Tonkin, the Navy and Air Force ran into a severe shortage of ordnance. With peacetime levels of production unable to supply the war's demands, the Pentagon resorted to buying back thousands of bombs that had been sold to our NATO allies, paying inflated rates. They took old iron bombs out of World War II–era storage. The carriers still had to fly many missions short on bombs. Instead of two planes carrying the available ordnance, six or eight would be used. That way, when

McNamara saw the daily numbers, he didn't see any drop in the Navy's performance.

When the war revealed these weaknesses, the Washington bureaucracy was so moribund it could not find solutions. It kept us doing the same thing over and over with the same results: The North Vietnamese doubled down in supporting the insurgency in South Vietnam while we flew ourselves to exhaustion.

This has been a fast summary of a pervasive, serious, multilayered crisis. I can assure you it was far harder to experience it than it has been to write about it. The problem has been well explained in many other books. But it was real. It was tragic. And it was a bitter experience for those of us who survived it.

The only difference in my telling is that I would be given the responsibility of doing something to fix the problem. I'll get to that story in a moment. But first I'll have to show you how a carrier air wing survived a tour on Yankee Station in 1968.

CHAPTER SEVEN

YANKEE STATION EDUCATION

Yankee Station, off the coast of Vietnam
Early 1968

I stood in the locker space next to our squadron ready room, donning G-suit, boots, gloves, and packing my survival gear for the next mission. I reached into my locker and grabbed my Ray-Bans. More than a decade old, they came with me on almost every flight. As I took my helmet from my flight bag, I found my little stuffed mouse. Still there in his nest, beaten up from transoceanic travel, he peered out at me with the same stoic expression that caught my eye in that unvacated locker at North Island.

Hey there, fella.

The mouse was my good-luck charm. Thousands of hours in high-performance jets. Combat over Vietnam. Night landings aboard old carriers—that critter saw me through all of it. I thought about giving him to Dana. She was eight now and would probably love him. Then I remembered his original owner. I had no right to gift this toy. His home would always be in my flight bag. I'd have to get my little girl something else when I got home.

When. Not if.

I gave the mouse another look, then returned the bag to my locker. Helmet in hand, I almost forgot my National Match Colt .45 pistol in its shoulder holster. Another good-luck charm that I had flown with ever since my father-in-law, Coronado's assistant chief of police, gave it to me. Retrieving it, I was good to go.

I wanted a MiG. Badly. All us fighter pilots did. But those North Vietnamese pilots were cagey and elusive, thanks to their radar ground control and the handcuffs that were locked on the wrists of those who wanted to destroy them. Weeks would pass without any American spotting a MiG. Then suddenly they would come streaking out of nowhere to tear into our thirty-plane strike formations.

I had yet to encounter one on any of my flights over North Vietnam.

Day after day, we flew missions from Yankee Station to hammer targets of questionable value. We bombed truck convoys when we could find them on search and destroy missions. They moved mostly at night in total darkness. We bombed supply depots and occasionally went after power plants, as well as military barracks long flattened by the squadrons who had deployed before us. We went after bridges and SAM sites. Very occasionally, we received permission from Washington to hit the MiG airfields around Hanoi.

The F-4 was designed from the ground up to be a Mach-plus interceptor. It was supposed to be the bane of all Soviet-built strategic bombers. Over Vietnam, the Phantom became perhaps the most versatile multirole aircraft America ever produced. Still with its interceptor heart, it functioned as an escort fighter, a utility strike bomber, and, south of the Demilitarized Zone, a close air support attack aircraft.

We were doing it all, learning on the job how best to carry out our missions. And they were never the same. But the two-a-days over the North, usually one at night, left us worn out. Lack of quality sleep also put our nerves on edge at times. We grew easily frustrated. Some people started to withdraw under the pressure, the exhaustion, and the grief over losing so many friends. This didn't happen in my squadron. Skank and the other senior pilots set the example by flying almost all the difficult missions with the junior crews, while never griping about the targets or the rules of engagement. They were great pilots as well as tremendous inspirations to all of us. Skank kept us focused and working as a team, taking care of each other as we flew daily into harm's way. In our air wing, all of the squadrons were led by example. It wasn't always that way, as some other outfits experienced.

We were losing guys to SAMs, flak, and even marauding MiGs whose pilots, well directed by radar, would launch slashing attacks into our formations. They were particularly adept at hitting the Air Force F-105 Thunderchief fighter-bombers, forcing them to jettison their ordnance and sparing the targets from being struck again.

Naval aviation and the Air Force will always be rivals as well as brothers in arms. In 1968, I felt for those Thud pilots, who took heavy losses over North Vietnam. Out of 833 F-105s built by Republic, 382 went down in Southeast Asia. Those Thud pilots were like our A-4 Skyhawk drivers—courageous and dedicated American heroes.

This afternoon, it was our turn to go beard the North Vietnamese lion. Dressed, armed, and ready to go, the pilots on the scheduled mission walked into the Strike Operations Center for the briefing. We usually went to the Strike Ops Center because that's where the ship's intelligence officers worked. We considered them lazy and figured they had no idea where our ready rooms were, so we made it easy and went to them.

As we entered, I caught sight of the day's map and my heart sank. No chance of MiGs on this run. The target area straddled the DMZ between North and South Vietnam at a place called Khe Sanh.

At the end of January, the North Vietnamese Army launched a major attack against a series of special forces outposts and the Marine firebase at Khe Sanh, which sat up on top of a flat-topped hill with all sides exposed. The embattled American and South Vietnamese troops were soon surrounded, deluged with artillery fire, and cut off from overland resupply. Helicopters and transport planes trying to get into the small airfield at Khe Sanh faced a gauntlet of antiaircraft weapons on their approach, then mortar fire as they touched down on the runway. A night assault by the North Vietnamese managed to break through the base defenses, but before they could exploit the penetration, a Marine platoon counterattacked into the charging enemy troops. In a swirling fight that evolved into a brawl with bayonets, rifle butts, and bare knuckles, the Marines threw them back.

They were holding on with sheer guts and firepower. Overhead, two Air Force B-52 Stratofortresses gave the Marines support by carpet-bombing the enemy's positions. Marine aircraft, other Air Force fighter-bombers, and now the Yankee Station air wings were joining the fight to save the firebase and the lives of the valiant men enduring the siege.

We launched late that afternoon and flew two hundred miles to our marshaling station above Khe Sanh. With the battle filling the surrounding valleys with gray-black smoke, we had only glimpses of what was happening below. The airfield was a scene of carnage. Burnt-out aircraft lay pushed to the side of the runway, victims of the mortar barrages. The base itself looked like a lunar landscape, with thousands of shell craters overlapping in the soft reddish soil.

I checked in with the Marine forward air controller whose job it was to guide us onto target. He was down there, right among those young American kids, enduring the artillery barrages and night assaults alongside them. With his radios and expertise, he was their fist of God. He was probably a Marine aviator as well, so he spoke our language and understood our perspective.

The forward air controller heard my check-in radio call and responded immediately. The situation sounded dire from his description. North Vietnamese troops were massing just beyond the wire for another night assault, and he wanted me to hit them with everything under my wings before darkness gave them the opportunity to attack again.

The late day offered a rare cloudless sky. The blue stretching above me contrasted with the ugly coils of smoke and flame filling the valley under my Phantom's nose. After receiving my instructions, I started down to begin my run.

"Keep your speed up, five hundred knots, four hundred feet, they'll be shooting at you," called the forward air controller. "Drop all your Snakes on my signal. Remember, there are Marines on the wire, just off your left wing."

I carried a dozen five-hundred-pound Mark 82 Snake Eye bombs. When we dropped these, spring-loaded air brakes or fins would deploy, and the bombs would fall virtually straight down at the point of release. It made for a very accurate weapon, plus it gave us aircrew time to get away from their explosions and fragment patterns when we were dropping from low altitude.

I leveled off at four hundred feet, going five hundred knots. The Phantom sped through clouds of smoke. From the hills to our right, small-arms fire erupted and my back-seater, Dennis Duffy, and I could see the muzzle flashes. Moments later, red-orange tracers laced the sky ahead and level with us.

With my high speed, I wasn't so concerned with taking hits from those North Vietnamese troops on the right of us whose tracers were horizontal, but I was terrified of blowing the run and dropping my Snakes on the Marines near the wire by accident. Earlier, an inexperienced Navy pilot did just that by accident and wounded some of our men.

The idea of killing Americans with a misplaced bomb? Well, I knew I would never get over that if it happened.

I listened carefully to every word the forward air controller said. If I wasn't exactly level, the bombs might fall right or left of the target area, depending on where my wings were to the horizon. Holding steady while every bad guy with an AK-47 seemed to be shooting at me was no easy feat. In fact, it was the toughest flying I'd ever done.

I checked my heading. Wings level. A split second later, the forward air controller called, "Drop! Drop! Drop!"

I pickled the Mark 82s. The F-4 lurched upward as the six thousand pounds of bombs came off our hardpoints and began falling toward the ground. Simultaneously, I pushed the throttle further and lit the burner. The Phantom's twin J79 engines responded and we pulled up with five Gs back to where we belonged—far above the fray.

Duff, my back-seater, said, "Let's haul ass, Kemosabe!"

As we climbed, my throat constricted, heart filled with dread while we waited to hear from the forward air controller. Toughest part of the mission is waiting for the results from the big grunt FAC.

Oh shit. Did I just kill a bunch of Marines?

No word from the controller. The altimeter needle spun as we speared through three thousand feet. The seconds ticked off. No word. Behind me, Dennis was probably twisted in his ejection seat, trying to see where our bombs had landed.

Oh shit...

The radio filled with static, then the forward air controller's voice shouted, "Great run! Great run! Right on target!"

I started to breathe again. Then a big smile formed under my oxygen mask. We'd done a few of these close air support runs in training, and a couple more over South Vietnam on our way to Yankee Station, but nothing like this. Those Marines were dangerously close to the release point.

One by one, my division of Phantoms made their runs, then we formed up and flew back to the ship, or home plate, as we called it. For days we flew these missions, supporting those desperate Marines. It felt good to be doing something useful. Every North Vietnamese we took out by our bombs was one less rifle pointed at our men below.

The Marines held. And as a joint Army, Marine, and South Vietnamese rescue force battled its way up Highway Nine to break the siege, the *Enterprise* air wing returned to its regularly scheduled programming over North Vietnam.

We flew day and night in any kind of weather. We flew alpha strikes, which were large, unwieldy raids of thirty or more planes. We F-4s provided escort against the MiG threat, or went in to suppress air defenses while A-4 Skyhawk attack planes struck the targets. We flew two- and four-plane armed recce missions, searching for anything worthwhile Washington allowed us to bomb.

Because we owned the airspace over their country, the North Vietnamese took to sending war matériel and men south to the war zone under the cover of darkness. To counter this, we flew at night, hunting for their vehicle convoys in hopes of catching them on the roads heading south.

The North Vietnamese guarded those truck convoys with light antiaircraft guns mounted on armored cars that looked a lot like the ones we built and supplied to the Soviets during World War II. With heavy machine guns or light cannon, they could hammer at us as we dove down to make our attacks.

The rules of engagement made it much easier for them to hit us. Washington dictated that we drop flares first, identify any trucks as military vehicles, then dive down under the flare light to deliver our attacks. The enemy quickly figured this out. Whenever we dropped a flare, their gunners would lace the illuminated area below it with tracers and exploding antiaircraft shells. We'd dive through all that incoming and get a split-second opportunity to release our bombs.

Once again, it would have been really nice to have had an internal 20mm cannon for such moments. We could have strafed our way in and suppressed some of the fire coming back at us. Instead, we just had to take it. There is nothing more frustrating than being a target that can't fight back until your bombs impact behind you.

One night, I was leading a two-plane armed reconnaissance patrol looking for movement on Highway One, which ran down the coastline. Near the port of Vinh, perhaps 160 miles from Hanoi, we caught sight of a couple of dim lights on the road.

There are no friends of mine down there, that's for sure.

Free from concern for a friendly fire incident, we looped around and decided to attack west to east along the road. Normally, either we'd make a pass and drop a flare, or one plane would drop the flare while the other attacked under it. Better yet, sometimes we delayed our attack until the flare burned out and most of the flak had stopped. We were a whole lot smarter than those rules of engagement writers back in D.C., and our being unpredictable gave the North Vietnamese gunners fits.

I'm tired of getting shot at. Screw the flares.

We carried cluster bombs that night. Think of these things as mother bombs that open up and released to spew dozens of small baby bomblets all over the area below. These hit the ground, detonate, and do their damage with thousands of whirring fragments of shrapnel. They were designed to kill troops in the open, but we found that they could cut through unarmored vehicles and set them afire. A good drop with a full load of cluster bombs from an F-4 would create a kill zone hundreds of meters in every direction. They were devastating weapons and much feared.

Down we went, my wingman trailing offset, just behind me. I released first. He followed a heartbeat later, and as we pulled off target and climbed into the dark night, two full loads of cluster bombs lit up a truck convoy filled with munitions and barrels of fuel. The fiery streaks in the air above Highway One could be seen for miles. Pilots patrolling the coast that night saw the fireworks on the horizon and asked, "What's happening down at Vinh?" That night we put a dent in the logistical train supplying the Tet Offensive in the South. These were moments to savor.

After we returned to the ship, I got a surprise. Following the debrief, some staff weenie stormed up to me and threatened to court-martial me for violating the rules of engagement. That flare I didn't drop? Yeah, that could have cost me my career, thanks to the rules of engagement and lockstep thinking of noncombat officers. I told him to pound sand. The attack was one of the most successful missions the squadron flew. It was also a reminder that in McNamara's war, the margin between a court-martial and a valor award was thin.

The missions continued, as did the losses. There were nights I got back to my bunk struggling with despair. Seeing friends die is never an easy thing. At times, you think you grow hard to it. Other times, their deaths open wounds that the heart simply cannot heal. On those nights, I would crawl under the covers and lay there, unable to sleep despite my exhaustion, mind racing.

*Could we have done anything different? Could he have gotten
out and we just didn't see the chute? Fortunately, none of them were
from my squadron.*

I'd try not to think about their families back home, but the faces
of the wives and kids would sometimes elude those efforts, and they
would come back to me in a rush. I found through my Navy career
that some men revel in the challenge and rush of combat. That
pace off Vietnam? It was their hunting ground. Me, I never got to
that point. Combat was a responsibility, even a sacred duty. That
moment as we passed the *Arizona* was a reminder of that legacy and
the connection we combat pilots shared in it. I took it very seriously,
of course, but I never liked it. Those men I would never see again,
those families I would see too soon again—they were the cost of that
adrenaline rush others craved. That was a burden I couldn't carry
and love at the same time.

The enemy always had a say, and that was the wild card in
combat. You could do everything right. Your division could do
everything right. Your chain of command could make every right
decision and lead from the front, like Skank did. Yet we faced a
cunning, devoted, and frankly courageous enemy who found ways
to surprise us with new tricks.

On those sleepless nights, my brain refusing to shut off, I would
think of those empty wardroom chairs. We lost some excellent
pilots. All the talent in the world was not enough when fate called
your number.

I didn't go to church much after I left home, but I never lost
my devotion. As the missions grew tougher and the roster of the
dead and missing grew longer, I relied heavily on that faith to see
me through. Knowing that there is a purpose, that it wasn't all
about capricious random acts of chance that could kill us, gave me a

measure of comfort that made getting into the cockpit every morning an easier task.

In those sleepless nights, which most of us out on Yankee Station had, we did our best not to think of home. It could make you cautious, hesitant in the air, get you killed. If you were wise, you never looked past the next dawn. Some combat vets would tell new guys, "Assume you're never coming back, truly believe it, and you will make it home." It was a psychological paradox of battle.

In my darkest times, I would think of Mary Beth. The heart loves who it loves. Nothing can change that. While I had not spoken to her or seen her in over a decade, I remembered every nuance of her face. I worked on my marriage every day I was home in California. I loved my wife and always would, whether we made it through the ordeals of combat and separation or not. But in my most honest moments, I knew Mary Beth would always be the love of my life, and it gave me comfort to know she was out there in the world. Most people never find their soul mate. At least I knew who mine was, even if I never saw her again.

After weeks of nonstop operations, we left Yankee Station and set course for Subic Bay for a rest period. We were wound as tight as humans can be. If you've ever watched the opening scenes of the movie *Das Boot*, you may understand the craziness we unleashed at the Cubi Point Officers' Club. These breaks from combat offered a chance to release the tension. It came out in spasms of partying, womanizing for a lot of the guys, stunts, pranks, and rivers of alcohol.

The club sat on a hill overlooking Subic Bay's mile-and-a-half-long runway. With a thatched roof, a concrete floor, and disposable plastic or metal furniture, the place pulled off the stereotypical tropical dive bar aura perfectly. We drank the beer that helped make

Andrés Soriano one of the richest men in history. His San Miguel beer cost ten cents a bottle and there was plenty to be found.

The place had catered to nearly every naval aviator who's ever done a WestPac cruise. The walls memorialized them, and in that respect our tropical dive bar was part museum, part memorial to those who came before us. Every squadron contributed plaques or photographs or memorabilia. It lent the place a hallowed feel, and in later years after Subic Bay closed down and the Navy left, the Cubi Point O Club was almost perfectly replicated back in Pensacola at the National Naval Aviation Museum. It was that important to us.

We had some unique features built into the place over the years. A local engineer and some junior officers built a small catapult track including an old aircraft cockpit with a tail hook release handle. Its propulsion system was nitrogen-powered and shot you down a short track. If you didn't get the arresting hook down to catch a wire you ended up in a tank of lukewarm water. Actually, it was probably mostly beer, though I suspected that late at night some junior officers had added other ingredients. Loud cheers followed any attempt, successful or not. The "cat track" was indifferent to the rank of the man in the cockpit. One night I watched the secretary of the Navy get very wet a couple of times.

The coiled tension sprang out of us in other ways. With lots of alcohol came an erosion of self-restraint, and those resentments built up on Yankee Station leached out of us at times. There were arguments and fights. Having learned on Yankee Station that rank alone did not make you a leader, we did not consider every superior as such. Leaders had courage, skill, and a willingness to set a good example. They took the toughest missions while working harder than everyone else. Those who did not measure up were obeyed only because of their rank and the fact that we were devoted to the discipline our Navy had instilled in us.

One night, an air wing commander who was roundly despised by his men somehow triggered his junior officers. Rank forgotten, the young guys started throwing punches. The air wing commander fought back, but, outnumbered, he was beaten to the deck. Still he refused to quit. He called out his men to bring it on, and they went at it again. Nobody intervened. That was an internal affair best resolved as warriors will. When the beatdown ended and the air wing commander lay on the deck, bloody and put in his place, his pilots looked down at him and one shouted, "Now we're even, CAG."

When you're asked to risk your life day after day for a cause that often made no sense, bound by rules that made it more likely you would die, poor leadership was often the final straw. That night, I felt grateful we had Skank Remsen leading us into the fray.

After about a week in the Philippines, we rotated back to Yankee Station, stopping along the way at a point off South Vietnam for a combat refresher. This was Dixie Station, from which we launched missions in direct support of the men fighting on the ground. There was little AAA, and no surface-to-air missiles here in the South, so these missions gave us a chance to get our heads back in the game before heading north to continue the Rolling Thunder campaign.

At the end of March, in a speech declaring that he would not run for reelection in November, Lyndon Johnson changed the entire dynamic of the air war. He announced an immediate suspension of all bombing attacks north of the 20th parallel. Just like that, Rolling Thunder was over, neutralized by a lame-duck president.

Up until then, the MiGs had been forced to operate from China, reducing their effectiveness. When LBJ told the world where we would not be bombing anymore, he essentially told the North

Vietnamese we were giving their fighter regiments a safe space again. At the same time, the new restrictions greatly reduced the Air Force's role in the air war over North Vietnam. The onus to continue it fell on the Navy.

The MiGs returned to their nests around Hanoi, the pilots rested and better trained than in the past. They studied our tactics and developed their own new ones to counter ours. It didn't take them long to come after us.

On May 7, 1968, five of our F-4s ran into what they thought was a pair of MiG-21 interceptors, one of which was piloted by Nguyen Van Coc, an ace with six American planes to his credit. The MiGs took off from Xuan Airfield and sped after an EKA-3B Skywarrior, an all but defenseless electronic warfare aircraft and tanker.

The plan was to use our Sparrow missiles and engage the MiGs once they'd been radar identified. With the airspace north of the 20th parallel essentially free of Air Force aircraft, radar could suffice to identify MiGs as they took off. No longer did we need visual identification to fire. We were going to use our interceptors as intended: missile platforms for beyond-visual-range missile shots.

The sky was hazy with broken clouds, making it perfect for our all-weather F-4s. Instead, the battle was a confused affair on both sides from the get-go. Our Phantoms raced to intercept and rescue the Skywarrior's crew, whose jamming efforts failed. As the F-4s closed, local ground defenses mistook the MiGs for American aircraft. NVA antiaircraft gunners lit up their own planes. They broke off the intercept and circled over Do Luong until their ground controller sent them after the Phantoms.

The MiGs spotted the F-4s in heavy cloud cover at about nine thousand feet. It turned out that the two lead MiG-21s tracked on American radar were bait. Trailing them were two other MiG-21s staying low over the treetops to hide from our sensors.

Four on five were the odds, and two F-4s encountered the MiGs first. A pair of Sparrows left the rails but lost their locks, missing their targets. As a cat-and-mouse game developed in the clouds, one of the F-4s got separated from the others. Nguyen Van Coc, low on fuel at this point, was about to turn for home when the lone F-4, flown by Lieutenant Commander Einar Christensen, a pilot from our air wing staff, and Lieutenant j.g. Lance Kramer, crossed in front of him. Nguyen Van Coc fired a pair of heat-seeking missiles— copies of the Sidewinder captured a decade before during the air battles of the Taiwan Strait.

One of the missiles struck home, knocking the F-4 out of the air. Christensen and Kramer managed to eject, and they were subsequently rescued. They were the North Vietnamese ace's ninth and final air-to-air victory.

Two days later, a pair of Big E Phantoms tangled with three MiG-21s, possibly four. The F-4 crews fired four Sparrows but did not score a confirmed kill. Fortunately, all of our aircraft returned that day. The MiGs were getting more aggressive, and I was getting more and more eager to encounter them.

On May 23, 1968, I led an element of two F-4s in Skank Remsen's division during a BarCAP patrol. BarCAP was short for barrier combat air patrol. It put us on station between our carrier task force and the North Vietnamese coast in such a way that we could quickly intercept any MiGs launching from the fields around Hanoi.

Usually these were boring missions where nothing happened. The MiGs made rare appearances, but never when I was up there. This day turned out to be different. A group of MiG-21 interceptors— those latest and greatest examples of Communist high tech donated to the North Vietnamese cause—sped off one of their runways and climbed out toward the coast, looking for trouble.

This was the moment every fighter pilot wants. While I never liked combat, I did want to find out just how good I really was. The years of hassling off San Clemente—the secret fight club that kept the art of air combat alive in the fleet—those moments of risking aircraft and career boiled down to what we could do with our aircraft when challenged by the enemy's MiGs.

Our ship-based radars picked up the MiG launch almost right away. The controller called us and gave us a vector. Skank pointed his nose toward the shore; my wingman and I did the same. Power on, J79s roaring, we sped toward the fight of our careers.

As we closed, the controller called out, "Bandits, bandits! You're clear to fire!"

It was a perfect intercept. Textbook. The MiG-21s appeared on our airborne radars. Our rear-seaters stared at the scopes, calling out targets and seeking a lock for our long-range Sparrow missiles. We'd been taught to shoot those AIM-7s at about twelve miles. Skank held our fire and narrowed the range, hoping to give us a better chance at a kill.

We achieved lock-on with good missile ready lights. We had our targets. They were coming at 12 o'clock, so it would be a perfect shot. Sparrows worked best when fired head-on.

Skank was about to fire when our radios squawked, "Silver King, this is Red Crown, Salvo! Salvo! Salvo!" It was an order to break off the attack and get out of the area.

We turned back toward the fleet, puzzled. A moment later, our controller amplified the warning. The guided missile cruiser USS *Long Beach* had been hiding offshore with its electronics shut down. Steaming in her place in our defensive screen was a smaller destroyer. The North Vietnamese knew the general range of our surface-to-air missiles and knew that the destroyers carried older variants that didn't have very good range. Thinking they were clear of any surface-to-air missile threat, they launched those MiG-21s. They ran right into that cruiser.

After we detected them, the *Long Beach* lit up its radar and weapon systems. From sixty-five miles away, they locked on to the MiGs—just as we were about to engage. A barrage of Talos surface-to-air missiles from that warship went streaking over us. We were forced to break contact. The MiG-21s ran for home. One was shot down and another one was probably hit as well. It was one of only three surface-to-air missile kills by the Navy during the Vietnam War.

I could have not cared less about that success. Those cruiser sailors had poached our MiGs and denied us a chance to see how good we really were. And they had actually fired, it seemed, with no regard for our presence, a dangerous roll of the dice. We landed on the Big E bitterly disappointed. If we had fired at twelve miles, maybe things would have been different. The missions continued, but I didn't see another MiG.

It was a tough cruise, but it left us all with an indelible lesson in what real leadership looks like. Some time later, leading a strike mission at low altitude, Skank Remsen took a rifle round through the cockpit, straight through both thighs. He took his leg restraints, slid them up both legs, cinched them tight, and used them as tourniquets. He then flew one hundred and fifty miles and successfully landed aboard the carrier. Flight deck medical staff got him out of the airplane and rushed him to surgery. He refused medical evacuation to a stateside hospital and remained on board to heal. Two weeks later that tough old hombre was back in the saddle, flying combat missions with his boys. Now that's my idea of real leadership.

On June 14, F-4s from our sister carrier, USS *America*, got into a scrap with some older MiG-17s. The Phantom crews tried to knock them down with Sparrows and managed to get four off in the short fight. All four missed. Two days later, the *America* lost an F-4 from VF-102 in a dogfight with MiG-21s. Four more Sparrows went downrange, but not a single one struck home. The crew ejected over North Vietnam. The pilot was captured, his rear-seater killed.

We'd lost two Phantoms in a month, fired more than a million dollars' worth of high-tech smart weapons, and suffered one KIA, one MIA. This was a shocking development, especially since neither the air wing from the Big E nor the *America* had managed to offset the losses with a kill.

A couple nights later, I was part of a flight of F-4s that provided air cover for a Navy helicopter searching for two Phantom crewmen from VF-33 off the *America*. They'd been shot down by a SAM deep inside North Vietnam, and the helo, piloted by Clyde Lassen and LeRoy Cook, ran a gauntlet of ground fire while skirting the treetops in the darkness.

My back-seater Duffy and I circled the scene. We carried air-to-air missiles and nothing else that night, which made us feel truly useless. A 20mm gun at least would have allowed us to dive down and strafe the enemy gunners shooting up the helicopter. No gun gave us no recourse but to stay above and help coordinate the rescue and communications while stewing over our helplessness.

Lassen couldn't find the F-4 crew, and the crew couldn't locate the helo. His rotors hit some trees on his first rescue attempt. Lassen decided to try again. Low on fuel, he flicked on his navigation lights. And every North Vietnamese soldier in the area opened fire on them. The jungle below was a web of muzzle flashes and tracers.

The aviators on the ground spotted the lights and tried to move toward the helicopter. John Holzclaw, the pilot, dragged his back-seater, Zeke Burns, to a clearing. The ejection and hard landing had broken Zeke's leg, and his survival depended on his front-seater's stamina and determination.

Lassen touched down in a rice paddy, his crew chief and copilot laying down fire to suppress the North Vietnamese with his M-16 rifle. LeRoy Cook, the copilot, fired his weapon through the helicopter's open side window. The downed Americans reached the helo and were helped aboard. The crew chief, Bruce Dallas, jumped in, and the battle-damaged bird sped for the coast. They made it to an offshore cruiser and landed on her helo deck with five minutes of fuel remaining. Lassen earned America's highest award for bravery, the Medal of Honor, for his actions that night. In my many months of combat on Yankee Station, it was the bravest and most selfless act I witnessed. After that night, I never forgave the Navy for failing to arm the F-4 Phantom II with a gun.

That rescue proved to be one of the last missions we flew from Yankee Station that June. We were getting ready to head home by this point, having been out since the beginning of the year. The MiGs were getting increasingly active, and in June we fought them three more times. Thirteen Sparrows were fired in those three engagements, but none of them hit.

We left Yankee Station in July, just as things reached a boiling point. On July 10, a VF-33 Phantom crew brought down a MiG with a Sidewinder shot. That helped ease the pain a bit, but a month later, the air wing that replaced ours launched off USS *Constellation* and was intercepted by MiG-21s. In the ensuing fight, a Sidewinder fired at a MiG locked on to a passing F-4 and brought it down. The crew ejected and reached the ground, only to be captured before the search and rescue helo could get to them.

As those two final summer acts played out, the Big E and Air Wing Nine returned to the United States. We were worn out, beat up, and bitter. Between the end of February and the end of June, our hundred-man air wing had lost thirteen killed or captured, ten bombers, an F-4, and a Vigilante reconnaissance plane. Something was very, very wrong.

If we were going to regain the dominance that was naval aviation's birthright, we would need to make changes. My orders were cut: I had been assigned to the Phantom fleet replacement squadron at Naval Air Station Miramar. As luck would have it, there, in the bustling enclave of Fighter Squadron 121, I would have the chance to help solve our costly, tragic problem.

CHAPTER EIGHT

STARTING TOPGUN

Naval Air Station Miramar, California
Fall 1968

Fightertown USA. That's the long-standing nickname of the naval air station whose Spanish name, Miramar, doesn't seem to suit the place. There's no "view of the sea" from its location fifteen miles north of San Diego, five miles in from the coast—at least not until you've gone wheels up and are flying west on what the air controllers call a Sea Wolf departure. No, the unofficial nickname painted on Hangar One is a much better fit. On the runways, ramps, and taxiways of the sprawling complex, the shriek of jet engines and the smell of aviation fuel was constant.

If my love of flight had been tested by the war, I still never shook the habit of lifting my eyes to the sky whenever a jet roared overhead. Who was it? How was he doing? What's going on? As an instructor, it was my job to keep track of my nuggets.

When I parked my sea bag at Miramar again, this time to serve as a tactics instructor at Fighter Squadron 121, I found the pace of daily life clipping along at a fast wartime tempo. The whole West Coast naval shore establishment had ramped up to support the war in Vietnam, and VF-121 was hauling a heavy load. As the fleet replacement squadron for all F-4 Phantom squadrons based on the West Coast, it had a clientele that included all the carrier air wings in the Pacific. As I mentioned earlier, we called it the RAG, based on its name during World War II, a replacement air group. Each type of aircraft had its own RAG squadron supporting it: the A-1 Skyraider, A-3 Skywarrior, A-4 Skyhawk, A-6 Intruder, A-7 Corsair II, F-8 Crusader, and various antisubmarine and early warning aircraft. Fighting 121 handled the F-4 community. Anytime a carrier lost a Phantom, we produced a replacement plane and a two-man crew. It was but a short flight from our runway to the flight deck of a carrier bound for Yankee Station. We understood the reality that loss and death were a part of our trade. A lot of good men never came home. Whenever word came of another aircrew killed, captured, or missing, it haunted us. In 1968, no one at Miramar was in the mood to fool around.

Our fighter squadron was the largest in the whole Navy when I was there. It had an average of about seventy F-4Bs and F-4Js assigned to it, and 1,400 officers and enlisted men, including administrative and maintenance staff. A squadron that big did not go to war. A home-bound training command, it made sure the squadrons that operated from our aircraft carriers at sea were at full strength and ready to go. Given how poorly the air war was going, the squadron's nickname, the Pacemakers, was apt. You might say the war was on life support as our losses mounted. So we did our part to keep the pipeline full, turning out new aviators as the war whittled away at our ranks. In 1969 the RAG would graduate more than 150 pilots and RIOs to fly the Phantom. No group of F-4 drivers, RIOs, maintainers, and mechanics that I ever knew had a stronger claim on their pride.

I was an instructor in the advanced tactics phase (or department) of the squadron. A good man, Lieutenant Commander Sam

Leeds, was head of tactics. Our students had been through the mill by the time they got to us. After they got their wings, ground schools somewhere had taught them how to fight fires; survive isolation on water, on land, and as prisoners; read and report air intelligence; use their cockpit instruments; and master the many systems of our McDonnell Douglas fighter aircraft. Basic air combat tactics was my area. Young pilots always had smiles on their faces when they got to our phase of training. With me, they got to do some real flying. At the same time, they were going through a series of intensive lectures; this flight phase had them learning basic aircraft aerodynamics, instrument flying, basics of air-to-air interception, weapons, navigation, electronic warfare, and carrier qualifications (it can't be said often enough: finding a moving carrier at night and landing on its flight deck is not for the faint of heart). The tactics we taught them were nothing advanced. The syllabus was standard Navy tactical doctrine, complying with all the restrictive published guidelines about how the F-4 Phantom should be flown. They learned how to fire their weapons, drop bombs, and use long-range radar to intercept a distant target. It was like an undergraduate education, about as advanced as Biology for English Majors, just the essentials of flying and maneuvering in an F-4 and using its weapons to defeat another pilot or destroy a target on the ground.

What kept us from pushing the aerodynamic limits was the attitude of risk aversion that commonly afflicts training. The worst thing we could do, as far as our higher headquarters was concerned, was lose a plane. So twice a day, when I took new Phantom pilots and their back-seaters up to fly, we played it safe. We did air combat maneuvering, or ACM, but always within strict safety parameters. We never let them fly below ten thousand feet. You might say the Navy didn't want to risk voiding the warranties on their new planes.

As a result, the program lacked combat realism. The first time RAG pilots saw the radical maneuvers that modern jets were capable of, tracers were flying. Their eyes had not been opened. That's not how you want to send a young man off to war.

Even still, by the time the students finished our phase of training, they were ready for further training, and ready for assignment to the fleet. The daily tempo of flight training was dangerous enough. The enemy took things to another level. He always gets a vote, a wise person once said, and in the skies over North Vietnam the enemy was voting in droves. Finally the time came for the Navy to do something about it.

Not long after my arrival, late in December, Sam Leeds called me into his office and showed me a thick document bound in a blue cover. It was a study issued by the Naval Air Systems Command. Its title, "Report of the Air-to-Air Missile System Capability Review," hardly sounded like a blockbuster. But this study, produced by Captain Frank Ault, the captain of the *Coral Sea*, was an impressive, consequential piece of work.

About two hundred pages long, it was a top-to-bottom exploration of the reasons for our failure in air-to-air combat over North Vietnam. Captain Ault's project had been a long time coming. It began in the summer of 1968, when he led a team that tackled the problem of the Sparrow missile. Building on that and other studies, he pulled in more than two hundred people to a symposium at the Naval Air Missile Test Center at Point Mugu, north of Los Angeles. There were pilots, commanders, and managers and technicians from Raytheon, Westinghouse, and McDonnell Douglas, all the major fighter weapons contractors. No one had put together the entire picture of the problem like Ault had. It was the first time the whole air combat system—our fighters, their missiles, and fire-control systems—had been studied holistically, from design and acquisition to operations and logistics. Ault wanted to understand weapons systems "from the womb to the tomb," as he liked to say. His conclusions were far-reaching.

Sam Leeds called my attention to one particular recommendation in the report. He flipped to page 37 and pointed to the eleventh of the fifteen items listed in paragraph 6, "Aircrew Training." It was there that Ault advised the chief of naval operations and the commander of Naval Air Forces, Pacific, to "establish, as early as possible, an Advanced Fighter Weapons School in RCVW-12* at NAS Miramar for both the F-8 and the F-4." These were the words that gave birth to Topgun. Apparently, the idea of such a school had already been under discussion at the RAG's parent command. Like any good idea, it required a brave soul to stick his neck out to become reality. Captain Ault's report put the idea front and center on some important desks.

Sam and I knew that any Miramar-based tactics training program would run through us. He looked at me and said, "Dan, why don't you take it?"

I suppose this was generous of him. He had both experience and seniority over me. He could have led the effort himself. But he already had a great job waiting for him. He was in the final running to command the first fighter squadron that would fly the new F-14 Tomcat. (Tom Cruise would help make that beautiful Grumman jet famous in the movie.) Sam could easily have taken the assignment to start the new schoolhouse and then handed it off to me when his time came to go fly F-14s. But he felt that the school should have the

---

* That's the acronym for Readiness Air Wing 12, which was VF-121's parent command at Naval Air Station Miramar.

same leadership from the beginning, for continuity's sake. He said as much, and strongly.

It was settled then and there. I made a quick, fateful decision: I'd do it.

When Sam and I informed our skipper, Commander Hank Halleland, that I had agreed to serve as the Navy Fighter Weapons School's first officer in charge (OIC), he had only one directive. "Don't kill anybody, and don't lose an airplane." That did happen from time to time, so we took the warning seriously. He also made it clear that the Navy was funding us on thin wooden nickels. We would have no classroom space, ready room, or administrative office, no maintainers and mechanics assigned to us, no airplanes of our own, only loaners. And, of course, we would have no money. The new graduate school would subsist by forage, hunting and gathering in the forgotten corners of Miramar. There was one more thing. Our deadline for preparing a curriculum and having it ready for the first class of students was short: sixty days. Aside from all that, I suppose the job was a real plum.

Soon we started calling the school Topgun. We weren't the first to use this fine nickname. There was an annual air weapons competition that used the name until about 1958. The aircraft carrier *Ranger*, which I would later command, called itself "the Top Gun of the Pacific Fleet." Our friends and rivals at Miramar who flew the older F-8 Crusader called themselves "the last of the gunfighters." Their own schoolhouse was established by the same paragraph in the Ault report that gave birth to us, but as that old fighter was on its way out, their tactics initiative did not last long.

I've often reflected on the sheer happenstance of how leadership of Topgun fell to me. I didn't know it at the time, but it was larger and more important than anything I had ever undertaken before. It was the chance of a lifetime to effect much-needed change. Its success would take the passage of years, requiring the work of the many fine aviators who followed me. But our new graduate school in fighter combat was greater than any one man or group of men. It would grow roots and flourish. It would transcend its own mission and stand for excellence and commitment of the purest kind. Its legacy would last for decades. None of that was expected in December 1968. It was a job to do.

The program almost seemed designed to fail. I say that because the Navy considers nothing very important that's not run by an admiral. I was a thirty-three-year-old lieutenant commander, three pay grades below flag rank. That the Navy gave leadership of Topgun to someone so lowly speaks to what it thought of our chances. We easily could have crashed nose first. We were going to disrupt the traditional way of teaching tactics. I'll say more on that later, but most real tactical aviation training took place out in the fleet. The skippers of the fleet squadrons thought they owned tactics. Topgun threatened that approach. Thus, we could easily fail.

In the Navy, the failure of any group can inflict collateral career damage on superiors in the chain of command. The damage was usually in proportion to the rank of the failing commander. If Topgun crashed and burned, my own career would take a hit. Yet my humble rank meant that the senior officers standing over us would suffer no blemish on their record. Our failure could be written off to the stumbling of youngsters who, while well intended, were not up to the task. That's probably why a guy like me got to be the first OIC of Topgun. It sounds like a much bigger deal today, knowing what we know.

Being in that dicey position, I took comfort in having Hank Halleland's support. He quickly proved himself a friend from the beginning, helping us find people and resources. The pedigree of the Ault report helped too. The higher echelons at Pacific Naval Air

Forces headquarters and at the Pentagon had to pay attention, since the CNO himself had endorsed the study.

But the war didn't care, not a lick. And the war was the reason Topgun was born. It awaited our return, ready to kill any of us who showed up unprepared. Next time we reported in for a WestPac cruise, we would need to perform a lot better. Lives hung in the balance.

I've always tried to keep in mind something that was famously well expressed by another fighter pilot in another day: God is my copilot. When I look back at how we pulled it together, it's clear to me that the acting hand was far mightier than my own. I prayed for the gift of discernment to make it work. It wasn't going to be easy, but everything we would need was at our fingertips there in Fightertown USA.

Captain Ault described what had to be done, but—bless him for his wisdom and foresight—he said nothing about *how* it should be done. He prescribed the creation of the Navy Fighter Weapons School but did not say what it should teach, how it should be taught, or how it should be set up. Today, an initiative like that would involve millions being spent on special studies and outside experts. Until they were unanimous in their conclusions, nothing would start happening. The paper pushing would take years. In 1969, I was left to my own devices. With the wise council of Hank Halleland and some other trusted voices around Miramar at my disposal, I thought I might have a puncher's chance. I went right to work.

Topgun was best understood as a graduate school. It functioned essentially like a teachers' college for fighter pilots. Our job was not just to teach pilots to be the hottest sticks in the sky. It was to teach pilots *to teach other pilots* to be the hottest sticks in the sky. Our first class of students, handpicked by their squadron commanders to join us at Miramar in sixty short days, would spend about five weeks with us and then return to their units to spread to their peers what we had taught them. In this way the Navy hoped to leverage a multiplier effect, seeding new ideas in a geometric progression as a class of eight went out to teach eight times sixteen more.

The way to true mastery of anything is to learn it to the point that you can teach it to someone else. My first task, then, was to find instructors with a talent for teaching, pilots with the gift for delivering a complex lesson in a way that made it stick. Our expectations were sky-high. Not just of our students, but of ourselves. With only sixty days to develop new offensive dogfighting tactics for the Phantom, redefine the way Sparrows and Sidewinders were used, write the curriculum and lesson plans, create a flight syllabus with briefing and debriefing guides, and recruit our first class of pilots from the fleet, there was hardly an hour to waste.

Around the time Sam Leeds showed me the Ault report, I hosted a group of Israeli pilots at my home in San Diego. Heading the group was Lieutenant Colonel Eitan Ben Eliyahu. He had a superb reputation as a fighter pilot and leader. Danny Halutz, another future head of the Israeli Air Force, was part of the group. When I met these guys, the IAF was making the transition from the French-built Dassault Mirage to the Phantom. They were visiting Miramar to learn what they could. I learned a few things from Ben Eliyahu in particular, and we became good friends.

Over good American barbecue, listening closely to everything they said, I discerned that Israeli fighter squadrons believed strongly in the power of technical specialization. In each technical area, Ben Eliyahu explained, one man was designated to serve as the lead specialist. Radar, weapons, ordnance, aerodynamics, tactics—each domain had its wizard. The division of labor would prove to be an efficient way to assemble a team and develop a technical curriculum on a short schedule. That was the approach I used in selecting Topgun's first instructors.

Reflecting on what the Israelis had revealed to me, I decided that eight men would be the right number to cover the subjects we needed to master. Four pilots and four RIOs would join me as Topgun's founding cadre of instructors. These eight dynamic, smart, persuasive, and articulate young officers would help me pull our program together ahead of our hot start in March. I didn't think I could manage more people than that while developing the school and continuing to teach and fly in the RAG—all of our instructors would have double duty—and doing everything that serving as the OIC entailed. There was little time to waste in assembling the team, designing a curriculum in collaboration with them, corralling assets, and finding a way to turn around the air war that was going south eight thousand miles away on the other side of the Pacific.

Look around any room and you'll realize that your people are everything. It doesn't matter if it's a business, a charity, a government agency, or a military unit. Your people are your destiny. We had to be successful or our careers and reputations would be finished. And that would be the least of it. If we failed, we would return to a war using the same tactics burdened by the same politically driven rules of engagement. That would just mean more of the same: lost friends and a brotherhood strained to the limit by the demands of war we were not allowed to win.

I didn't have to look far for good people to help me fulfill this unexpected charge. The pool of combat-seasoned talent at the RAG was deep, which was helpful because there was no time to do the paperwork necessary to transfer people to us from other units. The instructors who had been teaching with me in the tactics phase were all combat-experienced, with lots of flight time in the F-4.

They flew every day, putting new pilots through the paces. I knew all of them—and not just as pilots, but as *teachers*. Their reputations among the student pilots at Miramar were as important to me as their standing as warriors. When the time came to choose my "original eight," the right names came quickly to mind. I talked to each of them, had them read the Ault report, and described the enormous task we faced in building a graduate-level program with an advanced curriculum and preparing to teach it within sixty days.

I don't remember the exact words of my initial presentation, but it was based around the sentiment that we were being challenged to revive our heritage as naval aviators—to learn how to dogfight again. Captain Ault had empowered line aviators to have a voice. I was not surprised when I learned that the author of the section of the report that recommended creation of Topgun was a salty F-8 Crusader pilot, Captain Merle Gorder. In spite of the rivalries between the Crusader and Phantom communities, we were virtually the same tribe, going all the way back to World War II when our predecessors flying piston-engine, propeller-driven fighters had purchased our birthright in blood. With this as my message, I was able to get every one of my recruits to join me in the new venture.

The pilots I invited to join Topgun as instructors were Lieutenants Mel Holmes, John Nash, Jim Ruliffson, and Lieutenant j.g. Jerry Sawatzky. I called them into my office one by one and explained the idea of the Fighter Weapons School as referenced in the Ault report. To a man, they did not hesitate to sign on. We had long been vocal about the changes we thought were needed to win the air war in Vietnam. Here was the chance to do something about it.

Mel Holmes was a first-round pick in anybody's book. I had seen a lot of pilots fly, fight, and work. None was better than Mel.

I considered him to be hands down the finest F-4 Phantom pilot in the world in early 1969. Tall, handsome, and self-confident, he was a natural leader with strong opinions. He had been born and reared in northeastern Oregon, a rural outback that bred tough, independent people. One time when Mel was golfing at the base course at Miramar, he hit a drive into the weeds. That was bad news for the nest of rattlesnakes he walked into while looking for his ball. When his buddies saw him hacking away with his seven-iron, slaughtering those serpents in the grass, Holmes had his nickname: Rattler. He had one trait in spades and I strongly doubt it's teachable: a bone-deep, hardwired, electric-fire sense of aggression. It manifested itself on the basketball court, where he was hell on wheels. An athletic scholarship had paid for an education his family could not otherwise have afforded. But its biggest dividends were paid in the air. When Mel strapped himself into the cockpit of a fighter aircraft, whatever separated the flight surfaces from the man at the controls simply disappeared. He had as much natural talent as anyone I've known. No pilot I ever knew beat Mel consistently one-on-one. So he was a perfect candidate to specialize in tactics and aerodynamics at Topgun.

I chose John "Smash" Nash for the way his heart and mind worked together. Though he was the one member of the original eight who hadn't taught in the RAG's tactics phase, I knew him well from our early days flying McDonnell F3H Demons from the *Hancock* back in '63, a year that he and I were both lucky to have survived. John was at his best when he was pitted against a supposedly superior fighter pilot. Any suggestion that a mismatch was at hand triggered his competitive fire. His motto, "I'd rather die than lose," bore it out. Most combat pilots are wired that way. What made Nash special was the way he combined that fire with hyperattention to detail. Anyone who showed any degree of inattention to the fine points of something he was trying to teach got a hard dose of his Mississippi wrath. Most of our students were smart enough to avoid a second helping. Nash expected perfection from them and usually got it. He was as much an asset on the ground as in the air. His talent for technical research kept our ideas about tactics built on a deep base of fact. Nash was a systems guy. He told his students, "Automobiles, aircraft, and air-to-air missiles are built to fail. Expect problems and anticipate them." I considered his fusion of traits—detail-driven aggression—to be the best possible mind-set for a Topgun instructor.

Jim Ruliffson probably put out more pure intellectual wattage than any of us. No one understood the Phantom's electronic and avionics systems better than he did. With his superb technical mind and training in electrical engineering, he was a natural to spearhead our effort to master the Sidewinder and Sparrow missile systems. In the subtle differences in performance between these high-tech weapons, not to mention the optimal parameters of their use, was the critical margin between life and death. This was Jim's specialty. A fine stick and great tactician, he was a protégé of Duke Hernandez, a great one from the East Coast fighter community. "Cobra" Ruliffson distinguished himself with his superb gift for teaching this complex material to aircrews in a way that let them retain and use it.

Jerry Sawatzky, or "Ski Bird," as I called him, had played linebacker for Bear Bryant at Alabama. He was big, imposing, and highly energetic, but also very unassuming and one of the most likable people I ever flew with. He had survived a horrific fire on the carrier USS *Forrestal*, which claimed thirty-nine men from his squadron in July 1967. A born teacher, he was one of the first ensigns assigned to fly the Phantom when it was the fleet's hottest, newest ride. He knew the plane inside and out, and he was magic in an F-4. With his keenly aggressive way, he was known to "bend the jet," as we said. Jerry had great situational awareness, which was vital in fighter combat. It's very easy and all too dangerous to focus on the enemy you're about to shoot. A pilot has to stay alert to what's happening in the cube of air that extends several miles around him as all the players move at high speed in different directions. Jerry could teach others how to develop their awareness and retain it. He was also good at looking at an aerial encounter from the enemy's point of view. Holmes and Nash rated him very highly, which told me a lot. Ski Bird was a prince of a teammate. We appreciated him for being as reliable as gravity, usually showing up ten minutes early for a scheduled brief. He was just the kind of instructor we needed, since our job was to throw away the manual and push our aircraft beyond its factory limits.

Holmes, Nash, Ruliffson, and Sawatzky were my first four pilot instructors. But I hope I've made clear how important the radar intercept officers are. Without a good back-seater in his F-4, no fighter pilot gets far in an air battle. Topgun's four founding RIOs were the best that were available anywhere. At the head of the pack was John "J. C." Smith, whom I invited right away. He might have been the finest RIO there ever was.

In June 1965, flying from USS *Midway*, J. C. and his pilot, Commander Lou Page, scored the Navy's first air-to-air kill of the Vietnam War. The head-on tangle with a pair of MiG-17s was a by-the-book radar intercept, and their Sparrow performed as advertised. Moments later, their wingman, Jack Batson, shot down a second MiG. Of course the Pentagon was elated. As far as I know, these were the only "pure intercept" victories the Navy scored in the entire war. Soon thereafter the Vietnamese stopped playing our game and the radar-guided AIM-7 Sparrow seldom again delivered on the promises of its marketing brochure.

J. C. was colorful. He talked a mile a minute and at times never seemed to stop. That element of his personality made him a great RIO. A good back-seater never stops talking until his pilot issues the command "Go cold mike." J. C. was especially good with new pilots. Whenever I had one who needed some help, I'd prescribe for him a flew flights with J. C. in his rear seat. That always got him up to speed. J. C. lived the Christian life with his wife, Carol. Teaching others was his forte. He was a pretty fair negotiator too.

Another of my RIOs was Jim "Hawkeye" Laing. A youngster, just twenty-three, he was so quiet in person that you'd never know what a tiger he was in the rear seat. During his two combat tours in Vietnam, flying from USS *Kitty Hawk*, he and his pilot flamed a MiG-17 in a wild fight near Haiphong Harbor. Laing survived two ejections in barely a month. The second was harrowing in the extreme. Hawkeye and his pilot, Denny Wisely, landed well inland in a thick jungle, where they became the objects of an epic search and rescue mission. As the helo looked for them, John Nash courageously remained overhead, covering the rescue to the limit of his fuel while under fire from enemy gunners. He received a well-deserved Silver Star. Laing, with his notable history of survival against the odds, gave Topgun an element of moral strength and never-quit resilience that was enormously valuable. He took all of his hard lessons in stride and always came back for more. A deeply religious family man, Jim imbued Topgun with his never-say-die spirit. He was one of the steadiest, most stalwart, spiritual, and reliable men I have ever known. When he spoke, everybody listened. He was a generalist who contributed to each area of the curriculum. He could teach with the best and was a quality leader who was always ready to help anyone who needed it.

Our other Smith—Steve—had all the essential skills of a top-grade RIO but stood apart from everybody for his skills as a salesman, organizer, and grifter for all seasons. Steve-O could talk a Bedouin out of his camel, ride it to Alaska with a load of shaved ice, and sell it all at a premium to an Eskimo. He had a great laugh and darkly handsome looks that drew an enviable share of female attention. I guess we didn't begrudge him those successes, because he was a world-class organizer and had a work ethic that outdid mine. He was a self-starter, keeping a daily to-do list in his pocket, and it was a rare sunset when he hadn't scratched off every item. "Rebel" was at his best when I gave him free rein and didn't ask too many questions.

Our junior RIO, Lieutenant j.g. Darrell Gary, was the youngest man in our cadre of founders. He had every attribute I wanted in an instructor—mature (beyond his years), confident (beneath his years), and very hardworking. If Darrell looked a bit too much like a movie star fighter pilot to be an actual fighter pilot, we had to accept what God gave him and be glad for it. It was plentiful. Some pilots were smarter than he, and others were more experienced, but none was more driven. Though his after-hours activities were diverse and even legendary, as often as not they involved important professional work. In cadet training, while everybody else was asleep in their racks, Darrell would often be found sequestered in the head, sitting on a throne with a flashlight in one hand and a textbook in the other. That's part of the reason he graduated at the top of his class in naval flight officer school. He came to VF-121 in 1968, after two combat tours in the *Kitty Hawk*. It was hard to miss his extreme self-assurance. Because evolution tells us that birds with that trait tend to become extinct, we gave Darrell a call sign to match: Condor. It was designed to encourage him toward humility. But all these years later I can finally say it. Darrell was one of Topgun's sharpest lecturers, gifted with a probing tactical mind. He is one of the most aggressive, intelligent men I have ever known and is a natural innovator whom people followed willingly.

Our last find was an ace in the hole of sorts, even though he was a nonaviator. When Steve Smith met Chuck Hildebrand, Chuck was working as an intelligence officer, bored and unhappy, in one of Miramar's F-8 photoreconnaissance squadrons. Steve talked him up a little, recognized his useful talent, and helped arrange his transfer—all on the same day. Chuck was the perfect man to serve as Topgun's intelligence officer. He was a human vacuum cleaner. He got the inevitable nickname "Spook." Tall, studious, professorial in bearing despite his youth, he never stopped collecting documents for our reference library, detailing the capabilities of enemy aircraft and pilots. Without Spook, Topgun would have needed many more years to emerge as a research library for fighter pilots and the center of knowledge that it quickly became.

And that was our team. I like to think that their being in one place, the right place, at precisely the right time was the work of a power greater than me. With the team assembled, all we needed was a place to call home.

One Friday afternoon, Steve Smith, foraging in a remote part of NAS Miramar, near the base operations center, found an abandoned, dilapidated modular trailer. It was perfect. He chatted up an off-duty public works crane operator and offered him a case of scotch if he would make delivery to our area of the base. Later that afternoon, the ten-by-forty-foot structure was hoisted aloft and relocated to a space adjacent to VF-121's hangar. Over the weekend, we laid in new flooring, repainted it with bright red trim, and hung a sign on the door announcing the existence of the Navy Fighter Weapons School.

While the rest of us renovated our find, Steve went scrounging and stole a bunch of office furniture and a couple of classified document safes from God knows where. Legend had it he bagged some of it from the Air Force. Wherever it came from, we filled our formerly condemned trailer with all the trappings of a real classroom and called it home. By Monday morning, Topgun was officially in business.

CHAPTER NINE

THE ORIGINAL BROS

Miramar
1969

The famous movie that borrowed our name—and we all still love it—might make you suspect that we were a self-obsessed bunch, that it must have been a constant battle of egos between the students and even the instructors inside that stolen trailer and on our training flights out of Miramar. Television shows like *Baa Baa Black Sheep*, with its over-the-top portrayal of Major Gregory "Pappy" Boyington and Marine Fighter Squadron 214 as a gang of misfits, created that sense too.

Speaking for the Original Bros, I'll say that for six and a half days a week, we were scholars, even monks. No PhD in astrophysics ever worked harder to understand the facts of the physical universe than we did at Topgun ahead of the arrival of our first class of students in early 1969. Our mission was to master the full combat capability of our airplane and its weapons and turn around the air war. As skipper I set the tone and made decisions. But the Topgun instructors emerged as the intellectual drivers of our attempt to redefine the flight envelopes of the F-4 Phantom and its missiles. That was our most important work, and the foundation of the Topgun legacy.

Pilots were dying because our missiles were not designed to operate in a dynamic, high-G, high-angular-rate environment. That's a technical way of saying that an air-to-air brawl moves so fast that a fighter pilot should never trust a missile to win it for him. Certainly, the pilot had to be smarter than the missile. It was simply a killing tool, like a throwing knife. But a man must know how to use it perfectly, every time.

One thing we saw was that our missiles were taking a beating day and night aboard ship. Carrier ordnance personnel had to manhandle those heavy things, and they got knocked around. Whenever a pilot landed with his missiles still aboard, the weapons absorbed a stiff, debilitating concussion. You have to know your weapon and its limitations as surely as you do your airplane. So we went to school on them to uncover every shortfall. There were many shortfalls and some very technical solutions.

The forward thinkers in Washington who had eulogized the day of the dogfight knew nothing of what it was like to be part of an alpha strike arriving over Hanoi. They couldn't picture thirty Navy planes inbound, with sometimes fifteen enemy SAMs rising toward you. They couldn't see the crowd of unidentifiable radar and visual contacts in the sky swelling and commingling as MiGs reached altitude and approached us, or the surprise of an Air Force formation arriving unannounced over the target, right when things were getting sporty. The ever-present AAA and even small-arms fire made for a chaotic dynamic as you rolled along at six hundred knots.

As I've perhaps belabored, the rules of engagement required us to make visual identifications of targets before firing. Telling friend from foe meant getting close enough practically to see him through your windscreen. Good luck with that. By the time you got within recognition distance of a MiG closing head-on with you, your advanced radar-guided missile was about as useful as a fence post strapped to your wing. In the first three years of the war, our pilots had fired nearly six hundred missiles at enemy planes, scoring a kill on about sixty. If you're keeping score, that's one in ten. More often than not, those agile little MiGs, having ducked our first swing, would be on our tails showering us with explosive cannon shells sooner than our wingmen could shout, "Bandit on your six—break right!" Something had gone wrong. It was our job to follow Captain Frank Ault's suggestion and solve the problem from the ground up.

Some of the most productive hours of my professional life were spent in the trailer. A couple of cinder blocks were the staircase to the left-side door that put you in our operations center. It had a desk and a chair, some cabinets, a pair of safes that Steve Smith had liberated to hold our classified documents, plus the inevitable Navy coffee mess. For students there were six tables in two rows of three, flanking a narrow center aisle, and a dozen chairs. At the far end of the room was a chalkboard and a podium, with barely enough room for an instructor to stand. There was a small window on one end and two on the side. Armed with our youthful ideas about what the U.S. Navy was doing wrong, we went about rewriting the rules of tactical air warfare in the F-4 Phantom.

Mel took charge of our effort to deconstruct the aerodynamic capabilities of the F-4, revise its performance envelope, and discover its true capabilities in the air, well beyond the parameters set by McDonnell Douglas. We developed the Topgun curriculum in searching, impassioned conversations, illustrated by fast work at the chalkboard. To build a curriculum in air-to-air tactics, all you had to do was get Mel Holmes, John Nash, and Jerry Sawatzky talking a bit. The others would join in, and we'd be on our way. Once it got rolling, you'd better be strapped in with a five-point harness and taking notes fast, because it was going to be a wide-open discussion.

Rattler might lead off by discussing his thoughts on a trick of the tactical trade that was too advanced to teach in the RAG. By the time we were finished, we had something important in the making: an outline that became a lesson plan that became a flight syllabus and a curriculum, broken down and assigned to the instructor specializing in that technical area. All of it was reviewed over and over again as each instructor presented the material to the other Bros.

John Nash was my expert on air-to-ground tactics. Phantoms were, after all, sold to the military as "fighter-bombers," and we couldn't ignore the second part of its mission while going to school on the first. Nash was the best among us in that specialty. He was a master air-to-air tactician as well.

Cobra Ruliffson did a lot of his best work away from Miramar. He was a frequent visitor to the Raytheon offices in Massachusetts. Working with the engineers who built the Sparrow, he took apart the flight dynamics of our problematic missile. The actual parameters of the Sparrow's sensors and electronics had never seemed to inform the tactics. There were optimal times and places to fire a Sparrow, and if you didn't know the kinematics and the process times, or the shifting matrix of G forces, angular rates, and track crossing angles that your choice of moment to fire imposed upon your missile, you weren't going to hit anything. Jim grasped all the factors of time and space that defined the air-to-air missile's proper use. By the time his study was aligned with our new understanding of the Phantom's own performance parameters, its flight envelope, we had a better weapon on our hands.

Doing all of this on a sixty-day deadline meant for some busy days.

Our beautiful F-4 had some important things going for it. One of them was the pair of General Electric J79 turbojets that made the plane accelerate like a rocket. Earlier U.S. fighters had used their superior engine power to gain an advantage over the agile MiG, soaring high above a fight and diving back down when they saw a chance to kill. We called this tactic "using the vertical." Developing it for the Phantom, for which it had never been envisioned, would be one of our top priorities.

While we were preparing the curriculum, I joined Chuck Hildebrand and J. C. Smith on trips to Langley, Virginia. Only by visiting CIA headquarters, we discovered, could we get access to the highly classified air action reports from the carrier squadrons off Vietnam. It was funny that they were originally unavailable to us, seeing as the squadrons we had belonged to were their authors in the first place. Still, without top-secret clearances, we needed cooperation from our contacts at the CIA. On one trip from Washington back to Miramar, J. C. and I hand-carried two briefcases full of classified debriefs—reports that were full of valuable lessons that had been paid for with blood.

Before we could teach our material we had to study and learn it cold ourselves. We created, collated, and corrected the curriculum at a fever pace, working all hours to refine it, hunting and pecking with two fingers on manual typewriters, red-lining each other's drafts, and rehearsing our lectures to each other. This last part was key. As we took turns at the podium in the trailer, we faced withering scrutiny from our fellow instructors. In the military, this is known as a "murder board." No hiccup in presentation style, no slip of the tongue, no glitch in dress or personal appearance was too small to be seized upon and corrected on the spot. We knew we would be ineffective lecturing to our top-notch students if we were anything less than bulletproof. How would they believe in us at Topgun if we couldn't deliver a graduate-level lesson well? In the meantime, we began reaching out to the fleet squadrons to recruit our first students.

The founding class would consist of two representatives from four Phantom squadrons, a total of four pilots and four RIOs. Steve Smith, our best salesman, was put in charge with the guidance that he recruit from both the East and West Coasts. He had quite a time of it making these cold calls. He would ask for the executive officer, inviting him to nominate his best junior officers, one pilot and one RIO, to join us for a five-week class in advanced tactics. After Steve made his pitch, the XO usually said something like this:

"Sorry, who the hell are you?"

Steve would explain. If he ever suggested that the XO's higher headquarters might already know of our existence—"Sir, haven't you been briefed about our school by your air wing commander?"— he often found the situation escalating. The squadron CO himself would get on the horn. And that's when the inquisition really got going.

"I don't know who are, son. Do you really expect me to cut loose my best guys and send them to you? By the way, what makes you think you can teach tactics better than I can?"

At that point Steve would have to up the ante by explaining that participating squadrons were responsible not only for sending us two aviators, but also a Phantom and some maintenance people to keep it up. Sometimes this news was agitating.

Steve didn't close every sale. Often the CO, miffed, hung up and queried the Pentagon about Topgun's status and standing.

That's when our top cover paid off. The Navy Department's highest headquarters for air warfare, known as "OP-05," always set the skipper straight.

Steve's persuasive gifts paid off best when he was talking to East Coast guys. The fact that Topgun was based at the gateway to the Southeast Asian war zone was useful. "Are you aware of what's going on here at Miramar?" Steve would say. "We're considering inviting one of your squadrons to join us. Their chances will be better if they have combat experience. Do they?" With East Coast units the answer almost always was no. This had a way of building desire. Over time, Steve created buzz—and demand.

As the roster of Class One came together, we tested some of our finished lesson plans on students in the RAG. We were seeing them regularly anyway, because all of Topgun's instructors were still teaching the basics in VF-121. One day in the middle of February, Mel Holmes and I did a two-plane training hop, putting a pair of student RIOs through the paces in long-range radar interception. I was cooking along in full afterburner about a hundred miles off the California coast, approaching San Clemente Island, when I felt a thump. My warning panel lit up. There was a fire in my right engine.

As I shut it down, my back-seater, Lieutenant j.g. Gil Sliney, ran through the emergency checklist while Mel eased in close for a visual inspection, trying to see through all the smoke. We were about thirty miles from Miramar, off La Jolla, when the seven-liter liquid oxygen canister mounted in the tail of my Phantom exploded. It tore the tail section clean off my bird. End over end we tumbled. Time slowed down. We plummeted. In my headset I think I heard Mel's voice.

"Dan, you guys eject, eject!"

Gil pulled the handle and we rocketed out of the doomed jet. We fell in a parabola toward the ocean, strapped into our ejection seats at twenty-one thousand feet.

It's odd how time passes in a crisis. Inspired by the flood of adrenaline into my system, I had the time to look down over La Jolla and notice the scenic cove. My helmet visor was gone, but somehow my Ray-Bans were still hanging on. *I've got to save them,* I thought. Those sunglasses had been with me since my Pensacola training days. No way did I want to lose them now. I reached up, shucked them off my face, and stuffed them into a zippered pocket on my flight suit.

It was then that I realized, as I fell through space, that I was still attached to my ejection seat. This was a problem. The heavy apparatus was supposed to separate automatically by action of a powerful spring activated by a barostat at twelve thousand feet.

Falling toward the sea, I looked around for Gil's chute and was relieved to see it drifting down, behind and above me. Disengaging myself manually from the ejection seat and falling clear, I pulled the D-ring to pop my chute. Nothing happened. I yanked it again, harder, and the cable broke off in my gloved hand. I was falling at terminal velocity, fourteen feet per second or like a rock. Somehow, I had to get my hands on the chute pack.

Short on time and altitude, I pulled myself up the risers and reached my chute pack. I thought of my wife and kids and home and it was God who gave me the strength, I'm sure. Reaching the parachute pack, I opened it with my hands and the chute flew free. The beautiful white blossom swelled above me, jerking me upright and into a lazy but short descent. *Thank you, my dear Lord.*

Looking down at the cold water, I saw dark sleek shadows swimming just below the surface. There wasn't much time to think about what that meant. My chute had opened so low—Mel said it was about twenty-four hundred feet—that I had time only for two swings back and forth in the harness before I hit the drink. Almost at once, my small life raft deployed. When I climbed in, I did double time, because I thought I was avoiding the sharks. A moment later, a pair of large gray sea creatures launched themselves up against my raft, parking their snub noses on the edge of it. Dolphins. Chortling excitedly, they stayed with me until the rescue helo arrived from the carrier *Bonhomme Richard*.

As the rotor wash sprayed me with salt water, the helo crew hauled me heavenward. I wondered about Gil, and there he was, reclined on the deck of the cabin and beaming. The rescuers had been quick to snag him. As Gil, elated, gave me a sidelong man-hug, I warned him that I'd kill him if he tried to kiss me. He didn't. Clearly it was not the day for either one of us to die.

An accident investigation revealed a defect in the aging original bar springs of the Phantom's ejection seat. The Navy surmised that this problem, which was fleetwide, was the reason five pilots had been lost during night ejections. I doubt Gil and I would have made it if our mishap had happened after dark. After a medical checkup on the *Bonnie Dick*, we boarded a C-1 Trader and with a nighttime catapult shot were on our way home to Miramar.

It was just another day in the life, full of routine danger and little of what passes for glory. As for the nights, my young instructors knew how to blow off steam. The Topgun social circuit was in place from our first day at Miramar. It reached from Downwinds, the beachfront O club at Coronado, to Bully's in San Diego and all the way up to La Jolla, where Bully's had another location and where Condor and Hawkeye Laing rented a house that became famous. Right on the beach, at 259 Coast Boulevard, was a little white stucco house that we started calling the "Lafayette Escadrille." A refrigerated keg was always on tap and the doors were never locked. It and the two houses across the street, which were rented by other young Miramar pilots, attracted an entourage that included everybody from San Diego State coeds to members of the San Diego Chargers pro football team. Darrell never knew who he was going to have to throw out of his bedroom when he rolled in from Miramar on a Friday night. But all of us lived and breathed for the work we did at Topgun. Of course, anything we did off base was meant solely to keep our edges sharp for the work that really mattered.

A few days after my unprogrammed cold swim, I was back to work. Having finalized the Topgun curriculum and completed most of the murder-boarding, we were ready to receive our young sticks from the fleet. We would have to be on our game. Because we were going to make these guys into world-beaters.

On March 3, 1969, in our stolen trailer at Fightertown USA, Topgun's Class One convened. All eight attendees had come from Pacific-based squadrons, VF-142 and VF-143, just off a Vietnam deployment with USS *Constellation*. They were some of the finest junior officers in the fleet, all combat-experienced aviators, all graduates of the Naval Academy, career Navy. We didn't take reservists. Their names were Jerry Beaulier, Ron Stoops, Cliff Martin, and John Padgett. The RIOs were Jim Nelson, Jack Hawver, Bob Cloyes, and Ed Scudder. The instructors and I sensed quickly that their COs had chosen well. All were sharp and well prepared.

After fifteen years in the Navy, I had learned a few things about leadership. If you had not attended Annapolis or ROTC in college, you learned it not by express instruction, but by absorption of example. You got it on the job. Some of it came by negative example: "Don't be like Commander What's-his-name." But most of my role models were helpful and even inspiring. I've mentioned Gene Valencia and Skank Remsen. But many fine aviators were mentors to me. Their lessons always resonated. They taught me what kind of leader I needed to become.

When the legendary Swede Vejtasa was a wing commander at Miramar, he welcomed every new class in the RAG more or less like this. "Okay, boys, training command was fun, because each of you did well. You wouldn't be in fighters if you hadn't. Now the *fun's over*. When you finish, you are headed to war, maybe immediately. Pay attention! Learn everything you can about your aircraft and its capabilities, the tactics, and the standard operating procedures. They may well save your life. Dismissed."

Swede was telling those nuggets what they needed to hear. With advanced talents such as these eight, however, I felt no need to be heavy. I issued a heartfelt "Welcome aboard" and said we had been charged with an important purpose. I introduced my instructor team and told them who they all were. I explained that we would all learn together along the way. The main thing for any skipper to bear in mind is this: The troops need to know he's interested in their welfare. This is true regardless of the leader's personal communication style. Hard-asses can care, too. Some leaders give lip service to caring, but what a leader does to show it is far more important. I wanted my instructors to challenge them—but always constructively. We would aspire to build their confidence, not destroy it. They were professionals and future mentors in training. So we were going to show them how it was done.

I closed by saying, "There is an urgency here beyond anything we have ever done. We hold lives in our hands." These words still fill me with conviction today.

Our students had little time to settle in before we got to work. The first week was mostly lectures. Before the sun was up, at 0430 on the day after they arrived, we started the classroom work with a daily briefing. We reviewed the sad state of affairs on Yankee Station, talked about how we meant to change it. Our study of the after-action reports revealed one thing that all of us knew pretty well. Dogfights were over in a hurry. The critical moment was the Merge, when two jets passed a few hundred yards apart. The enemy's next move after that point told you a lot. Is he aggressive? Does he turn toward you sharply, confidently, put the pressure on you? Or does he hesitate for a critical second and a half and let you make the next move? The smart fighter pilot leads with his strength—his first best move. Because it's probably all going to be over in less than a minute. The elapsed time from Merge to kill was thirty to forty-five seconds. Everything you knew had to come together in that vanishing moment of life or death.

We flew a couple of times to let our students shake off the rust. There wasn't much of it to shake. Flying two-seat TA-4 Skyhawks as "aggressors," in the role of the enemy, we learned quickly that these were no beginners. They climbed the learning curve quickly. I respected their abilities, as I did with all my opponents.

The pace of the program accelerated once we began flying a lot. After the first week or so, we ran two or three training sorties every day. With instructors playing the role of aggressors, we would put the students in different scenarios, flying all the basic permutations—1 vs. 1, 2 vs. 1, 1 vs. 2, 2 vs. 2, 4 vs. 2, 4 vs. 4, and 2 vs. 4.

A dogfight is a true physical ordeal. When a fighter aircraft is flown hard, it shakes you like a plummeting roller coaster on the verge of collapse. You're buffeted from side to side, helmet hammering the Plexiglas canopy, harness digging into your shoulders and hips. G forces cause blood to surge and drain from your extremities, including your head. Our program tested not only a student's body, but his mind.

With four or even five separate test engagements on every flight, you can do the math and then imagine the strain this places on a pilot. It beats you up and sometimes, on the most instructive days, drains you to your core. ACM is a full-contact sport played on the edge of life and death. The fast pace of operations exhausted even well-conditioned aircrews. We were especially zonked after starting the day with an 0430 briefing. To allow for recuperation, we alternated schedules. After an early day in the air, the next morning we slept in, meeting in the classroom at 0630 or 0700. We worked almost around the clock, eating when we could, usually from a food truck that rolled onto the 121 ramp. We were that lady's favorite customers, devouring her sliders and hot dogs, heavy on the mustard and onions.

There were a couple of names for the MiG-killing new tactic we developed for the F-4 community. It basically involved flying a Phantom like a Saturn V rocket. Straight up. Sometimes we called it "using the vertical envelope." It was also known as the "high yo-yo." But the name we settled on was inspired by the shape of the airspace we used while flying it. J. C. Smith called it the Egg, and the moniker stuck. That was the shape our Phantoms traced, rocketing up and coming back down. I should point out that Topgun did not invent this maneuver. The guys in the F-8 Crusader community had been using "the vertical option" for years. Our breakthrough was applying it to the fighter of our day, the F-4 Phantom, an aircraft that was never supposed to perform such tricks but that proved very well suited for it thanks to its powerful engines.

The maneuver really did break new ground. In the safety-conscious cocoon that was the RAG, what little dogfighting we did stayed in the horizontal plane. The vertical was something that only a few rebellious instructors fooled around with from time to time.

You might guess the names. Mel, he was one. I had used it in my "fight club" days off San Clemente a decade before. The best pilots we encountered in those after-hours hassles always used the vertical. I learned from the best out there, just as Mel had when he was stationed at North Island.

None of our students had ever flown an F-4 Phantom like a space vehicle out of Cape Canaveral. None ever forgot his first experience of the "pure vertical." With the student in the rear seat we'd fly somewhere out over the ocean or the desert of El Centro, then start the demonstration. Lighting the afterburners, I accelerated to five hundred knots, then hauled the stick back into my gut. Since the Phantom had no trouble reaching Mach 2 in level flight, it wasn't hard to fly straight up. We sank into our seats as the airplane began to climb. With those twin J79s cooking away, we pointed our nose to the stars. I held it. And held it. And held it some more. Our nose was still pointed high. Despite the enormous thrust of the engines, the big brute eventually started to decelerate. That was when the student in the rear seat got worried.

As we lost speed, trading kinetic energy for the potential energy of altitude, the basic aerodynamics of lift came into play. Airplanes aren't engineered to grip the sky at very low speeds. The airfoil of the wing just can't do its work. A maneuver like this is a no-no in any RAG. At low speed but under full power, the airframe starts to vibrate ever so slightly.

At that point most aviators want to push the nose over and let gravity get them moving again. They want airflow rushing over that swept wing to resume giving them lift. But that wasn't what we were doing. Not yet. Both hands on the stick, elbows against my ribs, I kept the nose high with absolutely no aileron input.

As the Phantom sat atop that towering parabola, engines still putting out full power but with our airspeed feeling like it was near zero, we started what's known as a tail slide. It's an unnatural thing for a heavy jet to do. Properly done, though, it's safe. The engines hiccupped, belched some flame and smoke, but they never quit.

At this point, I'd often hear hollering in my headphones. "Do something!" The poor student was along for the ride, helpless. But I couldn't worry about that. I needed him to experience the physical sensations of this unusual "flight profile"—and know he could live through it. Because this was where the magic happened. Anyone who's tossed one of those little balsawood gliders into the air with the adjustable wing shoved all the way forward has seen how elegantly a three-ounce toy plane rises up and falls back. That was basically what we were doing here.

If this were a combat scenario, we would have left our enemy well behind as we rocketed heavenward. Now as we turned back over at the top, my RIO scanned the sky below to help me find him. It was hard for him if he wasn't tracking closely. It was tricky to keep an eye on your prey, sitting there upside down, G forces pulling you. But if you paid attention throughout the maneuver, you'd know where your target was. That was bad news for a MiG. We were going to turn him into a bag of dust.

Normally our Phantoms flew in pairs. The formation was known as the Loose Deuce—two planes flying in line abreast. As soon as we made contact with an enemy, one F-4 would attack, beginning a turning fight. The other would skyrocket into the vertical, as I have just described. While the enemy was busy with the wingman, turning and veering in the horizontal plane, he would have little chance of seeing the other Phantom as it rocketed to the top of the Egg. I would use these unbothered seconds to choose a flight path that put the enemy dead center in my missile envelope.

Technique was critical as I came off the afterburners, pressed my foot down on the rudder pedal, and fed in some rudder. As the nose of the plane began to fall through, pointing back down to earth, we began a dive that allowed us to regain airspeed. We took a vector to lead the enemy or latch on to his tail, keeping enough distance to set up a good missile shot.

This was the important tactical evolution we developed at Topgun. I would explain it to my rear-seater on the intercom system as we went along, and gave him a debriefing on the way back to base. Because his turn at the stick was just moments away.

By the time we landed back at Miramar and taxied to the octagon, as the rotary refueling facility installed there on the taxiway is known, my student was completely exhilarated, realizing that we'd just rewritten the rules. As I shut down the port engine for a hot refueling, ground crews hustling in our giant NASCAR-like circular pit stop, my student could hardly wait to try to fly the Egg himself. As soon as the refueling was done, we switched seats, taxied around, and took off again.

Out over the desert or the ocean, I'd coach him through the vertical maneuver. He had never dreamed a Phantom could do it, but our rugged machine performed the same way every time. Once the student decided he could trust it, he was exhilarated to fly the F-4 as it was never supposed to be flown.

Back on the ground, there was always a lot of laughing and hollering from the front cockpit. The student would be ready to beat his chest. And trust me on this: Once four or five twentysomethings have an experience like that, the energy level at the O club that evening is something to see. If you walk in and witness it, the buzz you'll hear isn't rowdy idiocy. It's the sound of people believing in themselves, in their aircraft, in their weapons, in their leadership, and in their ability to win a war when it all comes together.

The day to start worrying about your military is the Friday night you go into an officers' club and everybody's quiet, staring into their beer.

We knew that the RAG's emphasis on radar interception was not going to help us in Vietnam, where visual identification of a target was required by the rules of engagement. It especially worried us that the missiles were still treated as infallible when experience showed us they were anything but. So when nuggets were told that they could get a kill with their AIM-9B Sidewinder if they fired it within a thirty-degree arc of the enemy's tail—and that was the only parameter they thought they needed—we knew we had considerable work ahead of us. Truth was, a missile shot was exceptionally difficult when your target was maneuvering for his life and angles were sharp. Jim Ruliffson broke this down at the level of circuitry to show why targets needed to be led a little in order for the infrared sensor to have time to activate and acquire the target after the missile had launched from the plane. That short lag was causing a lot of missiles to fly uselessly around Southeast Asia. Out in the fleet squadrons, those busy COs didn't have a lot of time or space to troubleshoot and innovate.

Flying every day, we worked on all of this, and hard. We developed the Egg in a way that made excellent use of our two-plane Loose Deuce formation. As one Phantom tangled with the opponent at some lower altitude, the other Phantom soared heavenward to set up a kill on the next pass. Working in tandem against an opponent, two pilots could alternate turning and dogfighting and soaring to the top of the Egg, trading status as "free" and "engaged" fighters. It enabled them to keep constant pressure on a MiG, slowly running him out of altitude, airspeed, energy, and eventually fuel, until they could kill his ass. (That off-color language isn't what I was raised to speak. But war isn't pretty and killing is the name of the game. I see no reason to sanitize this reality.)

The Loose Deuce tactic reflected Topgun's culture, which empowered junior officers to act and speak freely. There was no leader/wingman hierarchy in our tactics, which left either fighter free to attack, depending on who sighted a bogey first. Loose Deuce was versatile and aggressive. Certainly it was a far cry from the Air Force's tactic, the Fluid Four, which in spite of its adjective was quite rigid, giving the initiative and most opportunities to the flight leader.

The confidence we invested in our students was well placed. They continued learning fast, and after three or four days of our brand of rocketry, the skeptics came around. Soaring and plunging to and from the top of the Egg, they got educated fast while squaring off with instructors flying as aggressors, and with guest pilots from other squadrons flying F-8 Crusaders, Air Force F-4s, F-86s, F-100s, and other types. The spirit of our tribe caught hold of them deeply, and they became the second generation of believers.

They were good, and their confidence grew. That had its own dangers. We had no alternative but to live dangerously and feel comfortable doing it. Some ego is essential. I considered our rivalry with the pilots of VF-124, the RAG squadron that flew the F-8 Crusader at Miramar, as healthy up to a point. Their long, sleek, gape-mouthed gunfighter was a heck of an older bird. We went head-to-head with them often and a couple of their guys were as good as it got. Moose Myers, Boyd Repsher, and Jerry "Devil" Houston come to mind. I never passed up a chance to fight them. God help the MiG driver who ran into their like on a clear day.

But technology is usually on the side of the newer airplane. A well-flown Phantom did not lose to an F-8 in a 1 vs. 1 contest. Mel went undefeated 1 vs. 1 against the Crusader after 1968, and he fought them constantly. One time I went 1 versus 2 with a Crusader squadron skipper and his wingman. Though they were both good sticks, I was up 3–0 at the end of the third engagement, flying our A-4E Mongoose, even though I was the "1." Feeling pretty good about it, I listened in on their radio conversation. The skipper said, "What the shit is going on here? Damn it, we have to go back and retrain." I'm sure they did, but training wasn't the problem. The problem was that their plane had seen its best day. It was on the way out. But the F-8 guys, bless 'em, never lost their attitude. A lot of them transitioned to the F-4 as the war dragged on. Some of us could not resist the impulse to keep them humble.

In their hangar at Miramar was a glass case containing a beautiful longsword. Its origins were dubious, but the squadron claimed it had been wielded by a twelfth- or thirteenth-century Crusader. They treated it as some kind of holy talisman and generally guarded it accordingly. One night we caught them in a lapse. Some of our guys staged a clandestine operation to liberate the relic. Our student Jerry Beaulier did the honors, sneaking in and taking the sword from its case. The next day at the O club, our guys led a show-and-tell with the blade during happy hour. Some F-8 guys were present. A fracas ensued. Somehow the Topgunners managed to escape with their prize.

We later showed mercy and returned the Crusader sword, with a finishing touch. Marland "Doc" Townsend, a senior instructor and future skipper of VF-121, attached a placard to it certifying that it had been carried aloft at Mach 2. That was a sore point because the Crusader maxed out short of that. I was briefed later on the fistfight that developed in the bar afterward, but neglected to write an after-action report.

Life at Topgun was a fight club every day. As the instructors flew against the students, it was natural for the students to want to take a scalp now and then. If one of them beat Rattler, Smash, Sawatzky, Cobra, or me, it could help his service reputation. They seldom did it. But by the end of the syllabus and its twenty-six flights, it did happen. There was plenty of pride to be taken in that. I tried to keep them grounded. Everybody gets beaten now and then, I told them. If you managed to beat Mel and were smart, you understood it was dangerous to pump up your ego. The lesson there was that if Mel could get beat, anyone could. I considered this attitude the heart of professionalism. And as for my instructors, from time to time I had to warn them, "No egos, fellas. We're here to teach."

All that said, I couldn't always keep Rattler and Nash from wanting a piece of each other. Though these guys were close, they were just so strong-willed. Nash was a real needler. He could piss off the pope. He was always working on Mel. Maybe he didn't like the consensus that Holmes was the most talented Phantom pilot we had. I understood this and watched them carefully.

One day during a 2 vs. 1 with a student, they mixed it up hard. Mel and the student were the 2, going against Nash, who was flying an adversary aircraft. It turned into the Rattler versus Smash show, a contest of greats. It happened more than once, and we had a serious offline discussion. I had to lay down the law once again: no dogfighting between Topgun instructors. We were there to teach, not to feed our egos. Too much was at stake. I was mindful of Halleland's warning. One accident could scuttle us, the skipper had said. If Nash and Holmes stayed on this course, very likely one or both would be making a long trip back to the trailer on foot, with a popped parachute bundled up under his arm. Losing a plane could number our days.

No, I didn't want my pilots living on the pride of whom they could beat. All of us were in the same fraternity. When, say, Jerry Beaulier was finished with Topgun, I wanted to be sure how he would do against a MiG—and maybe unsure how I would fare against him. If we did our job, we'd have made him pretty dangerous. That's where any good instructor will find his pride.

CHAPTER TEN

SECRETS OF THE TRIBE

Miramar
1969

Only in 2013 did the U.S. government finally declassify its reports on a secret Defense Intelligence Agency project to test actual MiGs. Part of the effort went by the name of Have Doughnut. That program was made possible after an Iraqi pilot defected to Israel in 1966, delivering his prize MiG-21 to the West. A bit later, a Syrian pilot mistakenly landed in Israel with his MiG-17 and another operation was born. The DIA called that one Have Drill.

We were in the middle of teaching Class One at Topgun when our friends up the highway at Air Test and Evaluation Squadron Four, or VX-4, let us in on the secret of the captive MiGs. The squadron's CO, Commander James R. Foster, often invited us to his base at Point Mugu, north of Los Angeles, to join the fun on their Friday "fight of the week" event. His guys, all of them seasoned test pilots, were always ready to try out some new tactic in a new plane. We tried never to miss the show.

One weekend Foster invited J. C. Smith and me to his ready room, where he showed us film of U.S. planes dogfighting against a MiG-21. This really got our attention. It was footage from an

American test range. Jim explained that he and his chief of projects, Marine major Don Keast, had been going to a forbidden zoo in the Nevada desert where these exotic animals were being tamed. The heavily restricted airspace had several names. Paradise Ranch. Groom Lake. Dreamland. Area 51.

Naturally, we expressed interest in having a turn. In the spring of 1969, Foster worked channels to secure approval for the leadership of Topgun to go to Dreamland for a week and see it for ourselves. The project was so secret that when we flew from San Diego to Nellis Air Force Base, near Las Vegas, we weren't allowed to tell our families anything about our destination, let alone what we would be doing.

From Nellis we took a cab into the city, where, across from the Las Vegas Hilton, there was a small hotel that was run by the CIA. The barkeeper at the watering hole there, known as O'Brien's, must have owned a security clearance. He had a professional's knowing attitude and never asked questions as we unwound during our overnight stay. The next morning before sunrise we would be back in the taxicab to the air base for a flight to the safari park where the MiGs lived.

It's probably not wise for me to describe a lot of what I saw at Area 51. The way the base was laid out, it was hard to see much. You'd man your airplane in the hangar and they'd pull you out. The hangars and taxiways seemed to have been arranged to block your lines of sight in most directions. That was fine by me. Highly sensitive programs went on there that I don't believe the public had an immediate need to know about. The CIA's A-12 Oxcart program— better known by its Air Force name, the SR-71 Blackbird strategic reconnaissance aircraft—was one. Other classified activities went on there at night, which may account for why we never stayed over on our days to fly. We clocked out at closing time and were back to O'Brien's by dusk.

But what we learned during the day was just invaluable. While the TA-4 and F-86H did a fair impersonation of a MiG-17, and the F-5 could stand in for a MiG-21, there was no substitute for the real thing. When I first saw the 17 up close, my instant feeling was trepidation, as I would soon be flying it. Sitting on its stubby nose and leaning over the windscreen to look into the cockpit, I was impressed for better and worse. It was old, rough, simple, heavy, and beautiful in its way. The avionics were crude, lacking the power-boosted controls of U.S. aircraft. I gave the fuel gauge a double take. This bird carried only eighteen hundred pounds of fuel, less than one-eighth of what a Phantom's tanks held.

I got six or seven flights in the adversary plane. It was agile to be sure, but I still felt like I was flying a very fast anvil. My frequent opponent at Dreamland was one of Jim Foster's crackerjacks at VX-4, Ron "Mugs" McKeown. He was a superb pilot. He concealed a considerable intellect behind his breezy self-confidence and ready willingness to do mischief. Tough, too. At the Naval Academy, he went undefeated for three years in the boxing ring. Mugs and I would spend most of a day flying head-to-head and swapping roles, Phantom for MiG. A former Air Force test pilot school graduate, Mugs was used to flying a lot of different aircraft. He was damn good in a MiG. The plane was so quick to run out of gas, even without using its afterburner, that you had to make your moves and score your points fast. You had to learn the rhythm of how to fight it. If you did, you could be dangerous.

Another pilot at VX-4, Lieutenant Commander Foster "Tooter" Teague, claimed that no Navy pilot who flew against the MiG-17 beat it 1 vs. 1 the first time out. That may not have been true, but either way, Major Boyd was right that the Communist plane had its advantages. Of course, we knew that already. It turned out that Doc Townsend, who had preceded Hank Halleland as skipper of the Phantom RAG, had, unbeknownst to me, flown against the MiG-21 at Dreamland a few years before we started Topgun. Townsend's work, though very highly classified, apparently had given the F-4 community its initial push to fly beyond prescribed boundaries in ACM. He seems to have passed down a lot of what he had learned to Sam Leeds at the RAG.

There was no better way to validate our tactics than to try them out at Dreamland. Once the Air Force guys got used to seeing us, we were allowed to fly straight to the base that did not exist from Miramar. We'd taxi in before sunrise, park our airplanes, go to the hangar, and sometimes grab a combat nap. We were in the skies at first blush of dawn. We never filed a flight plan. One day I flew a brand-new F-4J out to evaluate it against MiGs. Fresh from the factory in St. Louis, that Phantom smelled like a new car. It had, among other things, an improved radar and fire-control system that we were anxious to try out.

I should say here that the captured MiGs weren't supposed to be flown in dogfights. "ACM evaluation" was not the purpose of their Nevada residency. They had been obtained by the Air Force for "technical research." The blue suits were measuring engine temperatures, high- and low-end airspeeds, doing all the stuff they did in testing at Edwards Air Force Base. Accordingly, the three-star general who was in charge of the Air Force units at Groom Lake allowed no dogfighting. There could be no such risky behavior on his watch. We saw it differently. There were tactics to prove up. So we bent a few rules. If the Air Force chose to skip our flight briefs or debriefs, which they did, who were we to insist upon wasting their time? We got ourselves on the schedule and did our own thing. I suppose this was the closest we ever came to resembling characters in the old TV show *Baa Baa Black Sheep*. Forgiveness is easier to request than permission.

When Mugs met me at the hangar, enthused as he always was, he said he was scheduled to fight a MiG-17 and asked to borrow my airplane. It was still hot from my ferry flight, but I saw no reason to refuse him. He said something about wanting to test a new evasive maneuver when he flew that afternoon against one of the greats at VX-4, Tooter Teague, who had worked with Jim Foster in getting naval pilots' access to the MiGs. It was foolproof, he said, though adding that the maneuver had never been tried in an F-4. It was cheeky of Mugs to announce this after talking me out of that hot rod. As he taxied to the fuel pit, topped off, and accelerated down the runway, I suspected I'd been had.

Even if that was the case, I didn't want to miss the show. Mugs McKeown and Tooter Teague going 1 vs. 1 was always worth seeing. Both men were top-tier test and evaluation guys. You never knew what you might see. So I checked out another Phantom belonging to VX-4 and joined them in the airspace over Area 51.

Circling at a safe distance, with J. C. in the rear seat, I watched them merge and start a dogfight. Neither seemed to be getting an edge on the other and the tangle descended to lower and lower altitudes. Then Mugs tried his maneuver. He turned so sharply that his plane skidded and momentarily "departed controlled flight," as we say. Regaining it, he flipped over, inverted, and entered a stall once again. This was graduate-level flying, PhD sort of stuff. I can't do justice to the adventurous aerodynamics of it without moving my hands around a lot and using technical language.

After the stall Mugs was not able to regain control. Tooter broke character as an enemy aggressor and was trying to give Mugs some help over the radio. Mugs said something like "I got it." But he never saved his plane from its spinning descent toward the desert.

As the F-4J tumbled below five thousand feet, the hard deck through which we were never supposed to descend, Tooter and I both yelled, "Mugs, get out!"

Cool as a test pilot, he said, "I'm departing the airplane."

As if in slow motion, the Phantom arced toward the earth for the last time. Mugs or his RIO, Pete Gilleece, pulled the ejection handle.

Foom-foom! Two small rockets went off, two seats followed, and—thank God—two parachutes opened in the sky. And two million dollars' worth of factory-fresh Navy flying machine erupted in flames in the desert.

As Mugs and Pete continued their nylon descent, they drifted directly toward the churning fireball. Fortunately, the desert whipped up a breeze that carried them to a landing maybe two hundred feet from the flames. They felt a pretty toasty heat wave but walked away without a scratch.

I wasn't sure the same would be said of Topgun.

After a mishap involving a multimillion-dollar piece of equipment, Uncle Sam required an investigation. And that worried me. Any report of the loss of a VF-121 plane at Topgun would imperil the program as it struggled to make its way. Since I had checked that Phantom out of Hangar One, we were responsible for it. Hank Halleland's warning rang in my ears.

When I landed and returned to the hangar, I made the call to Hank to break the news. I was surprised to find out that Jim Foster had reached my skipper first. Jim explained to him that it had been his pilot who carried out the maneuver while doing VX-4 business. Hank must have smiled as he said to Jim, "Okay. If that's true, you just bought yourself an airplane." With those words, the test-and-evaluation squadron took the hit and Topgun was off the hook.

Jim, to his eternal blessing, took the additional trouble of reporting the incident directly to Washington, instead of to Pacific Naval Air Forces headquarters. By reporting it to Rear Admiral Edward L. "Whitey" Feightner, the chief of naval fighter studies, he saved Vice Admiral William F. Bringle at AirPac from having to deal with it. (I promise you Bringle knew of the incident about fifteen minutes after it happened.) That double trick made our crashed bird VX-4's loss and let everybody avoid a grilling from our West Coast headquarters. No one wanted to see Topgun shot down, for we had come so far in such a short time.

Taking our leave of Dreamland that evening and flying back to Miramar in a VX-4 jet, J. C. and I drank well at the officers' club. Topgun would see another day. Where do we get men of Jim Foster's and Hank Halleland's courage? They never seemed to forget that we were at war.

The Air Force was slow to get wind of what we were doing with those precious captive toys at Area 51. We kept no written records of the dogfighting. Routine maintenance paperwork was our only paper trail. The reporting and debriefs were all done verbally after each flight, safely back at Miramar, within our tribe, over a beer or two in the trailer late at night, or at the officers' club.

Mel Holmes and I were invited to visit the Air Force Fighter Weapons School at Nellis to brief them on what we were doing at Miramar. I was curious to check in at their gun shop and learn more about the General Electric M61 Gatling gun pods they mounted to their Phantoms. (We decided not to use them.) Nothing the Air Force was doing entered the homegrown Topgun curriculum. Our cultures were so different, and that was reflected in our tactics. We did know that Colonel Lloyd "Boots" Boothby, a USAF pilot at Nellis, was as aggressive as we were, but had to hide it. He and some other good men, including Windy Schaller, one of the chief test pilots, were deeply frustrated with the rigidity.

Topgun couldn't avoid a rivalry with the U.S. Air Force. It wasn't about politics to us. It was about flying and ideas. Sure, it bothered us to hear the Air Force claim it had created the first fighter weapons school. (If that was true in name, it wasn't true in substance—or result.) It's bad ideas that lose wars and get people killed.

The most vocal advocate of the Air Force thinking at the time was Major John Boyd. In 1969 he was making a lot of speeches promoting his "energy-maneuverability" theory of air-to-air warfare. Simply put, it's a mathematical formula that tries to reduce fighter aircraft performance to a single value based on the plane's speed, thrust, aerodynamic drag, and weight. First put forward in 1964, it had reportedly been used by the Air Force to design new fighters such as the F-15 Eagle and F-16 Fighting Falcon, outstanding planes, as we all know. When Topgun was getting launched, Holmes, Jerry Sawatzky, and I attended classified conferences to keep current, and we'd see Boyd at several of them. Eventually, after we were established, we were invited to make presentations of our own.

In 1969, Mel and Ski gave a talk at Tyndall Air Force Base in Florida. John Boyd followed them, pitching his theory. There was some good debate, and Mel remembers Air Force officers starting to challenge their catechism. A particularly brave captain once questioned the Fluid Four concept by asking why a wingman with more tactical experience than his flight leader should be forbidden from taking a kill when he had it. That one ruffled some feathers. In the Q&A, though, Major Boyd made an infamous remark. He said that no U.S. pilot should ever dogfight a MiG, because his theory proved mathematically that since the enemy plane performed better throughout the flight envelope than the F-4, taking on a MiG was a good way to end up hanging from a parachute or a whole lot worse.

The problem with any theory is the baggage of its assumptions. We thought Major Boyd was making some rather large ones and considered his analysis suspect as a result. In the base auditorium at Tyndall that day, Ski poked Mel in the ribs.

"Why don't you say something, Rattler."

Mel stood up and proposed to the Air Force officer that he was underrating a few things. Namely people. Mel said that while weapons might have parameters and airplanes theoretical values, no algorithm could predict much if it excluded the most important factor of all: the skill, heart, and drive of the pilot in the cockpit. The moment of truth was the Merge. It was then that you had your chance to take the measure of a man.

"Sir," Mel said, "I just don't think you can know anything about another pilot before the first turn. And if you don't know that, then you can't say that a MiG-17 will win every time."

That needed saying.

The best I can recall, Major Boyd didn't really engage. He replied by restating his claim. "Thank you for that view, Lieutenant, but you can't fight MiGs in an F-4. We'll lose wars that way."

We would see about that.

John Boyd was intelligent, patriotic, and good at a great many things. From this exchange, we concluded that one of them was deriving big ideas that aspired to universality but did not reckon with the human heart. In aerial combat, technical factors were important. Some of them could be modeled. But no model could tell the whole story. Major Boyd was not wrong. His theory was simply incomplete. He also completely misjudged the F-4. We were no slouches at the science, either. With Cobra Ruliffson's technical acuity and hard work, we had fused hard data with equally hard experience. It ended up showing exactly how a Phantom could smoke a MiG, almost every time.

The energy-maneuverability theory had little to say about tactics or the people who made them work. The pilot is the key part of the equation, though as a variable it cannot be quantified. Out at Miramar, as students and instructors bent the jet and flew beyond the limits, we were trying to turn the man in the cockpit into a weapon. As adversary pilots, Mel, Ski, Cobra, Nash, and I were enjoying the role, flying, debriefing, and adjusting from the enemy point of view. Day after day and flight after flight, we were helping our students meet the challenge. We were making them part of the equation.

Men surely are weapons, and, as I said, ideas matter. I'd venture to say that any engagement pitting Major Boyd and any of his handpicked three against Mel, Jim, Nash, and Sawatzky would have had an instructive outcome. (And okay, I guess I have to say it: I could have filled in for any of them to equal result.) Adherence to strict rules and restrictions meant almost certain defeat against well-trained pilots fighting under no such restrictions. And this is why we say Topgun never existed before the Navy set up at Miramar. No schoolhouse that required adherence to fixed ideas, reduced airplanes to numbers, or considered its instructors as "priests" could ever be Topgun in our book. The final tallies over Vietnam would eventually tell the tale.

While Topgun's forays to Area 51 were never discussed at Miramar (the handful of us who were cleared to go treated the classification seriously), those flights were incredibly valuable. Our experiences there went straight into our 0430 briefings, and from there were used to refine the Topgun syllabus. We learned some

In 1956, at Whiting Field, in Florida, I entered primary flight training to become a naval aviator. We flew the legendary North American SNJ. Those well-worn birds were usually oil-streaked, like this one.

Ensign Pedersen at NAS North Island, 1959, with my first operational squadron, VF(AW)-3. Flying the F4D Skyray, I learned from such great pilots as World War II ace Eugene Valencia.

Standing twenty-four-hour alerts with our "Fords," we were always ready to intercept a Soviet bomber attack before it reached the West Coast.

An F-4 Phantom intercepts a Soviet Tu-95 Bear somewhere over the western Pacific. These encounters were usually quite friendly.

America's first nuclear-powered carrier, USS *Enterprise*, became my home on Yankee Station in 1967. In four months, our air group lost thirteen of its hundred pilots.

An F-4 Phantom releases a load of Mark 82 bombs over South Vietnam. By 1967, the Navy was suffering from a shortage of bombs.

Four North Vietnamese pilots with twenty U.S. aircraft to their credit at a runway near Hanoi. We were not prepared for close-in dogfights against the agile MiG-17. Defeating the Russian-built interceptors became the founding premise of Topgun.

VF-121 ADVANCED TACTICS FLIGHT INSTRUCTORS 1969
Original "TOPGUN" Instructors listed in bold with "Call Signs"

Back Row L-R: Jerry Kinch, Dick Moody, Peter Jago, Tom Irlbeck, **Darrell "Condor" Gary**
Ross Anderson, **Jerry "Ski" Sawatzky**, Sam Vernallis, Don Sharer, **Jim "Hawkeye" Laing**

Front Row L-R: Joel Graffman, **Steve "Rebel" Smith**, **Mel "Rattler" Holmes**, Hank Halleland
Dan "Yank" Pedersen, Vern Jumper, **Jim "Cobra" Ruliffson**, John "Smash" Nash
J.C. "Mississippi Two-Five Thousand" Smith (not in photo)

The boldfaced names were my Original Bros at Topgun. I told them our mission would be the most important thing we did in our military careers. "We hold lives in our hands."

Jim "Hawkeye" Laing, one of our Original Bros, stands beside his F-4 Phantom prior to the first strike against Kep Airfield near Hanoi in April 1967. Laing was shot down during this mission and was later rescued by helicopter.

Jim Laing was the only Original Bro to eject twice as a result of battle damage over North Vietnam. This stunning photo, taken by Jim's wingman, shows him ejecting on April 24, 1967, after the strike on Kep. His pilot ejected a split second later.

Mel "Rattler" Holmes was the finest Phantom pilot in the Navy in 1969. Tough, relentlessly aggressive in the air and on the ground, Mel was a key part of Topgun's initial success as our tactics and aerodynamics specialist.

Darrell "Condor" Gary and Jim Laing aboard *Kitty Hawk* on Yankee Station, on April 24, 1967, hours before Jim and his pilot were shot down and later rescued.

Jerry "Ski-Bird" Sawatzky towers over Mike Guenther, one of our adversary pilots, as they stand in front of a pair of A-4 Skyhawks. Jerry was a natural teacher at Topgun and a superb aviator too.

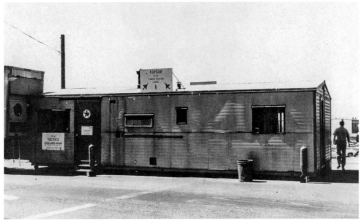

Once we had our team assembled, we needed an office and classroom space. Steve Smith found this abandoned modular trailer and paid a crane operator a case of scotch to deliver it to our area at Miramar.

Mel Holmes and Steve Smith designed the Topgun patch in the Miramar officer's club one night on a cocktail napkin. Complaints that it might offend the Russians soon ceased.

At Topgun, we painted our aggressor A-4s in camouflage schemes used by air forces around the world. Some of those paint jobs rendered the little aircraft almost invisible.

Here I am with J. C. Smith in a TA-4 Skyhawk belonging to Ken Wiley's VF-126. Ken's Skyhawks became Topgun's initial adversary aircraft.

A MiG-21 flies over Area 51. Captured Soviet aircraft played a key role in helping us develop the tactics to defeat them.

From April through October 1972, during Operation Linebacker, F-4 squadrons downed twenty-one MiGs, losing just four aircraft in return. The stunning success validated the Topgun program.

Though we learned to beat the MiGs, the war ended in defeat in 1975. Condor flew high cover the day the last Americans were evacuated from rooftops around Saigon. Meanwhile, the South China Sea was carpeted with hundreds of vessels filled with refugees fleeing the North Vietnamese Army.

After Vietnam, Topgun continued teaching new generations of fighter pilots. Here, a Topgun instructor demonstrates maneuvering an F-14 Tomcat against a MiG-21 during a class in the mid-1970s.

An adversary TA-4 painted in a Soviet Air Force scheme.

One of Topgun's F-5 adversary aircraft goes vertical off the California coast. The Freedom Fighter did a fine impression of a MiG.

After leaving
Topgun, I took over
VF-143 and in 1976
commanded the
Coral Sea air wing.

The F-14 Tomcat reached the fleet in the mid-1970s and served until 2006.
Made famous by the movie *Top Gun*, the F-14 was beloved by all who flew it.
I regret that I never did.

When the Navy promoted me to captain in 1978, my flying days were over. I commanded the fleet replenishment ship USS *Wichita* then took the aircraft carrier *Ranger* to the Persian Gulf.

At sea aboard the *Wichita*, I'm in the dark jacket surrounded by the bridge crew. The ship won several highly coveted Battle Efficiency Awards ("Battle E's") for superior performance in an operating environment.

The *Ranger* and one of her escorts replenish at sea. Taking command at Subic Bay in October 1980 was the capstone of my career.

Monroe "Hawk" Smith was my air ops officer on the *Ranger*. He was the skipper of Topgun from 1976 to 1978.

Mary Beth and me at my parents' home in Whittier, California. I flew home from flight training in Texas over Christmas 1956.

Mary Beth and I reconnected thirty-two years after our breakup. We were married in Denmark, in the church that had baptized my father. The ring on my finger is the one she gave me for Christmas in 1956.

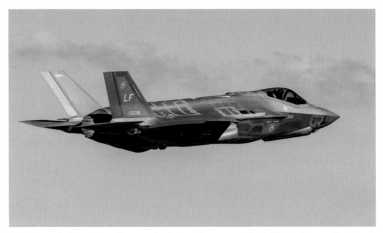

The Navy and Air Force have staked their futures on the F-35 Lightning II. Development of the so-called Joint Strike Fighter (some pilots call it the "penguin") began in 1992. Twenty-seven years later, we do not yet have a fully operational squadron and it is the most expensive weapons program in history.

Mel Holmes, myself, Darrell Gary, and Jim Laing at Condor's house in Southern California in April 2017, almost fifty years after we stood up Topgun.

important thing about the MiGs, and for that we were in debt to our friends at VX-4.

Slowly but surely, we were gaining confidence that when our junior officers went back to the war, they would be the dogfighters— and teachers—that their country needed in a desperate hour.

CHAPTER ELEVEN

PROOF OF CONCEPT

miramar
1969

Topgun's students became crisp, smart, quick, deadly, and confident. They knew the performance envelopes of their airplanes and missiles, maneuvered quickly to exploit them, and handled all the switch interfaces in the cockpit efficiently. They demonstrated their ability to fly the Egg tactics to perfection and use the high yo-yo out of a two-plane Loose Deuce formation to fillet and fry aggressor pilots almost every time out. Their final exam was a special treat: an unrestricted Sparrow and Sidewinder shoot against live maneuvering targets.

Steve Smith was in charge of our BQM-34 Firebee drone live-fire exercises, generously provided to us by Jim Foster's squadron up the road at Point Mugu. These remote-controlled jet-powered gunnery targets, built by the Ryan Aeronautical Company, had been around since the 1950s. Unlike towed targets and the more common drones, which did not maneuver, the BQM-34s were flown by an operator on the ground. They were capable of more than six hundred knots and could fly up to sixty thousand feet. In the hands of a Phantom instructor like Steve-O, well, that twenty-two-foot-long target had a fair chance of giving even a good pilot fits. While it didn't have the power to soar vertically, it was plenty maneuverable, capable of sharp twists and break turns. Though we were a little worried about the possibility of accidents flying such a hot rod from the ground in a live-fire exercise, we figured the risk was worth it. Topgun's students needed this experience against a thinking opponent before we sent them back to war. At the Pacific Air Missile Test Range, some of our young guys were so good that they destroyed the wildly evading drones, then shot some more missiles to pick off the falling parts. After a success like that, the confidence soared and they were on final approach to graduation day in early April. As it approached, we had another surprise in store for them—a flight out to Area 51 to take a turn against a real live MiG as I related in the previous chapter. For students, it was a crowning moment in their young careers.

One evening at the Miramar O club while Class One was winding down, we designed what has endured ever since as the official Topgun flight-suit patch. Steve Smith and Mel Holmes sketched it out on a napkin: a MiG-21 in a Phantom's gunsight reticle and pipper. In Washington, people who had time to worry about such things thought it might offend the Russians. I made one call to Vice Admiral Bringle's office and the complaint went away. The patch design perfectly reflected the origin story of Topgun, and it has survived basically unchanged for fifty years. Every graduate of the Navy Fighter Weapons School wears it with pride.

As that small emblem got around the fleet, people noticed. As the reputation of Topgun flourished and grew, the fleet squadrons began calling *us*. Very soon Steve had the pleasure of explaining that all our billets were full, but that he'd be glad to keep their names on file.

The story of the patch, like so many other stories about Topgun, suggested the wisdom of letting junior officers be in charge. If the Navy's decision to put a fresh-caught lieutenant commander in charge seemed like risk avoidance at first, I see now that our insurgency could have succeeded in no other way. Without the great creativity, focus, and pace of younger men, we wouldn't have gotten it done. We were never more openly controversial than we had to be, but we had to rock their boat. You can get away with it, if you know what your mission is and you're damn good. We were.

The graduates of Class One returned to the fleet with a changed way of thinking, a patch, and a Topgun training manual. It was a master document that captured everything we had taught them and made it teachable. As training officers, they were the evangelists of the Egg and the lords of the Loose Deuce, and they set to work remaking the fleet squadrons in our image. Meanwhile, Class Two showed up, and we started the cycle all over again, hustling hard to update the lessons and the program documentation. There was no time to breathe easy.

To think all of this came together in about ninety days and took root in a stolen trailer. On the day Steve got that crane operator to perform a little larceny in exchange for a case of scotch, we never imagined it would become the nerve center of the Navy's evolving effort to improve its fighter tactics and doctrine for the next fifty years. But that's exactly what happened. Never was a man more fortunate to have God as his copilot.

Right after Class Two graduated, Vice Admiral Bringle, as Com-NavAirPac, made a formal request to his boss, Admiral John J. Hyland, the commander in chief of the Pacific Fleet, officially to establish the Navy Fighter Weapons School at Miramar effective July 1, 1969. This meant everything to our fledgling graduate school. For the first time, we had explicit validation from the top of our chain of command, unprecedented for a project led by junior officers. Around the same time, that world-beating RIO, J. C. Smith, relieved me as Topgun's officer in charge. The handover was easy. He had been with me every step of the way. Continuity like that helped Topgun grow roots—just what Sam Leeds had ensured by letting me have the job in the first place.

In October, I went to Washington to brief the Pentagon on our experiences at the Topgun schoolhouse. Our syllabus was approved by the CNO himself. Later that year, Commander Richard Schulte relieved Hank Halleland as skipper of VF-121, our parent command. In Dick Schulte, Topgun continued to be fortunate in its friends. He personally arranged for the acquisition of four new adversary aircraft for our school. The A-4E Mongoose was far more capable than the two-seat TA-4s we had been flying as adversaries in "dissimilar" air combat maneuvering.

One Friday at the O club in the early days, Tooter Teague tried to sell me on using the Air Force's F-86H Sabre as our principal aggressor. The debate went long into the night and was settled the following morning in the air, F-86 versus A-4E. We bent those two jets hard. The moment of truth came when Tooter tried to match me in a vertical climb. He had no chance, not even in burner. It ended with his aircraft stalling, going into an inverted spin, and falling out of control like a dropping maple leaf. At that point he agreed with me that the Mongoose should be Topgun's aggressor of choice. No more borrowing aircraft from the RAG, in other words. We were free to soup them up as we wanted, removing all excess weight. The Mongoose's superior performance and constant availability enabled us to develop an expanded dissimilar ACM curriculum as well. A few months later, the Topgun curriculum got its first test in the crucible of war.

When our student Jerry Beaulier deployed with Fighter Squadron 142, the Ghostriders, on USS *Constellation* in March 1970, it continued to be a strange time on Yankee Station. The air war was still on hold while President Johnson's White House held peace talks with North Vietnam. Though the carriers were striking at enemy supply lines running into South Vietnam through Laos and Cambodia, targets in North Vietnam were off-limits. That meant U.S. planes weren't flying where the bandits were. As usual, there had not been much of a threat to our carriers from enemy aircraft. Not since September 1968 had a U.S. pilot killed a MiG.

In the twelve months since receiving his Topgun patch and returning to his squadron, Jerry had been serving as VF-142's weapons-and-tactics officer, teaching what he knew but enjoying little opportunity to see anyone use it. That changed in March, when it seemed the MiGs were ranging farther south than they had been.

On Saturday, March 28, Jerry and his RIO, Steve Barkley, were idling in their F-4J, standing on the catapult in alert five status, ready for a quick launch. When the radar control ship reported four bandits inbound toward the carrier that afternoon, Beaulier and his air wing commander, Paul Speer, were launched off the *Constellation*'s deck. Directed to take a westerly vector toward the oncoming enemy, still eighty-seven miles out, they were cleared to fire at once (they got a break from the usual rules of engagement requiring visual identification).

As the radar calls kept coming and the range closed, they saw no sign of the MiGs. The Phantom pair pressed ahead. It was Beaulier who first sighted the enemy fighters ahead and above him, at about twenty-five thousand feet. Following the Loose Deuce doctrine, Jerry alerted Speer and took lead, stoking his afterburners and accelerating into a climbing turn to intercept. The two MiGs spotted the Americans and separated, the leader climbing and his wingman breaking into a right turn. Beaulier took the enemy wingman while Speer went after the leader.

As he closed with the number two MiG, Beaulier realized, I suspect, in the space of those first twenty seconds, that his excitement had led him to stray from proper technique. He was fighting in the horizontal. In climbing to engage his enemy directly, he had lost too much airspeed to attack effectively. He dove again to regain it, pulling seven Gs at the bottom. He found the MiG descending with him. Looking to avoid a turning fight, he returned to what we had taught him. He pulled up sharply to initiate the Egg maneuver, rocketing vertically. The MiG had no chance to keep up.

Meanwhile, down below, Commander Speer had seemed to unnerve his own MiG. Its pilot turned wide and left the fight. Speer was turning back toward Beaulier to clear Jerry's tail when Jerry's MiG saw Speer. The North Vietnamese pilot fired a heat-seeking Atoll missile at the approaching Phantom. The head-on shot missed.

Up and up Beaulier's Phantom went. With RIO Barkley keeping him oriented, telling him the MiG shooting at Speer was no threat, Jerry focused on setting up his shot. Arcing over the top, he saw that their opponent was vulnerable. The MiG had lost sight of him. The enemy pilot banked right then reversed sharply left, as if looking for his pursuer.

This last maneuver was a fatal mistake. It gave Jerry a clean shot up the enemy's tailpipe. With the tone of a Sidewinder lock buzzing in his helmet earphones, he pressed the trigger and his missile left the rail. It tracked true and exploded underneath the MiG. A shower of steel fragments sliced into the enemy plane and set it on fire.

Trailing flames like a torch, the MiG sailed along, rocking its wings. Beaulier pulled up sharply to avoid running past him, slid in behind him again, and fired another missile. This one finished him. Just like he had done in the drone shoot at Topgun.

Back on the flight deck of the *Constellation*, the celebration started immediately. Paul Speer, a large man, gave diminutive Jerry a bear hug and lifted him off his feet. Champagne, strictly forbidden, flowed. Later that day a Hanoi radio broadcast confirmed the MiG loss. In Washington, the politics of the peace talks forced the Pentagon to make smoke. Other than a brief announcement of a MiG being downed—the kill was said to have been scored by Phantoms that were escorting photoreconnaissance aircraft—the Navy kept a lid on the story.

Back at Miramar, we wondered who the MiG killer was. We worked our private channels as best we could. When word came back that an unnamed aircrew from the *Constellation* had gotten it, we were thrilled. The carrier's two fighter squadrons had sent us Topgun's first class. We had wondered if there would ever be another dogfight over Vietnam, and were thrilled to think we might have a case study bearing out our tactics. When it was finally confirmed that the MiG killers were Beaulier and Barkley, we were ecstatic. It validated not only what we taught, but our school's very existence.

The highly classified after-action report of their engagement went back to the Pentagon, where the aviation and intel offices studied it in depth. Eventually we listened to the voice tapes of Jerry, Barkley, Speer, and his RIO. As we expected, there was no excitement there. They sounded like they were discussing a particularly important grocery list. Jerry went on to fly 220 missions in the F-4 Phantom. Topgun never taught a better one. Some said his success produced the impetus, then and there, to begin the process of turning Topgun into a proper naval command.

As our humble detachment within VF-121 saw its influence grow, we attracted some interesting visitors. Some very good foreign pilots served on exchange at the RAG. Foremost among these, in terms of talent and experience, was the British contingent. As their Fleet

Air Arm had been transitioning to the F-4, the Brits sent some capable pilots and back-seaters to train with us. They passed through VF-121 much as other foreign exchange pilots did, serving in the RAG tactics section at the time we were forming Topgun. Their senior man was Commander Dick Lord, who was exceptional in the air. All of them, including Dick Moody, Peter Jago, and Colin Griffin, were very professional. While I could not involve them officially in Topgun—Dick had returned to England by the time we started—the Royal Navy exchange pilots performed valuable service within the RAG, especially flying as adversaries.

And they were great fun on the ground. As Condor sums it up, "What we learned from them was how to play mess rugby in our whites at the Admiral Kidd O Club in San Diego; how to pass out in our plates at a dining in; and how to leave our breakfast on the ramp and still make our takeoff times." Contrary to headlines in the British press a few years ago, British pilots had nothing to do with the formation of Topgun. The revisionist history has been disappointing. But it never diminished our affection for the exchange Brits, whether it be in a tavern or in the air.

In 1970, the Great One himself came for a visit to our trailer: Brigadier General Robin Olds. His fighting days were behind him now, but what glorious days they were. In World War II, he became an ace in both the P-38 Lightning and the P-51 Mustang, something no one else ever did, finishing the war as a squadron commander at the age of twenty-two. In 1966 and 1967, his fighter wing was so prolific that the comedian Bob Hope called it "the world's leading distributor of MiG parts." Robin led the way with four kills—a record that stood until 1972. He walked on water as far I was concerned.

When Dick Schulte and I invited Robin to be a guest of honor at one of our monthly Super Happy Hours at Miramar, Olds was

serving as commandant of cadets at the U.S. Air Force Academy in
Colorado Springs. He quickly accepted, but on one condition. He
said he would come only if we let him fly. Though he was a second-
generation West Pointer, he had none of the high attitude you often
find in academy graduates. Robin cared only about results. It didn't
matter what ring you wore. But we were happy to give him this little
perk. We put him on the schedule for an ACM hop in an F-4.

I didn't know whether Robin was current in that aircraft. We
figured he had never flown a Navy model. He arrived with flight
gear and was clearly ready to go. After we gave him a quick cockpit
checkout, away he went. J. C. Smith was his rear-seater and Mel
Holmes flew on his wing.

The first engagement was a 2 vs. 1. The skilled duo of Robin
and Rattler made short work of the aggressor. Rattler went low and
got the bogey turning, leaving Robin to fly free and get the kill. So
far so good. In the next engagement, a 2 vs. 2, Robin and Mel took
on a pair of A-4Es flown by Dick Schulte and T. R. Swartz, a MiG
killer from the A-4 tribe. (T.R., a former F-8 pilot, scored the only
air victory of the war by a Skyhawk pilot.)

It was Mel who located them. Mel and Robin had briefed in
advance how they would use the Loose Deuce formation, and Mel
took the lead, turning toward them, reaching the Merge, and beginning a turning horizontal dogfight against the closest aggressor
plane. The other A-4 wasn't to be found at the moment. Mel, as the
"goat," was setting up his A-4 enemy to be bagged by Robin. That's
when things fell apart.

The Air Force legend did not show. Having spotted the other
Mongoose, he went tearing off after it. As Mel radioed to Olds,
"Hey, I'm engaged," Robin was on the chase, leaving Mel in favor of
trying to get his fangs into the second bandit.

Meanwhile, Swartz gained an edge on Rattler, conducting the dogfight expertly at low altitude, exploiting all the dancing ability of the lightweight, fast-rolling, tightly turning, rapidly accelerating Mongoose. It ended with Mel getting bagged. Believe me, that didn't happen often. It happened here only because his partner quit the tactical plan.

Back on the ground Robin climbed down from the cockpit, enthused. He had enjoyed the chance to wring out a fighter again and get a kill. But he pulled me aside. "Your back-seater talked the entire time. He never shut up!" He was right. J. C. usually never stopped talking. Especially when there was a serious mistake to correct. I still have to laugh. If a triple ace wearing a star was doing it wrong, Lieutenant Commander Smith would not be too shy to tell him. It was part of what made him the best RIO of his day.

At the debrief, J. C. Smith continued talking to Robin—just the way junior officers always talked at Topgun. He was just reviewing our rulebook, dogging his superior officer for not staying with Mel. If Robin ever got his wing out of joint over it, we saw no sign. Despite his deeply ingrained ideas about fighter tactics, and his commitment to the Air Force's Fluid Four, he finally conceded the wisdom of our tactic. "You've got it right," he told me. I doubt the Air Force ever adopted our formation afterward, but it did me a world of good to know that Robin Olds seemed convinced. He would eventually upset the wrong people with his outspokenness on the errors of his service over Vietnam. I would have done anything to persuade this brilliant tactician, warrior, and disruptor to transfer to Miramar. Major command should have been his due.

Handsome, well spoken, and charming, he filled the bill like a rock star that evening, drawing a huge crowd. His speech was superb and very well received.

*   *   *

In May 1971 Commander Roger Box succeeded J. C. Smith as officer in charge of Topgun. A two-tour combat aviator and Navy test pilot, Roger had an agenda. He believed the time had come for Topgun to become a stand-alone command. At the time, it was still just a department within the Phantom RAG. The RAG had the authority to move aircraft and people in and out of Topgun at its discretion. Without control of its own assets, the school in theory could have been out of business overnight if the RAG decided its needs were more important than the Fighter Weapons School's.

But Roger had an ace up his sleeve: the sympathy of the commander of Fleet Air Miramar, Captain Armistead "Chick" Smith. Roger, having served on his fighter wing staff, enjoyed good relations with him and approaching him for help springing Topgun free of control by the RAG. But there were problems. The CO of the RAG squadron at the time was Commander Don "Dirt" Pringle, a highly capable, well-respected officer who could overwhelm people merely with his presence. Under pressure to keep the RAG producing, Pringle didn't want to lose any of his prized aircraft to a separate Topgun command. He needed the A-4Es especially for his tactics shop. He was also hoping to begin doing what Topgun had been doing.

A key player in the fight for Topgun independence turned out to be Lieutenant Commander Dave Frost, one of Roger Box's instructors and a brilliant tactician who succeeded Cobra Ruliffson as schoolhouse specialist in the Sparrow missile. He was member of the Annapolis class of 1963, and had graduated in the second Topgun class.

Dave and his fellow instructors wanted to build on what the first generation of Topgun had accomplished. The manual needed updating, particularly because of all the real-world data the fleet was sending back as they began bagging MiGs. With our program getting results over North Vietnam, there was increased demand as well. We needed more adversary aircraft and skilled pilots than ever. But those resources were being pulled in three directions: training RAG students; supporting Topgun classes; and working with the fleet's adversary training program to prepare deploying squadrons for combat. Something had to give.

On the way back from a tactical conference at VX-4, Frosty and fellow instructors Dave Bjerke, Goose Lorcher, and Pete Pettigrew stopped for dinner in Malibu. They compiled their notes and drew diagrams on paper napkins. The changes that emerged from the "Malibu Conference" were used to update the F-4 tactics manual and maintenance plans.

They thought that as the school evolved it could have a greater impact as an independent command. But Pringle resisted. Scarcity of resources wasn't the only reason. There was also the issue of prestige. Though the public didn't know about Topgun yet, the wider Navy certainly did, and the Air Force had taken notice too. Whichever command "owned" the Navy Fighter Weapons School stood to play a large role in defining the direction of tactics and training. Its officers stood to have their careers enhanced.

That spring Roger Box's influence with Chick Smith began showing some promise. Like all good leaders, Chick usually got people to work together. He directed a ninety-day trial period in which Topgun would operate semi-independently. At the end of that period, Chick would hold a conference to evaluate whether the trial balloon rose or popped. They blocked out some aircraft and people as their own and moved forward independently. Roger managed the ninety days without a hitch. Before the evaluation could take place, he was selected to command a fleet squadron. Dave Frost was left to represent Topgun at a showdown with the Miramar brain trust. Roger's absence wasn't going to help the schoolhouse's cause at that meeting, which was bound to be contentious.

The evening before the decisive meeting, Commander Pringle called Dave to the VF-121 headquarters, where Pringle and his exec pressed him to declare the three-month test a failure, so that everybody could simply continue business as usual. But Frost had done his homework. He came loaded with data showing how much better Topgun had performed when it was operating separately. Though he realized it might hurt his career, he held his ground, defending Topgun like an accomplished attorney making his case. The meeting broke up in disagreement at 9 p.m. They all knew they would reconvene the next morning to finish their arguments, then it would be up to Captain Smith.

The next morning, neither side conceded anything and temperatures rose. Having heard enough, Smith pounded the table, stunning the participants, who had never seen the Fleet Air Miramar commander so agitated. Smith and his aide left the room. After what seemed like hours they returned, and the temperature in the room seemed to drop about ten degrees. Because the verdict was in: Topgun would become a separate command.

It was a quiet celebration at Miramar. I was away on a cruise, and most of the other Original Bros had gone to new duty stations too. Until the decision could be implemented, Topgun's instructors would continue to have responsibilities at the RAG. But the school was now in a real official competition for operating assets, people, aircraft, and funds. It would take a strong team to make it come together.

In January 1972, Captain Smith cut the order. Topgun became a permanent detachment, appearing on the RAG organizational chart with a solid line instead of a dotted line connecting it to Chick Smith's headquarters. That little tweak to the org chart made all the difference. Suddenly we were assured of adequate staffing, equipment, fuel, and operating funds. Our program was free of its former parent organization.

Roger Box became Topgun's first commanding officer, rather than "officer in charge." His tenure was brief. When he was transferred to the fleet on short notice, Mugs McKeown picked up the torch. He had the seniority, charisma, and talent to handle the job well. But he too was set to deploy to Tonkin Gulf. With his departure, Dave Frost, Roger's advocate extraordinaire, became the skipper, serving until Mugs returned from the fleet and relieved him.

In the spring of 1972, after President Nixon restarted the aerial bombing of North Vietnam, Topgun's graduates started tallying victories. By the time Operation Linebacker began, we'd graduated several more classes and were loaded for bear when the air war resumed in earnest.

One afternoon Frosty got a call from Washington. It was his old rival, Dirt Pringle. The former skipper of the RAG had moved on to an influential billet: executive assistant to Admiral Elmo Zumwalt, the chief of naval operations himself. For an upcoming meeting of the Joint Chiefs of Staff, the CNO wanted to present a review of the air-to-air box score. Frosty was to address an Air Force group at Nellis Air Force Base to discuss tactics and organization as well as demonstrate the use of our adversary program. As he put it, "The Navy was going to poke the Air Force in the eye." Dave worked up a presentation of the new Navy tactics. As he and his guys had just revised the Topgun manuals, it was a fairly easy assignment.

The room was crowded—obviously word had gotten around. Dave explained how Topgun operated, and noted the cautious approach the USAF took to air combat training. All of their dogfighting was F-4 against F-4. Never did an Air Force pilot see a plane imitating a MiG.

He got a lot of pushback during the question-and-answer session. A couple of accented voices stood out at the back of the room. As it happened, the Air Force Fighter Weapons School at Nellis had some Israelis among their foreign exchange pilots. One of them was my friend Eitan Ben Eliyahu. He and his cohort, the talented and cerebral Asher Snir, who had twelve and a half kills, had fine reputations that preceded them. Impatient, I suppose, with all the discussion of a matter they considered settled, one of them stood up and said, basically, "We agree with the Navy!" That seemed more or less to end the argument for the moment.

Some Air Force pilots were catching on in the meantime. Junior officers were alive to the dynamism of the Navy's Loose Deuce cruising formation, and the offensive potential of exploiting the Egg. The USAF also began to understand the value of dissimilar combat training, as well as the tactics and culture of the Loose Deuce. The blue suits learned fast, and the training environment became one of mutual respect with a healthy exchange of ideas.

The Air Force sent two Nellis instructors to fly with Topgun for a week. Major Richard "Moody" Suter, who had flown with us at Area 51, and Captain Roger Wells were experienced tacticians. The two pilots spent a week flying in the front seat of the TA-4s, seeing everything from 1 vs. 1 up to 4 vs. 4. Quickly absorbing the nuances of Topgun's syllabus, they returned to Nellis to start urging the Air Force's leadership to come around. Moody, like the great Steve Smith, could sell sand to an Arab. In late 1972, within a few months of the Miramar visit, the "junior service" stood up its first dedicated aggressor squadron, eventually maintaining a force of two dozen T-38 Talons and F-5 Tigers to mimic enemy planes and tactics. The cross-pollination of Topgun's tactics into the Air Force's training would not bear fruit in time to help it reverse its fortunes in the Vietnam War, but the foundation had been laid for a longer-term, mutually beneficial relationship.

Topgun would influence the development of the next-generation fighter, the F-14 Tomcat. We were consulted on new aircraft requirements and weapons acquisition as well. But the future of fighter aviation seemed a distant concern in 1972 as the ground war in Vietnam took a turn for the worse.

CHAPTER TWELVE

TOPGUN GOES TO WAR

Yankee Station
Spring 1972

After the Tet Offensive and the siege at Khe Sanh in early 1968, the U.S. presence in Vietnam diminished, both on the ground and in the air. By the spring of '72, with President Nixon's policy of "Vietnamization" requiring South Vietnam to handle its own defense, only ten thousand American troops remained in country. About a hundred aircraft were on hand in the country to support them. Another hundred or so planes were based in Thailand. Two carriers on Yankee Station fielded another 140 aircraft. Watching this drawdown in U.S. forces, our enemy prepared a massive ground offensive against the South.

On March 30, thirty thousand North Vietnamese Army soldiers, supported by a hundred tanks acquired from Red China, invaded South Vietnam. A few days later, another twenty thousand troops, also supported by tanks, struck South Vietnam from Laos. They were the vanguard of a Communist army that would ultimately field three hundred thousand troops and six hundred armored vehicles.

The South Vietnamese Army, caught by surprise, buckled. When desperate Allied soldiers called for ground support, the Air

Force and Marine Corps squadrons in country were hamstrung by the monsoon season. What aircraft did get through faced shoulder-fired SA-7 missiles, which took a heavy toll. Within a week, the situation grew dire.

To stem the tide, President Richard Nixon unleashed the full weight of American airpower. Air Force F-4 squadrons flew in from all over the world, and the rotation plan that kept two carriers on Yankee Station was replaced by a full-on surge. Soon the *Coral Sea*, *Hancock*, *Kitty Hawk*, and *Constellation* were operating in the Gulf of Tonkin, with the *America*, *Midway*, and *Saratoga* ready to deploy. It would be the largest concentration of naval airpower since World War II. With the restrictive rules of engagement rescinded or modified, it was a different war.

On May 10, President Nixon ordered the mining of Haiphong Harbor and other North Vietnamese ports, putting a stop to Soviet deliveries of MiGs and surface-to-air missiles. Meanwhile, Air Force, Marine Corps, and Navy planes hammered North Vietnamese supply lines. Bridges collapsed under a barrage of first-generation smart weapons, including laser-guided bombs, delivered by Navy Grumman A-6 Intruders and A-7 Corsair IIs. Air Force B-52 Stratofortresses struck MiG airfields around Hanoi.

The enemy tried to defend these important targets. Flying MiG-21 and MiG-19 interceptors, the North Vietnamese pilots found themselves in wild dogfights with USAF F-4 Phantoms. On May 10, three MiG-19s went down to air-to-air missiles, but the North Vietnamese pilots scored two kills. The Air Force continued to use the old-style World War II–era tactics that we found so limiting. During the climax of the morning's air battles, a three-kill F-4 pilot named Major Robert Lodge and his rear-seater, Captain Roger Locher, had just fired a missile at a MiG when another one slipped behind them. Lodge's wingman called out a warning, but it was too late. The MiG pilot opened fire with his cannon and tore the Phantom apart. Major Lodge stayed with the aircraft to give his back-seater a chance to escape. Locher ejected and was eventually rescued after an epic escape and evasion experience. Lodge was killed in action. The Air Force pilots were brave men and good aviators; yet their service's failure to learn the lessons of Rolling Thunder's air battles cost them. On day one of Operation Linebacker, the Air Force barely topped a one-to-one kill ratio in air combat.

The Navy was on a different path. North Vietnamese MiGs encountered a new Navy. The alpha strikes included electronic countermeasures aircraft that jammed the radio frequencies the North Vietnamese pilots used. When they ran into Topgun-trained pilots, the tactics we developed at Miramar changed the game altogether.

The *Constellation's* air wing hit the Haiphong area on May 10. Thirty jets sped over the beach, the pilots determined to inflict maximum damage on a vital target area that had been off-limits for virtually the entire war. Flying escort in an F-4J Phantom was Lieutenant Curt Dosé, who had finished second in his 1971 Topgun class, where he represented my old squadron, VF-92. When Dosé returned from Topgun, he became the weapons training officer. His knowledge and experience percolated throughout the squadron and changed how it fought.

As Dosé and his section leader, Austin "Hawk" Hawkins, orbited between the enemy airfields and the target area, the MiG-21s began to rise. Our radar picket ship, USS *Chicago*, detected the enemy activity at Kep airfield. In the past, we would have been forced to wait for the MiGs to come to us and pose a threat. Now, with the handcuffs removed, the U.S. pilots could break straight for Kep. The Navy planes took only a few minutes to arrive.

At five thousand feet, Curt Dosé spotted two MiGs waiting to take off on the north end of the runway, plus a few more in revetments in the dispersal area. Dosé called to Hawkins, "Silver Kite, in-place turn port. Go!" Both Phantoms went to burner and dove for the deck, breaking the speed of sound on the way down. The MiG-21s, alerted now, lifted off the runway and jettisoned their external fuel tanks.

Dosé in the lead, the Phantoms streaked right over Kep's patchwork asphalt and concrete runway at Mach 1. The sudden switch from the cooler air at altitude down to the humidity down low caused Dosé's canopy to fog, obscuring his view of the fleeing MiG-21s. He shut off the air-conditioner system, which cleared the cockpit almost immediately, and picked up both MiG-21s again.

The chase took them down the treetop level and below. More than once, Dosé lifted a wing to avoid hitting branches. They wound around rolling hills as the MiGs played for time, trying to get their speed up while their fellow pilots launched from Kep to come to their rescue.

Behind the MiGs, with more energy and speed, Dosé and his leader controlled the fight. As the range narrowed and the MiGs passed through thirty degrees in their left turn, Dosé pulled the stick back and maneuvered from a lag pursuit into a perfect setup behind one of the MiGs. His Sidewinder growled in his ear and he fired the missile at about fifteen hundred feet. It missed, exploding behind the MiG. He fired a second missile. This one streaked straight into the MiG's tailpipe. A moment passed before the enemy plane blew apart, killing its pilot.

The lead MiG remained. Hawkins had expended his Sidewinders at it, which either lost tracking or malfunctioned. By now, the pursuit had taken the F-4 pilots back around toward Kep in this left-turn chase. Down to his Sparrow missiles now, Dosé asked Jim McDevitt, his back-seater, if he could get a lock on the MiG. They were too low; the ground clutter kept interfering with the missile's ability to track the enemy aircraft.

For a brief few seconds, the Americans and North Vietnamese were at an impasse. Without guns, the F-4s couldn't finish off the MiG, and with their remaining missiles outside their performance envelope, they would either need to break contact or figure out something else, all while blasting over the treetops at 550 knots.

Dosé, an aggressive and instinctive pilot, was not about to break contact. Instead, he pitched up into the vertical in a sort of barrel roll to try and fire a Sparrow in front of the fleeing MiG. He knew it wouldn't hit, but he hoped to spook the North Vietnamese pilot enough to get him to abandon his turn and give Hawkins a good shot at him.

While inverted at the top of the barrel roll, Dosé automatically checked his six. The other pair of MiG-21s on the runway were right behind them at their five o'clock and closing.

Dosé called them out, and both Phantom drivers broke hard right, toward their attackers, then went to full burner again. They broke through the sound barrier on their way to almost a thousand miles an hour. That sort of maneuver would have left a MiG-17 in the dust. A MiG-21? That Russian fighter possessed exceptional power and speed, and of course the always worrisome guns. A MiG-21 was climbing right up Hawkins's six. The enemy pilot looked to have the F-4 cold.

There was still one trick in the Topgun toolbox. The classified Have Doughnut program at Area 51 had taught us that at such speeds, the MiG-21 couldn't maneuver like an F-4. The two Americans broke hard into each other in a crossing turn, making an X in the sky. The Loose Deuce tactics worked beautifully as the cross turn cleared each other's tails.

Just then, the MiG pilot launched one of the Sidewinder copies known as the AA-2 Atoll missile. Hawkins's tight break defeated the missile—it exploded behind his F-4. The miss combined with the F-4s crossing maneuver convinced the MiG pilot he couldn't stay in this fight. He fled for Kep after Dosé stuck his nose at him and went after him. The Topgun grad gave up the pursuit and rendezvoused with Hawkins for the return to the *Constellation*.

The next day the phone rang at Dosé's parents' house in La Jolla. Captain Robert Dosé had served as a naval aviator during World War II and had experienced his own dogfights in the western Pacific. The caller, a Navy insider who knew the significance of what had happened, told Dosé's dad, "Bob, your boy got a MiG yesterday."

Bob and Curt Dosé became the only Navy father and son pilots to down enemy aircraft.

That fight over Kep was just a warm-up for the rest of the Navy's day over North Vietnam on May 10. The *Constellation*'s air wing refueled and rearmed for a second alpha strike set for the afternoon against the railyard at the port of Hai Duong. The air wing flew straight into a mass MiG intercept, creating the largest single dogfight of the Vietnam War.

The MiGs raced into the strike group, initially blowing past the escorting F-4s. A pair of MiG-17s caught an A-7 Corsair down low and gave chase. The frantic American pilot called out, "MiG on my tail! I've got a MiG on my tail!"

Overhead, Topgun graduates Matt Connelly and his RIO, Lieutenant Tom Blonski, were covering the strike just north of the target area. They heard the call for help, but without any context, they couldn't rush to the rescue.

"Where are you?" Matt called out over the radio before banking hard to check the sky below. Sure enough, he and Blonski caught sight of the two MiG-17s hard on the heels of a lone A-7. The Corsair driver was trying to shake them with a hard left turn, but the MiG-17s stayed with him.

It would be a race to see who got into position to shoot first. The A-7 fled, the MiG-17s in hot pursuit. Matt rolled right and dove nearly inverted after the MiGs, keeping them on his nose. As he approached their altitude, he rolled left and pulled in behind them. It was a masterful maneuver, but he still ended up about sixty degrees off the lead MiG's tail and he couldn't get a good tone with his Sidewinder.

He fired anyway. The MiG pilot saw the launch and reacted instantly, pulling straight up and flipping inverted in an Immelmann. The 17 flashed right over Matt and Tom's canopy and vanished behind them.

The Topgun grad leveled out and lit his burners. The F-4 extended away from the fight, then Matt used the vertical, intending to get above the MiGs before dropping like an anvil on them for a second pass.

Instead, as his F-4 streaked into a near-vertical climb, both pilot and RIO discovered they had just flown into the middle of a wild dogfight involving almost fifty friendly and North Vietnamese aircraft.

A MiG sped right across their nose, bending into a right-hand turn. Matt rolled after him and turned hard to pull enough lead to get a missile shot. The MiG started to roll slowly left. Knowing from our Topgun curriculum that one of the MiG-17 Fresco's weaknesses was its roll rate at high speeds, and also knowing that its pilot had a blind spot directly to his rear thanks to the bulky ejection seat, Matt exploited the situation. As the MiG rolled out of the turn, the F-4 slid directly behind his tailpipe about a mile away. Unable to see the F-4, the MiG pilot began rolling left. Connelly nailed him with a Sidewinder. He felt the heat of the blast as his aircraft flew through it.

Another MiG-17 sped across Matt's nose in a shallow right bank. He gave chase, and suddenly the North Vietnamese pilot started rolling left in a near duplication of their first kill.

Matt stayed in his blind spot and triggered another Sidewinder. This one lost lock briefly, then reacquired the target and blew its tail clean off. After a brush with another MiG that ended up almost flying wing on them at one point, Matt and Tom lit out for the *Constellation*, their weapon rails empty and two kills to their credit.

In the fight that day were other crews with Topgun experience, including Randy "Duke" Cunningham. While Randy had not graduated from the Navy Fighter Weapons School, he'd sat in on so many classes and flown so many aggressor missions with us in the backseat of a TA-4 that he might as well have been a grad. Everything he learned in our trailer he brought with him to Air Wing Nine's VF-96, the Fighting Falcons. He even took my call sign. I had chosen "Duke" because so many people said my voice sounded like John Wayne. Some even said I looked like him. When Randy came along he said he wanted the moniker for himself. I had no problem with it, so I changed to "Yankee." Shortened to "Yank," it served me well.

That day over Hai Duong, Randy and his back-seater, William "Irish" Driscoll, knocked down three MiGs using our vertical tactics. As they tried to leave the area, a surface-to-air missile shot them down. Both men were picked up in the water not far from the coast. Duke and Willy had scored two kills earlier in the year, making them the first Navy aces of the Vietnam War.

Altogether, the first day of Operation Linebacker highlighted just how far we'd come since 1968. The Navy's F-4 crews flamed eight MiGs without loss, while the Air Force got three for two

Phantoms shot down. The death of Major Lodge came as an especially difficult blow to the Air Force units based in Thailand. He was one of the best pilots in the theater, the weapons guru for his F-4 wing, with three kills to his credit.

The Topgun training made a significant difference, as testified by most of the participants of the day's action. Our Navy crews still faced some of the same deficiencies we had encountered four years before during Rolling Thunder—malfunctioning missiles and the lack of an internal gun being the two most significant—but with the right tactics and training, the F-4 became a true MiG killer.

Eight days later, Topgun grad Lieutenant Henry "Black Bart" Bartholomay and his RIO, Oran Brown, shot down a MiG-19 while flying with the *Midway*'s air wing. The MiG-19 was not an aircraft we had trained against at Dreamland, but many of the same rules applied to it as to the other MiGs.

The following month, Tooter Teague of VX-4 ended up in a wild fight. Though Tooter was not a Topgun instructor or graduate, he had worked closely with us as we stood up our graduate school. He had spent time at Area 51 while flying the MiGs, so he knew the enemy's rides intimately.

On June 11 Tooter led his squadron, VF-51 off the *Coral Sea*, on an escort mission while the rest of the air wing pounded targets around Nam Dinh. The MiGs defending the area often used a ridgeline to mask their intercept approaches from radar. The intel guys on the *Coral Sea* figured this out, and radar control set up Teague to bounce the MiGs should they try.

Sure enough, they caught four MiGs as they hugged the far side of the ridge. Teague and his wingman surprised them and shot two of them down. The crews worked as an integrated team, one F-4 pressing an attack while the other covered him, then reversing roles to take down a second one.

By mid-June, the Navy's kill ratio during Linebacker stood at almost twelve to one, a 600 percent increase over what we had managed during Rolling Thunder. The Navy's high command was ecstatic; the North Vietnamese Air Force clearly was demoralized. That spring, a MiG-17 pilot encountered a Navy F-4 and ejected on the spot before he even came under fire. They had no answer for our new tactics and teamwork. By the summer of 1972, the MiGs focused on attacking the Air Force while avoiding U.S. flights originating from Yankee Station. Our MiG-hungry Topgun grads didn't like it, but the tactical switch provided stark testimony as to which service they thought they could score against. Sadly, the Air Force fought the 1972 air campaign essentially as it had Rolling Thunder. Adherence to the Fluid Four formation cost them aircrews. Of the fifty-one aircraft the Air Force lost during Operation Linebacker, twenty-two went down to the guns and missiles of the North Vietnamese MiGs. During the same time, the Navy lost just four birds to MiGs. The Marines lost an F-4 to a MiG and scored one in return. From the start date of the Topgun program to the end of the war, the Navy's overall kill ratio was twenty-four to one. Its ratio for the entire war, beginning to end, would stand at twelve to one.

The Air Force crews voiced their opinions on the formations and tactics, wanting to make changes, but their chain of command proved inflexible. It cost them dearly in June, when the MiGs shot down three Air Force F-4s without a loss, the single worst air-to-air engagement of the war for the United States. The MiGs scored two more kills against the Air Force before the end of June. The Air Force failed to score in return. At the start of July, the Air Force F-4s had claimed seventeen MiGs in 1972 for the loss of ten aircraft in those dogfights. It was a valiant performance by some very brave men. Sadly the poor loss ratio, 1.7 to 1, could be traced to inadequate training and inflexible tactics.

*   *   *

While the Air Force struggled, I was in Washington overhearing a lot of buzz about Topgun and its success. Our little trailer with its stolen furniture truly became the nexus of a revolution that, once started with that first class back in '69, spread through our entire fighter force. Before Linebacker ended in October, 60 percent of the MiGs flamed by our men on Yankee Station went down at the hands of Topgun grads, or fleet F-4 air crews trained by the initial cadre of graduates of NFWS. The results blew all the bureaucratic opposition to Topgun right off the map. Of course, there always remained some latent animosity or jealousy by other factions of the Navy, including the attack aviators. (It only got worse when the first *Top Gun* movie became so popular a decade later.) For a few years, the naval aviation fraternity wasn't as strong as I had thought. Individual careers seemed to be more important than the satisfaction of building a winning team.

That June, I called Miramar and talked to Jerry Kane, who was running the show then. I told him that eyes had been fully opened in D.C. They saw the value of Topgun at last. Even better, there was talk of making Topgun an independent command.

On July 7, 1972, it finally happened. I missed the ceremony at Miramar, as did most of the Original Bros, but we were there in spirit. Our bond was formed back in 1968 and '69, at Miramar. What we did in those two years was the most important thing we would ever do for our country. One look at the Air Force's experience in '72 convinced me that Topgun saved a lot of lives. I thought of the families, the "cruise widows," and the kids at North Island missing their dads, and I felt like I'd played a role in making sure they would have a homecoming.

Our successes over North Vietnam were tempered by those losses. Don Hall, an A-7 Corsair squadron commander on *Kitty*

Hawk, was among them. My old buddy from VF(AW)-3 suffered engine failure during a night landing and was killed in the ensuing crash out in WestPac. Suzy, his widow, raised their two boys and never remarried. That beautiful lady passed not long after her sons graduated from college. How many more would have suffered like her if we had adhered to failing ways?

Meanwhile, the situation in South Vietnam stabilized as a result of the success of Operation Linebacker. The strikes up north choked off between 60 and 70 percent of the supplies the enemy needed to sustain their offensive against our forces. Hanoi agreed to begin peace negotiations in Paris in October, and Nixon suspended the air campaign while those talks proceeded. You have to wonder how many lives could have been saved had Rolling Thunder been carried out the same way from the beginning. The war would have taken a very different course had we done things in 1964 the way we learned to do them in 1972.

As Linebacker unfolded, I was stuck stateside, wanting only to get into the fight and bag my own MiG. After years of training to do it, seeing friends go off and succeed or die trying, I went to bed some nights thinking about Yankee Station. Our signals intelligence guys—the ones who listened in on North Vietnamese radio chatter—believed they had identified a MiG pilot with over ten American planes to his credit. Known as "Colonel Tomb," he was said to fly like the Red Baron had in World War I—above the fray, lurking to pick off American stragglers as they sought refuge back over the sea. Years after the war, we discovered that Colonel Tomb didn't actually exist. The top North Vietnamese MiG ace of the war was Nguyen Van Coc with nine kills.

In the moment, though, as the war raged, I wanted to meet this Colonel Tomb in the air and make him test his ejection seat. It became a personal goal. I wanted revenge for all my friends he had killed or forced into the torture camps. But mostly I was looking to prove I was better than their best.

In December 1972, the peace talks broke down. The Hanoi contingent walked away from Paris and refused to set a date to return. Furious, Nixon ordered a renewed bombing campaign, throwing the full weight of Strategic Air Command's massive B-52 bombers against the North. As the fighting flared again in what would be called Linebacker II, or the Christmas Bombings, I was mere days from getting a new assignment that would send me out to Yankee Station with one of the best fighter squadrons in the Navy. Perhaps I would have a chance at personally extending the Topgun winning streak.

CHAPTER THIRTEEN

THE LAST MISSING MAN

Yankee Station
January 1973

Home with my family for a rare Friday night together, I was barbe-
cuing steaks, thinking about taking an after-dinner swim with the
kids, when the phone rang. I went to pick it up, sensing something
was wrong. As it turned out, I was right. The executive officer of
Fighter Squadron 143, the Pukin' Dogs, was missing in action in
South Vietnam. That pilot, Harley Hall, was a friend of mine.

The squadron was in a state of shock. It also needed a new XO.
Which accounted for my emergency orders to pack up within twenty
hours and begin the long journey out to the *Enterprise*.

Harley's fateful mission, I couldn't help but think, might well
have been the last of the entire war. With the Paris peace talks
showing progress, it figured to be over soon. Harley made sure he
led what he knew could have been naval aviation's swan song over
North Vietnam. He never came home.

I first met Harley in 1966, when we were going through the
Phantom RAG at Miramar. He became one of the most gifted pilots
of his generation, and had commanded the Blue Angels. He'd just
gotten married to his girlfriend, Mary Lou Marino, in a little church

in Santa Barbara. Crossed swords. Dress whites. Gloves. The works. They were a great-looking couple, so devoted to each other. They had a five-year-old daughter and were expecting their second child. I never really got to know Mary Lou, but Harley—I would have followed him anywhere. Most everyone who flew with him felt he would become chief of naval operations someday.

His junior officers flat-out worshipped Harley H. Hall. A charismatic leader, he always took the toughest missions. He mentored the younger guys and looked out for their well-being. He was scheduled to take command of the squadron when it returned to Miramar, and I was to become his exec. The only change now was an acceleration in the schedule.

Eventually I learned the whole story behind his disappearance. That strike from the *Big E* launched on the afternoon of January 27. Ernie Christensen was one of the last men to speak to Harley. Ernie saw him on the flight deck and offering a quick greeting, then climbed into his plane. The Dogs were going to hit a river harbor about fifteen miles off Quang Tri.

Guided by a forward air control aircraft, Harley rolled in to hit some barges, then made two runs on a cluster of trucks. As he pulled up after his second run, his F-4J shuddered from repeated shrapnel strikes. Calmly he reported to his wingman, "Mayday, Mayday. I'm hit. Heading 'feet wet.'" Turning for the coast, he hoped to reach the water before he and Al would have to eject. The closer to the coast they bailed out, the better their chance to survive.

His Phantom flew sluggishly and Harley reportedly struggled to keep the aircraft under control. His wingman, Terry Heath, spotted him a few miles from the target area, staggering along at about four thousand feet.

"I've got you," his wingman said. "But you're on fire." Flames streamed from the port wing, spreading toward the fuselage. Still,

Harley stayed with it, fighting for every second. Then the fire reached his hydraulic system. When he lost control of the plane, Harley and his back-seater, Phillip A. "Al" Kientzler, were out of time. They ejected. Harley's wingman saw them swinging in their chutes, descending about a half mile apart onto an island at the confluence of two rivers.

The area was crawling with enemy troops. As the two naval aviators swung in their chutes, ground fire erupted below them. Al was wounded in the leg as he descended. Harley was seen to reach the ground and start running for cover.

Harley's wingman swept over the area, trying to establish contact. An enemy soldier fired an SA-7 that barely missed. A moment later, a second missile streaked out of the jungle. Only hard maneuvering saved that F-4, and the brave pilot refused to leave his exec.

Racing to the scene to coordinate the search and rescue operation was the Air Force forward air controller. Flying an OV-10 Bronco, he and his back-seater were not so lucky. An SA-7 leapt up out of the tree line and struck their aircraft. As it went down, the two men ejected. Their chutes opened, and though enemy ground fire reached up at them, they too hit the ground safely. At length the pilot was heard on the radio saying, "Looks like I'm going to be captured." His radio circuit clicked back again as the North Vietnamese troops shot at him. "Oh my God! I'm getting hit. Oh my God!" Then silence. The enemy finally tied them to a couple of trees and decapitated them. A South Vietnamese special operations team found their bodies a few days later.

Harley Hall became a POW, but unlike Al Kientzler he was never released. And so in the last hours of the war, the men of Fighting 143 had their hearts torn out one final time.

The first night of peace since 1964 was no time for celebration. I struggled to make sense of the loss of one more friend as I told my kids that Dad had to go away again. As I pulled my gear together, I found my little mouse still in his nest in my flight bag. Through fifteen years and countless stations, he had seen me through. *Hey, little fella. We're heading back to the* Big E. *I'm gonna need all your mojo for this ride.* I found my old Ray-Bans, carefully tucked away in their case. As I packed them with the rest of my gear, it struck me that they'd been with me through my entire career. *Who keeps a fifteen-year-old set of sunglasses? Maybe it's time for a new pair.* The distractions were welcome, because they kept me from dwelling on my larger concerns. I had tried to be a good husband and father, but these constant separations took a toll.

The next morning, I shared yet another goodbye with my family. My wife and I knew the chance of combat was probably pretty low, given that the peace accords were signed and our prisoners of war were soon to be returned. If all went according to schedule, it would be only a few weeks instead of months this time. We were pros at this by now.

My oldest, Dana, was in her first year of high school that winter. Through all the other goodbyes, she had learned to be tough and stoic. After recovering from the shock of my impending emergency deployment, she handled it like a superstar. My little guy, Chris, was a different story. Almost five now, he looked up at me with tear-streaked cheeks, letting it all out. I gave him an especially long hug as we waited for my friend Jack Bewley to take me to the airport in his antique Bentley sedan.

At Lindbergh Field, I caught a flight to SFO, then Seattle, where I secured a seat on a mostly empty Pan Am 747 bound for Manila. I curled up across three seats and slept for most of the trip.

Twenty-four hours later, a Navy C-2 took me aboard at Cubi Point and flew me out to the carrier. The squadron's CO, Gordon Cornell, met me on the flight deck. Gordo was a warrior's warrior, a man who'd flown everything from F9F Panthers to F-8 Crusaders and F-4 Phantoms. Wounded in action over North Vietnam in 1966, he went on to earn two Distinguished Flying Crosses and seventeen Air Medals.

"Really glad to see you, Yank. Sorry it had to be under such terrible circumstances."

I shook his hand and asked how the Dogs were doing.

"They're Dogs, Dan. They'll always be okay. They're a tough bunch. Bonded, as Harley would have wanted."

Still clutching my hand, he seemed to reconsider this. He added, "They're hurting, badly. Some of the guys can't wait to get home and help out Mary Lou and the kids."

There was sadness in his eyes. The shooting war was over, but we all had wounds to heal.

CHAPTER FOURTEEN

THE PEACE THAT NEVER WAS

**Yankee Station
February 1973**

The Dogs were a quiet lot when I joined them in the ready room. Their anguish was palpable as they discussed how they might intercept Harley as the North Vietnamese moved him north to Hanoi. If we could pinpoint his location, maybe we could combine a strike package with a combat search and rescue mission and get him and Al out of there. With the war theoretically over, of course, neither Washington nor our admiral would have ever authorized such a mission.

Was the war really over? It didn't feel like it. Sure enough, the fragile cease-fire broke down. Both sides were at fault, and at times the flare-ups were serious enough to endanger the peace accord. Of course, the North Vietnamese supply influx into South Vietnam continued through Laos, where the fighting became intense. The Communist rebels stood a good chance of overrunning the pro-American government there, and they sensed the time was ripe now that we were, as our ambassador to Laos put it, "cutting and running."

The North Vietnamese used a road that ran through Laos and into South Vietnam. This supply route, which we had bombed for years, was known to us as the Ho Chi Minh Trail. Dubbed Operation Barrel Roll, the air campaign stretched from 1964 into 1973 and continued after the peace accords were signed. American aircraft, including B-52s, flew hundreds of sorties in support of the crumbling Laotian army.

Back home, the Paris Agreement was hailed as a victory. Our POWs were coming home. Our troops were pulling out. South Vietnam would survive and have the right to determine its own fate.

But only the U.S. troop pullout was real. The war in Laos continued, and the *Big E*'s air wing went back into the fight, bombing Communist insurgents and their lines of supply. Far from celebrating the war's end, we found ourselves in the midst of another one that nobody at home even knew had gone on for nine years.

Well west of the Vietnam border, we hit a truck convoy on the Ho Chi Minh Trail. Flying low and slow, an Air Force forward air controller marked targets for us with smoke rockets. We rolled in and hammered them with bombs. During another pass, the forward air controller's plane took a critical hit from ground fire. When he crash-landed on a small dirt road, we had another rescue mission to cover.

Far from the coast, we were going to have trouble getting him out, but we stayed over him, wishing yet again that the F-4 had an internal gun. We could have killed a lot of bad guys with a 20mm Vulcan Gatling gun that day. At last, another aircraft from his unit arrived and managed to land in a patch of open ground. When they hauled their comrade aboard, we thankfully avoided a repeat of what happened the day Harley and Al ejected.

As the weeks wore on, the squadron's mood shifted from shock and grief to stubborn resolve. The guys carried out their missions, flying in an air corridor that took us past Quang Tri practically every day. I could not have been prouder. Gordo and Harley had selected

and trained well. Lieutenant Terry Heath ranked among the best, a
pilot who thoroughly understood the F-4 and could take most anyone in a dogfight. Having been on Harley's wing that day over South
Vietnam, he was affected by the loss particularly hard. He'd risked
his life repeatedly to find out what happened to Harley and Al. His
poise and character helped keep things together.

If only the larger war had followed his example. All around
South Vietnam, the Americans were turning out the lights. The
final prisoner release took place in March. On the twenty-ninth,
the last of the American combat troops climbed aboard transport
aircraft at Saigon for the long journey home.

Before crossing the Pacific for Pearl, we stopped at Subic Bay.
Those nights at the Cubi Point Officers' Club were the wildest, hard-
drinkingest I'd ever seen. The guys really unleashed, like dozens of
overwound springs suddenly releasing their tension. In retrospect, it
was probably the first real act of healing for the squadron.

On June 7, 1973, the *Enterprise* arrived at Pearl Harbor. During
our arrival salute to USS *Arizona* in 1968, we were filled with antici-
pation of what combat would be like. Now we had names to mourn.
As I stood rendering another salute to our lost battleship, I thought
about our POWs such as Jim Stockdale and Harley Hall, Ron Polfer,
J. B. Souder, Arvin Chauncey, Robby Reisner, Coal Black, and
Dieter Dengler, to name a few. They were tortured, beaten, and
psychologically run down. They were forced to sign confessions,
starved, denied medical care, and, to add a final insult, used as prop-
aganda tools when actress Jane Fonda showed up in Hanoi, with
television cameras rolling, to fawn over our enemy. Some of these
men never came home.

In March, most of these POWs returned to America. Harley was
not among them. The mystery of his fate was never unraveled. Al
Kientzler was told by a guard that his pilot had died in his chute, but

Lieutenant Heath saw him running from his landing spot into some nearby trees. We'd received intelligence tracing his handover from unit to unit all the way to Hanoi.

The worst fear for all of us wasn't death. It was ending up like some of the Korean War crews shot down over enemy territory. Never handed back at the end of hostilities, they simply vanished. Rumors abounded over the years that some ended up in Soviet gulags, wasting away in Siberia, forgotten by everyone but their families. When we heard that Harley had not been released, the nightmare we all feared became his reality.

We were different men when we arrived at Pearl that spring day. It would take time for each of us to sort out what that meant. I guess that process started in Hawaii. Few of our squadron took the chance to go on liberty there. It was the only stay at Pearl I ever made where most of my men remained aboard. We caught up on sleep and considered our futures. With the war over, did we want to stay in the Navy? The airlines were paying well for good pilots. A peaceful, lucrative, and far more family-friendly career waited for them on the other side of the gate. Gordo would be moving on to another command. That meant I'd be moved up and given the squadron.

Just before we arrived at Pearl, we received a priority message ordering VF-143 and our sister fighter squadron on the *Enterprise*, VF-142, to turn around and redeploy in fifty-one days. Breaking the news to our men was going to be tough. And it could cost the Navy some good people. Honestly, I wouldn't blame any of them for getting out. Already we were due for a mass exodus. As we faced other threats—the Russians, the Chinese, more chaos in Southeast Asia and the Middle East—we needed to keep our talent. That would be a major leadership challenge in the weeks ahead.

We sailed out of Pearl a few days later, California bound. When I came aboard, the guys told me stories of the ship's last view of home.

When the *Big E* was set to sail from Alameda in the Bay Area, anti-war activists tried to storm the base or delay the carrier's departure by swarming the boat basin with small boats. The Navy and Coast Guard fended them off, and the *Enterprise* sailed on schedule. But a sour feeling prevailed when the carrier steamed under the Golden Gate Bridge. The country was poorly led and bitterly divided. A good portion of the public simply hated the military. I like to think those who felt that way were just ignorant. If they knew us, perhaps they would have come around. Maybe peace would bring some perspective and understanding. Or maybe that was asking too much of people who called us baby killers and spat on returning veterans in airports. We felt our universities were playing a role in spreading this poisonous, hateful view among younger Americans.

Halfway home, Gordo and I broke the news to the squadron of our quick return to sea. This time, the Navy was sending us to the East Coast to deploy on USS *America* for operations in the Mediterranean Sea. Cruises in the Med usually meant we would operate near the Middle East, the other major flashpoint of the Cold War. We promised to do our best to make it a "vacation cruise."

Four hundred miles from the California coast, the *Big E* launched her air wing. The attack squadrons flew to Whidbey Island, Washington, and Naval Air Station Lemoore, in central California. While some of the Dogs sped for Miramar, the rest of the squadron came home on Navy DC-9s when the ship made port in Alameda.

Those of us who flew into Miramar were in for a treat. We landed, taxied to the ramp, and parked our Phantoms side by side, arrayed before our families. Waving American flags, holding our kids on shoulders and cheering, they were a sight that stirred us all. We climbed out of our planes to meet a herd of kids. Many of them put on their dads' big flight helmets and were lifted into the cockpits so that their fathers could patiently explain what the myriad instruments and switches did. As Dana and Chris found me, their mom trailing after them, my family was reunited again. Steak and baked potatoes were on the menu that night. Afterward, I made sure we finally took the swim that got derailed on the last night of the war six months earlier. It was a long one, with a lot of joyful splashing.

Every fighter pilot wants command of his own squadron. When I learned I was to become the skipper of the Pukin' Dogs, I made sure to bone up on squadron lore. It began in 1953, at the end of the Korean War. The insignia of VF-143 was a winged griffin, a mythological predator with the body of a lion and the head and wings of an eagle. During a squadron function, one of the pilots tried to craft a snarling griffin out of papier-mâché. It ended up looking like a dog with wings, hunched over in the throes of misery, coughing up something it had eaten. Seeing it, one of the wives exclaimed, "My God, it looks like a puking dog!" Ever after, VF-143 had its proud nickname. For all the challenges ahead, I relished the opportunity.

The change-of-command ceremony was a formal affair with full dress whites, VIP admirals, and well-rehearsed speeches. When I parked and got out of my car, I heard something tear. The rear seam of my pants had split open, exposing my white Navy briefs. I couldn't believe it. There was no time to bolt for the base tailor shop. Gordo, whom I was relieving, was ready for our joint entrance, and all the guests and troops were waiting. When I walked to the platform, I hoped nobody would be checking my six.

When my turn came at the podium, I made a point of keeping my tail away from the crowd. As I began my speech, I heard a stir behind me. Though the crowd was none the wiser, the small group of VIPs had a clear view of my loose deuce. I heard a few quiet cheap shots in their muffled hilarity. I made my remarks in spite of my mortification. At that point the air wing commander took the mic and said, "Well, ladies and gentlemen, it sure is a bit breezy today!" I could only laugh. After a quick turn at the base tailor, I hustled to the reception at the O club.

With less than two months before deployment, the squadron went right to work. The leadership lessons I'd learned in the fleet and applied at Topgun were my basis for everything we did. Lesson one: Above everything, take care of your people. My men needed to feel valued. After the shared hardships out on Yankee Station, the grief over Harley's loss, and the chaos unfolding in the streets back home, beyond the front gate, we closed ranks. With those outward pressures pushing in on us, we became one of the tightest bunches I've ever known.

Another lesson was to take good care of your aircraft. Among the first things I did at Miramar was make sure the squadron kept the aircraft it had flown on the *Enterprise* on its most recent deployment. Usually a returning squadron sent its planes through a maintenance cycle and took new aircraft from inventory. The crew chiefs, maintainers, and plane captains hated this. Out on the *Big E*, they had gotten to know their current aircraft like family. Each Phantom has little quirks that make it perform just a bit differently from the others of its type. Some have issues. Some are unusually reliable. Once our maintainers figured all this out, they knew how to dote on them and the squadron gained a performance edge. At the end of the cruise, our F-4s had the most beautiful paint jobs and were free of corrosion. I pulled strings that let us keep these same aircraft as we prepared to go to the Mediterranean.

We broke for a trip to Las Vegas at the end of August for an enormous reunion of American aviators of all services who had flown in Vietnam. We would unofficially welcome back the 166 men taken prisoner by the North Vietnamese. Some three thousand of us and our wives gathered at the Hilton. There were many spontaneous mini-reunions that night as old friends saw each other for the first time in years. The happiness touched everyone. The war over, the years of hardship in the rearview mirror at last, our former POWs were ready to pick up their lives and careers. What an enormous challenge. Some came home knowing nothing of the Summer of Love, the Watts riots, the Kent State shootings, or the assassinations of Martin Luther King and Robert F. Kennedy. Their last experience of America predated acid rock and Woodstock. Fitting into the here and now and getting to know their families again tested the former POWs all over again.

I was chatting with old friends and our wives that night when somebody wrapped his arms around my shoulders and said, "Hello, Yank." I turned in my seat to see Ron Polfer. "Pompadour," as he was called by the guys at VF-121, was shot down flying a Vigilante reconnaissance plane. Punching out at about seven hundred knots cost him his eardrums, a few broken bones, bruises to his whole body, and capture by the North Vietnamese. But he survived to return and become chairman and president of Zeiss International. Arvin Chauncey, an attack pilot and liberty buddy of mine, greeted me in the same warm fashion. I had not seen him since the day he was shot down too. Throughout the evening, Bob Hope and many other friends of the military entertained us and turned it into a night most of us will never forget. The song of the evening was "Born Free," which few managed to sing without tears rolling down their cheeks.

Shortly after our Vegas interlude, the Pukin' Dogs said farewell to Miramar one more time. Yet another goodbye with our families. Chris clung hard to me again. Every time he did that it became harder to leave. No matter how tough the man, no matter how much combat experience and passion for flying he has, the sight of your little boy brokenhearted by your departure never fails to hit home.

At least we weren't being sent to Yankee Station.

We climbed into our Phantoms and flew east to Norfolk, and the rendezvous with our new home, the carrier USS *America*.

The Mediterranean, home of the U.S. Sixth Fleet, became a powder keg on October 6. That was the day our Israeli friends awoke to the greatest crisis of their lives: an imminent Arab invasion. The nation of Israel responded to that gathering storm with a massive preemptive strike.

When the Yom Kippur War started, I was at Norfolk with the Dogs. All I could do was hope my Israeli friends, Eitan Ben Eliyahu and Dan Halutz and the rest of them, were out there knocking MiGs down and laying waste to ground targets. I'm sure they felt the same as their American friends at Miramar headed to Vietnam in 1969. We all knew that the proxy nations we fought were but tentacles of a common enemy: the Soviet Union.

Our deployment to the Med was undertaken in this light. In January 1974, the *America* and its battle group sailed across the Atlantic to join the Sixth Fleet, then began a series of port-of-call stops from Barcelona to Athens. The pace was slow and easy. We flew, but not too much to wear us out. The ports we visited—it was indeed a vacation cruise. We explored the ruins of classical Italy; we saw Sicily and the Greek islands of Corfu and Rhodes. After the strains of Vietnam, this Med cruise turned out to be exactly what the Pukin' Dogs needed.

We would make periodic sweeps through the eastern Med to show the flag, then return to Athens for some time ashore. The guys in the squadron pooled resources and rented a beach house in a resort town called Glyfada. That became our base of operations when ashore, and the pilots would crash in every nook and cranny of the place at night. We'd have to step over each other to get to the head in the middle of the night. Psychologically, the Mediterranean cruise prepared us for peace better than anything could have.

I ran the squadron as best I could with men like Skank Remsen and Gene Valencia as my inspirations. One of the things I did was get hold of a theater-grade popcorn machine. Our maintenance guys found a place for it in their area, and we charged ten cents a bag. The money we made went into a squadron fund to be used for the morale and welfare of the Dogs. Twice on the deployment, guys lost a family member back home. Both times, we secured emergency leaves for them, using the popcorn fund to buy their plane tickets. The popcorn fund also bought all the pilots and naval flight officers a white or blue turtleneck, a blue blazer, gray flat-front slacks, and cordovan loafers to wear during our nonuniform time ashore. (As we were in Europe now, not the Cubi officers' club, I insisted that my men be sharply dressed.) We looked superb, and in a crowded club we could spot each other a mile away. It was a great way to boost our sense of pride.

Every great leader I knew made a point of taking care of his chief petty officers. This was important, as the chiefs oversee the nuts-and-bolts operations that keep the squadron functioning. The enlisted crew worked directly for the chiefs, not for the officers— a point that good officers never forget. I made a point of getting to know our chiefs, drinking coffee with them from time to time to hear the view from the hangar deck. Their input was vital to the morale and effectiveness of the squadron. At times, the chiefs invited me to eat with them in their mess. I was grateful for those opportunities—and took the opportunity to return the favor when we were on deployment in the Mediterranean.

I had asked Vice Admiral Bob Baldwin at AirPac if the Navy would consider chartering a 747 for us. The idea was to fly out our wives and girlfriends to enjoy a mid-deployment break while we were in Greece. Such a gesture would help improve retention, I said. And Admiral Baldwin went to bat for us, recognizing the high cost of training someone to replace any of the high performers in my squadron in 1973. Halfway through our cruise, a United Airlines 747 landed in Athens with the squadron's wives and fiancées. We spent ten days in Glyfada together. The family that celebrates together stays together. Of all the experiences I had in the Navy during my career, this interlude in Greece ranks as one of the best. There would be no airline pilots coming out of this deployment, thanks to Admiral Baldwin.

One day at the fleet landing at Athens, I watched our chief warrant gunner, Bob King, dive into the water. He swam all the way to Glyfada to wade ashore and surprise the gang at the beach house. He had been a SEAL in Vietnam. Though he was always tight-lipped about his time out there, he did once tell me how he had escaped a jam by crawling to a river at night and floating downstream as patrols of North Vietnamese troops searched for him. Along the way, a snake wrapped itself around him and began warming itself. He drew his Ka-Bar knife and cut the snake's head off as he drifted along. He was a great man who was revered by every man in the Dogs, including me. Imagine having men of such capability and deep experience at your disposal every day.

Our chiefs were uniformly superb. My own plane's crew chief, Tony Baker, set the example every day with his work ethic and attention to detail. My aircraft was always well prepared and ready to go, thanks to him. All that hard work, yet it turned out not one of our chiefs had ever flown in an F-4. At the end of our seven-month cruise to the Med, as we were preparing to return to Norfolk, I realized that because several of our naval flight officers lived on the East Coast and didn't need to fly home, our squadron would have five or six empty seats. Why not let the senior chiefs fly back with the air wing? I put out the word, and the chiefs pounced on the chance to experience a catapult launch and a fast ride home.

As we passed through the Strait of Gibraltar and began the long transatlantic crossing, the squadron completed seven months on deployment without a single accident, a remarkable achievement. Morale, at rock bottom the previous year, was sky-high. The Dogs were walking tall with our swagger back, ready for whatever the Navy threw at us.

A few hundred miles from Norfolk, our F-4s began launching for the cross-country flight back to Miramar. With me in the backseat of my F-4 on this flight was our J79 specialist, Chief Jim "Frenchie" Ireland. He was nothing short of a prodigy. He knew more about the inner workings of our power plants than any other man I ever met in uniform. As we chatted over the intercom during our flight, I could hear the excitement and happiness in every word he said to me. We refueled in midair over Tennessee before heading on to Roswell, N.M., for an overnight.

The next day, our sixteen Phantoms entered the pattern over Miramar. Fightertown was abuzz. Flags were waved, signs were held high. As we touched down, taxied to the ramp, cut our engines, and opened our canopies, our families surged toward our birds. For the chiefs who had never flown before, this was an incredible moment. To the surprise of their families, they climbed out of the cockpits in full flight gear. Frenchie's wife reached him just as our brown shoes touched the ramp. She wrapped her arms around him and gave him one hell of a kiss, then grabbed me for a thank-you-skipper kiss that left me mirroring Jim's smile.

Quickly on her heels was my son, Chris, giving me a little-man bear hug. My daughter, Dana, pushed right in for a long hug. My girl, always a bit more reserved, was halfway through high school now, and I'd missed much of it. I needed to be there for her. Finally, Maddi reached my side. We'd had ups and downs over the years. Our marriage had taken big hits during my time at sea. But I was in it for the long haul and wanted to make it work. Our embrace on the ramp made me think we had a chance.

My Dogs, surrounded by family, were headed home. Wrenched by the experience of Vietnam, they seemed reenergized and ready for more. When the *America* reached Norfolk the next day, the remainder of the Dog crew flew home in Navy C-9s. Everybody celebrated in their own way, but the joy seemed universally shared. It was the best homecoming I ever had.

CHAPTER FIFTEEN

END OF THE THIRD TEMPLE

Tel Nor Air Base, Israel
October 6, 1973

I would learn only after returning from the Med how the Yom Kippur War threatened the Middle East with Armageddon—and that Topgun had played a small part in averting what could have been a worldwide tragedy of the first order.

On October 6, 1973, as I explained earlier, Israel faced down an Arab army almost a million soldiers strong. Dan Halutz lay in bed that morning, unaware that these troops, supported by thousands of tanks and armored vehicles, were poised to strike against the Israel Defense Forces. His first indication that something was amiss came when an A-4 Skyhawk blew over his house at treetop level.

Dan belonged to the legendary 201 Squadron, known as "The One." Colonel Ben Eliyahu was its deputy commander. The One was considered the elite outfit of the Israeli Air Force, and as such received the latest and most technologically advanced fighter in the Jewish state's inventory: the F-4 Phantom. The Miramar RAG would play a vital role in the squadron's survival in combat.

In the Six-Day War of June 1967, the Israelis had responded to the imminent threat of an Arab invasion with a preemptive strike.

Now, while Prime Minister Golda Meir wrestled with how to deal with the geopolitics of what Israeli intelligence could clearly see coming, the head of the Israeli Air Force ordered all squadrons to be armed and ready to carry out a strike. But when Henry Kissinger, the U.S. secretary of state, made it known to the Israelis that they would not receive any American support if they attacked first, Meir made the decision to absorb the Arab onslaught. At midday on October 6, the air force countermanded the original order, telling the squadrons to be prepared for air defense. While the ground crews pulled bombs and air-to-ground missiles off Israel's fighter-bombers, the Arab invasion began. Waves of Egyptian and Syrian fighters and bombers thundered over Israel, attacking airfields, antiaircraft batteries, headquarters, and other command facilities. Our friends from the Miramar RAG days suddenly found themselves in dire straits.

Those who got aloft fought with almost superhuman tenacity. Two F-4 Phantoms from 201 Squadron rose to meet an incoming raid that included twenty-eight Egyptian MiGs. Outnumbered fourteen to one, the two crews maneuvered wildly, shooting threats off each other's tails in a desperate, sprawling dogfight. When it ended, seven MiGs were smoking holes in the desert. Both Israeli F-4s landed safely back at base.

There was a swagger to the Israeli Air Force, born from repeated victories over the Arab nations that had attacked them since the War of Independence in 1948. When the IAF rose to attack the advancing Arab armies, however, they had some of the swagger knocked out of them when they ran into a brand-new threat: the mobile SA-6 surface-to-air Russian-made missile launcher.

As they rushed to support three thousand forward-deployed Israeli troops against ten times that number of Syrian troops on the Golan Heights, the Israeli Air Force was unprepared for the SA-6.

Phantoms and Skyhawks exploded in the flames as missiles knocked them out of the sky. By the end of the day, the Israelis had lost forty planes—almost 10 percent of their entire Air Force.

The next morning, the Skyhawks and Phantoms went after those SA-6 launchers, which the Syrians had moved forward to defend their frontline troops from air attack. Unable to detect the SA-6s' new radar emissions, the Israeli crews could only eyeball the incoming missiles. By then, it was usually too late. Dan's squadron, The One, was shot to pieces over the Golan Heights. In five wild minutes, a Syrian SAM battery was annihilated at the price of four Israeli F-4s shot out of the sky.

At the same time, the Egyptians crossed the Suez Canal and invaded the Sinai with almost two hundred thousand troops, supported by tanks and armored vehicles. The surface-to-air missile batteries of the invaders also took a heavy toll of Israeli planes on this southern front.

Colonel Ben Eliyahu and his squadron attacked the Egyptian bridges thrown across the Suez Canal that day. To avoid the missile threat, they flew right down low on the dunes before climbing suddenly to release their weapons. They hit the bridges with surprising accuracy.

When a dozen Egyptian MiG-17s bombed the Israeli headquarters for the southern front, Ben Eliyahu and his men turned and went after them. In the ensuing dogfight, Ben Eliyahu scored his second confirmed kill, sending a MiG-17 into the desert sand. His wingman flamed two more, and a fourth crashed into the ground while maneuvering against Colonel Ben Eliyahu.

For all the air-to-air success, the Israeli Army could not stop the Arab offensive, and the Israeli Air Force was taking losses it could not sustain or afford. It was a dreadful situation. On the ground,

Israeli frontline units were simply being overrun. One unit defending the Golan Heights was down to its last half dozen tanks. The Syrians arrayed hundreds against them.

Israeli defense minister Moshe Dayan went to see Golda Meir. In a sober tone, Dayan said to her, "Prime Minister, this is the end of the Third Temple."

In other words, Israel was about to be overrun and crushed.

Prime Minister Meir ordered thirteen Hiroshima-sized nuclear warheads to be assembled and placed on surface-to-surface missiles and under the wings of an F-4 squadron based at Tel Nof. The nukes were deployed out in the open, so that American intelligence satellites could see it happening. In later years there was debate over the degree to which this impressed Nixon and Kissinger. Some accounts say the threat of a nuclear war in the Middle East was a powerful impetus to what followed.

Nixon ordered a full-scale emergency resupply effort for the Israelis. From U.S. Army bases in Germany, stocks of latest-generation antitank missiles were loaded into Air Force transports and flown to Israel, even as the air battles raged. It seemed my country, which had done so many things wrong in Southeast Asia, finally did something right.

In the United States, Phantoms and Skyhawks were pulled straight out of Air Force and Navy squadrons and forwarded to Israel to replace the planes lost to those deadly SA-6s. The majority of our NATO allies lent exactly zero assistance. Cowed by the threat of an OPEC oil embargo, NATO refused to help Israel in its hour of crisis, though the Dutch and the Portuguese, to their credit, allowed our flights to land and refuel in their countries.

On October 14, Colonel Ben Eliyahu led his Phantoms on a deep strike against the Egyptian MiG-21 base at Mansura. A wild fight erupted down on the deck as MiGs clashed with Phantoms and the base was pummeled with bombs. Ben Eliyahu locked on to a MiG-21, whose pilot maneuvered wildly, trying to buy time as his wingman came to his rescue. Ben Eliyahu's navigator twisted around in his seat and spotted that second MiG-21 sliding into firing position behind them.

Rather than breaking off his pursuit, Ben Eliyahu stuck with his MiG. He opened fire with his 20mm cannon—the latest version of the F-4 came with an internal gun—and watched as the MiG exploded in flames and augered in. A split second later, his RIO shouted, "Break! Break!" Ben Eliyahu bent the Phantom into a tight turn. The MiG-21 driver behind him, obviously inexperienced, tried to follow and pushed his aircraft too far. It spun in and crashed not far from the Israeli's first kill. Once again, it was considered a squadron kill. In any other air force, Ben Eliyahu would have become an ace that day.

As he took over the squadron command, he and Dan Halutz flew nonstop. In seventeen days, Dan flew forty-three combat missions. The pace was so intense that a major general came to Colonel Ben Eliyahu and recommended the squadron stand down and get some rest.

"Under absolutely no circumstances," came Ben Eliyahu's response. A warrior to the core, he would help save his nation or die trying. There would be no rest until one or the other happened. In this intense war of survival, only winning counted.

The squadron went into action day and night. They led attacks deep into Egyptian territory. On one mission against a communication center, MiGs intercepted them again. Colonel Ben got on the tail of one panicky MiG-21 pilot, who saw the writing on the wall and ejected. The squadron received credit for that one too.

The days of flying and fighting wore The One down. They lost brothers in nearly every fight, and each day fewer and fewer planes and crews remained. Yet the bombings and destruction of MiGs helped blunt the Arab advance. Finally, Israeli ground forces retook the Golan Heights, and drove into Syria, too, smashing the Syrian Army and leading Iraq and Jordan to send troops to defend Damascus.

As the tide turned, the first American F-4s and A-4s started to arrive to replace the near-crippling losses. Topgun played an unheralded role in this pivotal moment.

Mugs McKeown was the skipper of the Navy Fighter Weapons School at the time. After Roger Box stood it up as an independent squadron, and Dave Frost held the reins in the summer of '72, Mugs arrived from Yankee Station to run the shop. One Friday, halfway through the current class, word came that the Israelis needed his aggressor A-4E Mongooses. The maintenance people spent all weekend repainting them in Israeli markings and camouflage. Some F-4s were also promised to the Israelis, and a call for volunteers went out to fly them from Miramar to the combat zone. Every naval aviator present at that meeting volunteered.

Almost a hundred F-4s from Air Force units headed east to join the Israelis. More Navy Phantoms soon followed. A half dozen Israeli pilots arrived at Miramar three days after Mugs got orders to give up the shop's A-4s. A serious, secretive bunch, the Israeli pilots expressed profound gratitude for the help.

The Israelis flew the Topgun A-4s across the country and crossed the Atlantic, tanking en route before stopping in Portugal or Spain. For the American crews who delivered aircraft straight to Tel Nof, they discover not just an air force at war, but an entire people. The families of the flight crews lived in tents around the runways. Wives hung laundry out to dry next to missile batteries. Their country and lives were threatened. There could be no greater stakes for any patriot. The dynamics of the situation were so very different from the Vietnam War. More than a few of the U.S. pilots would have gladly stayed and flown into combat with the Israelis.

Three weeks into the war, a Russian cargo vessel carrying nuclear weapons steamed out of the Black Sea into the eastern Med, bound for Alexandria. Soviet-manned Scud missile batteries operating in Egypt included at least one tactical nuclear warhead each. American intelligence discovered that fact when overflights spotted the unique trucks the Soviets used to transport such deadly weapons. As a result of these discoveries, senior U.S. officials—apparently without the approval or foreknowledge of President Nixon—took the country to an upgraded nuclear alert, DEFCON 3.

The Russians saw the U.S. response and interpreted it as a panicky overreaction. After a series of long internal discussions in Moscow, the Soviets decided Syria and Egypt were not worth a global thermonuclear holocaust. The ship carrying nukes dropped anchor in Alexandria, but did not unload. The Kremlin's diplomats started leaning on its Arab allies to end the war.

Peace broke out on October 23, 1973. The Israeli counteroffensives cleared the Golan Heights, captured significant chunks of Syrian territory, drove the Egyptians largely out of the Sinai, and even established footholds on the west side of the Suez Canal. In that sense, it was a catastrophic defeat for the Arab alliance. But in truth it had been a near-ruin thing. The Israeli Air Force was battered and exhausted, with just seventy or so Phantom crews left standing. The Israelis admitted to the loss of over a hundred aircraft—almost a quarter of their entire complement of combat aircraft. With only a few exceptions, these planes went down to latest-generation Soviet-built missiles.

Those three weeks were rough ones indeed. They were worse for the Arab air forces, whose fighter pilots found themselves completely overmatched by the better-trained Israelis. Boyd may have had his equations, but at Topgun, we trained to the man in the cockpit. The better pilot will almost always win, no matter the odds, situation, or planes. The Israelis fought savage air battles against ridiculously long odds—and tore the guts out of their enemies. The exact kill ratio will never be known, as the Egyptians concealed the extent of their losses, as did the Israelis. Our Israeli friends claimed more than 440 Arab aircraft destroyed, most of them in air combat. Current sources show the number of Israeli air-to-air kills at around 83. The American influence was significant, but it boiled down to the men in the cockpit. They had performed as well as fighter pilots ever have.

Meanwhile, the Yom Kippur War precipitated a crisis at Topgun. With only a single aggressor A-4 remaining after the transfers to the Israelis, the school could not function. The October class graduated on schedule, but Mugs canceled the next one while they scrambled to solve this problem.

Since its inception, Topgun had faced ongoing jealousies and bureaucratic hostility. We fought our battles for resources and respect early on, and slowly gained both through any means necessary. The year before, thanks to Dave "Frosty" Frost making his career-risking stand, Topgun became an independent command with its own aircraft. Now, with our war in Vietnam over, some careerists above and around Topgun began to question the need for such a school, especially one that was an independent command. This is where it hurt Topgun to be run by junior officers. Lieutenant commanders and lieutenants usually do not have the political horsepower to fend off serious threats.

Fortunately, Mugs McKeown was a special kind of skipper. He intuited the threat. If Topgun owned no aggressor aircraft, the school would have no way to function independently. Bill Driscoll, Duke Cunningham's back-seater and the only Navy RIO ace of the Vietnam War, was a Topgun instructor at the time. He and the others running the school all sensed a pivotal moment was at hand. The Navy either refused to buy new jets or had no aircraft to spare in the aftermath of Vietnam. The animosity toward Topgun from the staff officers who came up through the ranks of attack aviation led to many closed doors. If Mugs didn't fix his aircraft shortage, Topgun might just dry up and blow away. Death by bureaucratic atrophy.

A fighter to the core, he'd earned his nickname while boxing at the Naval Academy. He also played running back for Navy in its glory year of 1960, when the team was ranked fourth in the nation and beat the number one Washington Huskies. Thanks to his time training with the Air Force, Mugs knew a lot of people outside Navy circles. He networked with men who became members of Congress and Air Force leaders who ended up in key commands.

While working the phones, Mugs learned from an old friend at VX-4 that the Air Force just stashed a pair of broken-down T-38 Talon fighter trainers at the Navy test facility at China Lake, where they were to be turned into target drones and blown up.

Mugs and his executive officer at the time, Jerry Sawatzky, went down to China Lake to take a look. The planes were in bad shape. The engine intakes were full of desert dust; the ejection seats were nonfunctional; they were missing parts and even had flat tires. Still, they were better than nothing.

With the help of Northrop, Topgun got those aircraft ready for flight. Mugs and Jerry flew them to Miramar, where the school's maintainers discovered that none of their support equipment would work with the new planes. Basic things like engine stands, hoists, and a cache of spare parts would be needed to get the birds functional. The mechanics improvised, pulling the engines out by hand and laying them on mattresses inside a hangar, but that was a stopgap. They needed a proper logistical setup for these planes.

It became a race against time. The school could not afford to keep canceling class. That would attract too much attention from the wrong crowd above Topgun. So Mugs reached out to an old friend from his test pilot school days, Major Richard "Moody" Suter, who played the central role later on in establishing the Air Force's big multinational exercise, Red Flag. Mugs made a backroom deal with Suter, trading a shipment of stylish USN leather flight jackets for the parts and equipment Topgun needed.

An Air Force C-130 flew the gear into Miramar, which caught the eye of an AirPac admiral, who reportedly began asking questions.

"Is there an Air Force detachment arriving?"

"No sir, all that gear is for Topgun."

"*What?*"

Mugs embodied the attitude that had played a foundational role in Topgun's history: Don't ask for permission—get it done and beg for forgiveness. Quickly the T-38s were up and flying, filling the gap until other aircraft arrived.

Not long after, in January 1974, Mugs lost his executive officer. Jerry called him one night and told him he couldn't hack the pace anymore. He was a former enlisted pilot who had become an officer like I had, through the Naval Aviation Cadet (NAVCAD) program. He was trying to finish college and had just gotten married. Too many balls in the air, and he knew Topgun needed an XO with his entire heart in the job. He asked to be relieved, and Mugs let him go.

The next morning, Jack Ensch walked into the Topgun offices to find Jerry cleaning out his desk. Jack had just come off nine months of medical rehab for his wounds and injuries incurred during his shootdown and imprisonment in North Vietnam.

"What's going on?" Jack asked his friend.

"I quit," Jerry answered. "You're the XO now."

The news caught Jack by surprise. He had come to Topgun as Mugs's special projects officer, a slot created for him so he'd have a place to work until his next assignment.

The connection between Mugs and Jack is one of the finest examples of the bond naval aviators build with each other. Mugs was an only child growing up, and in his most serious moments, he told Jack, "You know, you're the brother I always wanted and never had."

The two men flew in combat together, knocking a pair of MiG-17s out of the sky in May 1972. During one fight, as they were vectored after some MiGs, Jack called out from the RIO's position in their F-4, "Let's go get 'em, Mugs. I'm right behind ya."

Chuckling, Mugs told him, "Knock that shit off. This is serious."

Thirteen days later, Mugs left Yankee Station to take over Topgun. Jack stayed on the carrier. He was flying with another pilot, Mike Doyle, when they took a SAM hit and ejected. Doyle was killed. Jack suffered grievous injuries during his ejection, and was captured and taken to a North Vietnamese prison camp.

As Mugs heard the news, he had just learned that they were to receive the Navy Cross for their two-kill engagement in May. It was the second-highest award for valor that existed. Mugs said he would accept it only with Jack by his side. Eight months after Jack was released, he and Mugs stood shoulder to shoulder in a ceremony attended only by their families and a few VIPs. Together as brothers, they received their Navy Crosses.

Now at Topgun, Jack would be right behind Mugs again. The two would help usher in a new era for the school and its capabilities, ensuring that Topgun kept Navy fighter aviation the best in the world during some difficult years.

In the spring of 1974, I was still in the Med with the *America* and my Dogs. I was in Palma de Mallorca, Spain, during a port of call, having a drink in a waterfront hotel, when I noticed an airline flight crew entering the lounge. They were from El Al, the Israeli airline. One of the flight attendants approached me.

"Are you Commander Dan Pedersen?"

"I am."

"I have something for you from your friends in Israel."

She handed me a small box. No note. No card. Just a box. She walked away without another word.

Inside, I found a beautiful fourteen-karat gold Star of David attached to a gold link chain. The gift was completely anonymous.

How did they find me?

I thought right then of the barbecue at my place in San Diego, where I met Colonel Ben Eliyahu, Dan Halutz, and the other Israelis for the first time. No-nonsense, secretive, eager to learn. Professional to the core. Then I remembered a conversation we had had. I asked Ben why his people were so serious.

"Daniel, you will understand when you are in combat, getting ready to fire at your enemy, and you realize you are flying over your home, where your wife and children are."

They had lived our worst nightmare and prevailed.

I resolved to visit Israel someday to renew those friendships. Maybe I would even find out who had sent that beautiful gift.

I put it on and wore it for the rest of my Navy career as part of my basic kit. Little mouse. Fifties Ray-Bans. Star of David on my chest, reminding me that friendships can sometimes help save nations.

CHAPTER SIXTEEN

RETURN WITH HONOR

Forty miles off South Vietnam
April 29, 1975

For naval aviation, the problem of Vietnam never seemed to go away.

Lieutenant Darrell "Condor" Gary stood before the assembled pilots and RIOs of VF-51. In Darrell's short career, he'd been thrown into the air war over North Vietnam before completing his RAG training back in the late '60s as an F-4 back-seater. Two tours there and he came home in time for me to pull him into Topgun as one of our instructors. He subsequently went to flight school, became an F-4 pilot, and went through Topgun as a student before heading out to the carrier USS *Coral Sea* and his first overseas deployment as a fighter pilot.

In 1975, he was a young lieutenant tasked with delivering one of the most painful briefs the squadron would ever receive: It fell to Condor to bring them the news that we were abandoning our allies once and for all.

The disaster began the previous month, when North Vietnam launched a new offensive against our allies in the Central Highlands. For the past eighteen months, Congress had steadily whittled down U.S. military aid to South Vietnam. Suffering shortages of spare parts, ammunition, and lubricants, the army of the Republic of Vietnam was in a deplorable state of readiness. America was partially responsible for that.

The North Vietnamese offensive threw eighty thousand troops into the Central Highlands. Our allies buckled under the onslaught. As we pulled out in the early 1970s, we tried to train the South Vietnamese Army, but never overcame the corruption, malfeasance, and frequent cowardice of their officer corps.

Prime Minister Nguyen Van Thieu appealed to President Gerald Ford for $300 million worth of emergency military aid. Congress balked, in part because everyone could see that the South Vietnamese Army was coming apart at the seams.

Thieu ordered the army to stage a strategic withdrawal to defend key cities and strategic locations. Under heavy pressure, the South Vietnamese Army found roads clogged with fleeing refugees. The withdrawal bogged down. Officers panicked. One general told his troops, "Every man for himself." It became a rout.

This surprised the North Vietnamese. Sensing an opportunity, the Communist army converged on Saigon, overrunning our former air base at Da Nang and capturing dozens of South Vietnamese Air Force aircraft.

Chaos descended on the South. By April Fools' Day, it was clear our allies were doomed unless the United States came to the rescue. No amount of money could save the South Vietnamese military by this point; only a massive employment of airpower and ground troops could turn the situation around. We flew in dozens of heavy transport aircraft to Tan Son Nhut Air Base to extract as many people as possible.

There were horrible tragedies as the evacuation unfolded. On the fourth of April, a C-5 Galaxy, the largest aircraft in the world, suffered mechanical failure with 250 orphaned children aboard.

The crew turned around and crash-landed at Tan Son Nhut, killing 153 children and adults. The Communists marched on the air base as the evacuation gained steam. As the North Vietnamese advanced, commercial airliners were thrown into the effort. Should Tan Son Nhut become unusable, helicopters would be our only other option to get our people out of harm's way. The air base was soon untenable as the NVA closed.

The U.S. task force off the South Vietnamese coast, anchored by the carriers *Enterprise*, *Coral Sea*, *Midway*, and *Hancock*, were the evacuation's last best hope.

On April 29, Darrell briefed his squadron as it prepared to serve as MiG combat air patrol (MiGCAP) for the last-ditch evacuation off rooftops and makeshift helicopter pads around Saigon. At the American embassy, the final embarkation point, personnel chopped down trees to create a second helicopter landing zone. The situation was chaotic in the extreme.

Darrell reviewed the latest intel as dispassionately as he could, but beneath the façade he felt an overwhelming sense of disappointment and grief. The war that had consumed his youth was coming to an end with America abandoning her ally. We were finally about to quit on the conflict that had spanned his entire adult life. The mood at VF-51 was somber. There was none of the usual wisecracking. If the Communists took over, the consequences would be horrific. Tens of thousands of innocents would be rounded up and shot or thrown into labor camps. With four U.S. carriers offshore, why should we let it happen?

Darrell went over the rules of engagement. As ever, Washington-style thinking prevailed. We could not engage unless our planes or helicopters came under direct fire first. If MiGs attempted to intercept the rescue effort, Fighting 51 was cleared to shoot only if they posed a threat. The eighty helicopters used in the evacuation would fly to USS *Midway*, the receiving ship. The other carriers would support. The surface fleet formed a barrier between coast and carriers, ready to help in any way they could. When Darrell was finished, the aviators rose from their seats and headed toward their aircraft.

The helicopters began arriving over Saigon as the lead elements of the North Vietnamese army reached the outskirts of the city. Yet the Communists did not interfere with the evacuation. Fearing it could trigger full-scale American intervention at the eleventh hour, the North Vietnamese held back. The MiGs made no appearance, nor did the attack aircraft they'd captured at Da Nang. The biggest threat to the helos came from rogue disgruntled South Vietnamese troops. Small-arms fire raked them as they landed on rooftops and at the embassy tennis courts.

Overhead, Darrell and the other aviators of Fighting 51 could see smoke rising over the embassy in downtown, where the last of the staff burned top-secret documents and millions of dollars' worth of cash. Toasted hundred-dollar-bill ashes rained down on the crowd from the incinerator's smokestack. Helicopters touched down on rooftops, picked up loads of people, and turned for the fleet.

Some neighborhoods under curfew looked empty. The only vehicles on the streets were ambulances that had been pressed into service. Mobs of people hauled their luggage and all the cash they could scrounge up, desperate to get out of the city with their children before the Communists stormed the palace gates. Streaming out of every inlet, moorage, and slough came boats, sampans, luggers, rafts, scows of every sort, hundreds flowing into a great exodus, looking like ants on leaves as they rode the waves in search of salvation. It was a humanitarian crisis unlike anything since the final days of World War II. Millions would be consumed by it.

Darrell and the rest of his flight loitered as long as fuel allowed, then turned for home as another group of F-4s arrived to take up station. The flight back to the *Coral Sea* was one that the youngest of Topgun's Original Bros would never forget. Below his F-4, the evacuation armada carpeted the ocean to the horizon, pushing through the swells toward the Navy task force. It represented one thing: freedom. The sight of it was heartbreaking.

Toward midmorning, the first South Vietnamese Army helicopters appeared above the fleet. Flown by pilots who knew their country was in its death throes, they sought now to save themselves and their families. As the boats struggled along, the helos raced back and forth, delivering refugees to the *Midway* before turning around and going back for more.

As Darrell landed aboard the *Coral Sea*, steaming about ten miles from the *Midway*, he headed to debrief, helmet in hand, sobered by what he had witnessed. This was the end. We had never been allowed to win. He had a bird's-eye view of the consequences of it that day. They would be felt for decades to come.

The next morning, at 0500, the U.S. ambassador to a country that no longer existed climbed aboard a CH-46 Sea Knight helicopter and departed the embassy in Saigon. Three hours later, the last Americans—U.S. Marines—were pulled out and carried out to the fleet. That was it. South Vietnam surrendered unconditionally later that morning.

One Memorial Day, years after the war, Jim Laing and Darrell Gary were drinking a beer at Bulley's together. Both were well into their civilian lives. They started wondering about their old friends and how many in their circle they really lost back in those days. They grabbed a cocktail napkin and started writing down names. The first three names belonged to fallen aviators from the nine guys they had rented beach houses with in the early days of Topgun at the Lafayette Escadrille. From there, the list grew. They reached for more cocktail napkins. By the time their memories ran out, forty-three names filled a small pile of napkins. Those were just their friends. Half had been lost in combat, half in training. The personal cost of a war lost will always be the names and faces of friends. The larger consequences beggared the imagination.

With the last flight to the *Midway* from the embassy grounds, 1,373 Americans and 5,595 Vietnamese were helicoptered to the naval task force. Another 65,000 fled by boat, later to be picked up by one of the forty ships offshore. The fixed-wing airlift from Tan Son Nhut pulled out another 50,493, including almost 2,700 orphans. They were the lucky ones. In the immediate aftermath of South Vietnam's collapse, more than 150,000 civilians vanished, most either executed outright or thrown into concentration camps. Saigon was renamed Ho Chi Minh City, a memorial to the unknown masses of dead. Somewhere between 1 and 4 million Vietnamese perished from 1955 to 1975. In Cambodia, another 300,000 were killed. Laos lost between 20,000 and 60,000. In the years ahead, the killing would continue as Communist insurgents toppled the governments of Laos and Cambodia. From 1975 to 1979, the Khmer Rouge, a regime that swept to power in the wake of America's exit from the region, murdered or starved to death about 2.5 million people out of a population of 8 million—more than 30 percent of the entire nation. When Americans look back at Vietnam, we remember the domestic unrest. We think, too, of the 58,000 names memorialized on that long black marble wall in Washington. Those are important to remember. But few want to discuss the other consequences of America's lost war.

As the naval armada covered the evacuation off the Vietnam coast in April 1975, I was headed for the Philippines. The honor of serving as squadron commander had prepared me for a higher command. At Subic Bay, I caught up with the *Coral Sea* and went aboard as the prospective commander of Air Wing Fifteen.

I won't belabor the mood aboard ship. Everyone was ready to forget. Fortunately, the ship was scheduled to steam south for Perth, Australia, to celebrate the Battle of the Coral Sea, the 1942 naval victory that helped save Australia from Japanese invasion.

The air wing needed the lift of a friendly port of call with one of our closest and most loyal allies. The Aussies always treated us sailors with tremendous affection and kindness, even when our own countrymen didn't. It was also a good way for me to get to know the men and make the transition from the current skipper, Commander Inman "Hoagy" Carmichael.

We departed Cubi Point after only a short stay, steaming through the Sunda Strait, where the heavy cruiser USS *Houston* had made its epic last stand a generation before. The men were looking forward to the excitement waiting for them in Perth. Each morning, I saw Condor running on the flight deck, getting back in shape for the merriment ahead.

It was not to be. As Darrell put it, "One morning, I woke up and went for my run, and realized the sun was on the wrong side of the ship." Another emergency had developed, and so the president had asked where the carriers were. The *Coral Sea* was the closest, and we received orders sending us racing north at flank speed.

The Cambodians had seized an American-flagged and -owned cargo container ship. Now the ship was in Khmer Rouge hands, and the crew was somewhere ashore, locked up in what looked like an exact repeat of the 1968 *Pueblo* incident.

Would we never be free of this place?

The ship was named the *Mayaguez*. It had departed South Vietnam with cargo that included almost eighty containers full of military equipment and material from the American embassy in Saigon. The skipper of the *Mayaguez* was supposed to sail to Thailand. En route, he accidentally passed inside Cambodian territorial waters. On May 12, 1975, as we headed south for Perth, a small boat crewed by Khmer Rouge forces sped out to the *Mayaguez* and fired a rocket-propelled grenade across its bow only a few miles off the island of Poulo Wai. The captain of the *Mayaguez*, Charles Miller, ordered full stop and began broadcasting an SOS. The Khmer Rouge boarded the ship and ordered the vessel to Poulo Wai.

The next morning, two U.S. Navy patrol aircraft discovered the *Mayaguez* and took ground fire while making a low-level pass to confirm the ship's identity. The Khmer Rouge moved the ship to an anchorage just north of Koh Tang island, where our planes found her.

President Gerald Ford announced to the world that he considered this an act of piracy. The *Pueblo* incident in 1968 had become an open wound for the United States, for months embarrassing the Johnson administration. After the humiliation of South Vietnam's defeat and the blow to American prestige it inflicted, the president was in no mood to show weakness. He ordered the ship seized and the crew rescued. The *Coral Sea*'s air wing would provide air support and strike targets on the Cambodian mainland.

By rights, I should have been leading the air wing, but Hoagy Carmichael was not about to give up his command when we were going back into combat. I don't blame him; I would have done the same thing. I would ride this out beside our task force commander, Rear Admiral Bob Coogan.

Around WestPac, a rescue force was cobbled together under Seventh Air Force command. The plan called for Air Force helos to stage the Marines out of an air base in Thailand. En route on the night of the thirteenth, one of the birds crashed, killing twenty-three men. That put the operation on hold, at least until the *Coral Sea* reached the area.

The next morning, Air Force F-111s and A-7 Corsairs discovered the captive American crew aboard a fishing boat. The Khmer Rouge planned to take them to the mainland, making rescuing them far more difficult. The planes bombed and strafed in front of the vessel and shot up several patrol boats, sinking one, but that failed to dissuade the Khmer Rouge. The fishing boat continued on its way, and the planes overhead eventually lost sight of it. There were conflicting reports as to exactly where the crew was taken. Some thought they'd been taken back to Koh Tang. Other sources thought they were on the mainland.

On the afternoon of the fourteenth, President Gerald Ford ordered the Seventh Air Force to execute a helicopter assault on Koh Tang island and the *Mayaguez*. The forces landing on the island were to find the crew, if they were there, while another team helicoptered onto the *Mayaguez* and steamed it out to international waters.

Just before the rescue force went in, Admiral Coogan received a direct call from President Ford and Secretary of State Henry Kissinger. I was with him in the *Coral Sea*'s flag quarters and listened with great interest. President Ford ordered the carrier to strike targets on the Cambodian mainland, including port facilities and a nearby naval base.

"Admiral," the president said, "go get our ship and crew back. It's your show. Use all available means, but no nukes."

I wondered how many times our commanders on Yankee Station had heard such a command. Not even Nixon had ever expressed such a clear and explicit willingness to let us fight.

The rescue mission began at dawn on May 15. As the strike aircraft catapulted away and Marines in Air Force helicopters sped toward Koh Tang, I led a dozen F-4s on a fighter sweep over the mainland. Approaching Phnom Penh, we increased speed and dove down to the deck. Two dozen J79s shook the streets as we rocketed along at five hundred knots at just five hundred feet. We were there in case some MiGs wanted to make trouble. None showed up. Meanwhile, the size and suddenness of the air strike let them know America was serious.

Darrell Gary, who was scheduled to fly later in the day, climbed up the ladder to the *Coral Sea's* flight deck. Because the initial strike quickly obliterated the targets so completely, Darrell's flight was scrubbed. We meant business—and showed it.

Unfortunately, these were the days before a unified Special Operations Command and quick-reaction forces. The hastily thrown-together rescue group from multiple services operated with inaccurate intelligence and a complete misread of the situation on the island. The CIA believed Koh Tang was lightly defended, if at all. In fact, more than a hundred Khmer Rouge troops held the island to deter their Communist brothers from North Vietnam, who had laid claim to these patches of turf off the Indochinese coast.

Our Marines rolled into hot landing zones laced with machine-gun and rocket-propelled grenade fire. From the ship, Darrell watched as several CH-53 heavy transport helicopters took hits. One crashed offshore after receiving two RPG hits. The survivors were in the water for hours until a gig from one of our escorts pulled them to safety. Included in those survivors was the Marine forward air controller, who somehow found an Air Force survival radio that he used to call targets for the A-7 Corsairs overhead. Clinging to wreckage, the radio's batteries slowly failing, he gave everything he had to try and secure help for the embattled Marines pinned down in the landing zone.

Three CH-53 Jolly Green Giants went down during the rescue operation. Fifteen Marines were killed on Koh Tang and fifty more wounded during the fighting that raged throughout the day.

Meanwhile, our attack aircraft saturated the *Mayaguez* with tear gas. An American warship raced into the anchorage with a company of Marines aboard. An hour after the assault on the island began, the Marines, clad in gas masks, swarmed aboard the cargo ship and found it abandoned. We had our ship back. Where was the crew?

The Khmer released them, sending them back out to sea, where a Navy patrol plane spotted them. Another American warship steamed to the vessel and pulled the crew aboard just before the lunch hour.

The final act played out through the afternoon as the Air Force tried to extract the Marines from the landing zones. Heavy fire repeatedly drove them off, and one battle-damaged Jolly Green force-landed on the *Coral Sea*'s deck. Our maintainers swiftly patched it up. A few hours later, it went back into action.

The fighting raged, and our frustration level grew. The birds kept taking hits, and the Marines were reporting heavy casualties. By dinner, the Air Force brought in an AC-130 gunship and five C-130s carrying fifteen-thousand-pound bombs known as BLU-82s, nicknamed Daisy Cutters. They were the biggest, most destructive conventional weapons in the American arsenal.

The first one detonated as Darrell and others watched from our deck. Darrell saw the enormous explosion followed by the shock wave the blast unleashed. It obscured the island and swept right across the *Coral Sea*, causing the huge carrier to shudder from its impact.

As darkness fell, another Jolly Green staggered out of the moonless night. The massive helicopter carried a crew of five and managed to pull aboard thirty-four Marines before suffering engine trouble. The crew set down on the carrier's deck, and when its ramp dropped, almost three dozen wounded Marines tumbled out onto the flight deck.

Our ship's corpsmen raced to help them, triaging the wounded and lining them up on one of our elevators. The air wing's senior master chief went from man to man, offering water and words of support, giving them anything they needed. Even those who weren't wounded suffered from dehydration after twelve hours of combat in the tropical heat. The wounded on the elevator were lowered to the hangar deck, then carried by corpsmen and volunteers to our medical facilities, where surgeons operated through the night. They saved every one of those wounded Marines.

That night, a young second lieutenant was given a bunk in Darrell's stateroom. He was shocked and exhausted, with a *What in the hell just happened?* expression on his face. Forty-eight hours before, he was living an easy life on Okinawa. He woke up, ended up in a hot LZ, and watched some of his men die.

During the last part of the evacuation, that officer saw a C-130 make a run right in front of his position, dropping a BLU-82. A parachute opened above the bomb, and it swung down to land practically on his Marine platoon. It didn't go off. The mother of all bombs turned out to be a dud. Thank God.

In less than three weeks, the *Coral Sea* and her air wing had witnessed the final evacuation of South Vietnam, then taken part in what is now called the last battle of the Vietnam War. The fifteen Marines killed on Koh Tang island became the final men whose names were etched into the wall in Washington a decade later. Three more Marines, declared missing in action on the island, were captured by the Khmer Rouge and later beaten to death.

Though the cost was high, we got our ship and crew back. There was no repeat of the *Pueblo* incident. The Communist Khmer Rouge did not have time to inspect or offload the cargo, which meant whatever secrets lay inside the containers from our embassy remained safe. The U.S. government has never divulged their contents.

Aboard the *Coral Sea*, we were heartened by President Ford's willingness to let us off the leash. My new air wing performed brilliantly, destroying all of its assigned targets. It would take time and years to figure out how best to handle crisis situations as this one. The aborted attempt to rescue our hostages in Iran in 1980 would be another case study in how not to conduct such operations. They became the catalyst for changes that gave our military the flexibility to handle any such task the world might throw our way. For now, President Ford had shown our adversaries some of the strength and resolve that might have helped us during the LBJ years.

After we took our wounded Marines to Subic Bay, we steamed south for Perth and a ten-day port call. The Aussies welcomed us with a great hospitality. We were treated like family everywhere we went. The crew drank and laughed with our friends from down under and put the scars of the war in their rearview mirrors. By the end of it I was so exhausted from all the free drinks and parties that I crawled into my bunk and slept the sleep of a free man. The world was at peace for the first time in ten years.

CHAPTER SEVENTEEN

TOPGUN AND THE TOMCAT

While I was out with my air wing aboard the *Coral Sea*, the Navy began its first major evolution into the post-Vietnam era. The renaissance centered on a new and potent fighter aircraft whose design Topgun helped influence, the Grumman F-14 Tomcat.

Our work at Topgun in 1969 and 1970 continued to spark a rethinking of naval aviation and its role. Thanks to the efforts of so many dedicated commanders and junior officers, Topgun would not only survive the transition to peacetime, but would undergo a new golden age that helped shape how we would fight for the next twenty years.

In combat aviation, no aircraft is forever. Our beloved Phantom served a long and useful service life. But the future was within view even on the day that I accepted the assignment to lead Topgun in 1969. My old friend from Miramar, Sam Leeds, took command of Fighter Squadron One, the first unit that was assigned the new F-14, in October 1972, based on USS *Enterprise*. Later that year, VF-124, the Crusader fleet replacement squadron whose sword we stole and hauled around at Mach 2, stopped training pilots to fly the obsolescent F-8 and began training the first Tomcat pilots.

The last of the carrier-deploying Phantom squadrons made the transition to the Tomcat in 1987—a fifteen-year overlap during which both F-4s and F-14s served well and capably at the same time.

One of my few regrets is that I never had the pleasure of being part of the Tomcat tribe. When I had the chance, I would log some time just sitting in that Grumman-built bird, daydreaming about the things I could have done with someone like J. C. Smith or Hawkeye Laing in my rear seat.

Of course, the F-14 Tomcat almost never made it into the world, thanks to Secretary of Defense Robert S. McNamara, who loved to think he knew people's business better than they did. In 1968, he tried to force the Navy to adopt the hulking F-111 fighter-bomber for use on aircraft carriers.

Imagine SecDef's chagrin when a mere three-star admiral, the head of naval aviation at the Pentagon, decided to stand in his way. That truth-telling sailor, Tom Connolly, testified to Congress, "There isn't enough thrust in Christendom to make that airplane into a fighter." And he won. The Navy avoided being saddled with the "Flying Edsel," so named by its unhappy Air Force pilots because its chief advocate, Secretary McNamara, had been president of Ford Motor Company. McNamara took his revenge, denying Vice Admiral Connolly a deserved promotion to a fourth star. But the last word belonged to the Navy. It paid tribute to a great man by naming its new world-beating fighter aircraft after him. The legendary Tomcat was born. Though it fell right in line with other Grumman felines in history—Wildcat, Hellcat, Bearcat, Tigercat—the name was the artful final act in a Pentagon dogfight.

Where the F4D Skyray was like a Porsche and a Phantom like a muscle car, the F-14 Tomcat was a supercharged Cadillac: big, comfortable, the plushest ride in fighter aviation. It had a roomy cockpit, and the instrumentation, controls, and switches were well laid out, placing its systems easily to hand. A long bubble canopy offered visibility for the pilot and RIO vastly better than the F-4's. Grumman even thought to install a "hassle handle" on the rear instrument panel. During combat, the rear-seater could grab hold of it, gaining leverage to twist in his seat and check for a threat astern, between the Tomcat's twin tails.

The Tomcat, like the Phantom, was a twin-engine interceptor, designed mainly for fleet defense. But unlike the Phantom, the Tomcat was saved by Grumman's attention to its heritage: Their designers found a way to mount it with a powerful 20mm Gatling cannon. Topgun had a hand in that particular development. When the Navy's project officer from the Pentagon showed up at Nellis to pitch the F-14's coming glory as a missile shooter, future Topgun CO Mugs McKeown and I were on hand to ask, "Where's the gun?" I admit, we knocked around that projects officer pretty well that day. Ultimately the Tomcat was built with that Gatling gun tucked in the fuselage below the cockpit. The hollow moan of the six-barrel Vulcan rotary cannon can never be forgotten by those who've felt and heard it. Six thousand rounds per minute has a useful effect on an enemy pilot's psychology, too. Vice Admiral Tom Connolly was the one who took our input at the Pentagon and made a gun-armed Tomcat a reality.

The gun was great to have, but the advanced AIM-54 Phoenix air-to-air missile could really reach out and touch someone. Tracking up to six targets simultaneously with her Hughes AWG-9 multimode pulse-Doppler radar, one F-14 could destroy them out beyond one hundred miles with the Phoenix. At nearly half a million dollars apiece, the Phoenix blew through budgets nearly as fast as it chased down targets at Mach 5. Considerations of weight would leave the typical Tomcat weapons load-out short of the six it was designed to carry. The more typical load-out was four Phoenix carried on mounts on the aircraft's belly, and two Sparrows and two Sidewinders hanging from the wings. The final Tomcat variation, the F-14D, was known as the Bombcat. The versatile machine could carry the GPS-guided precision bomb known as a Joint Direct Attack Munition, as well as Paveway laser-guided bombs, a centerline reconnaissance system, or an infrared targeting pod. With that Gatling gun added in, Navy air wings were equipped to deliver a heck of a lot of firepower.

The Tomcat had a variable-geometry wing. It could retract, sweeping back almost flush with the fuselage, twenty degrees off the tail, or extend to nearly full stretch at sixty-eight degrees for takeoff and slow flight, adjusting automatically to maximize performance at any airspeed. With the wings swept back, she resembled a lethal bird of prey, but was still surprisingly maneuverable (the fuselage itself was shaped to produce aerodynamic lift). Once her Pratt & Whitney engines were replaced by the more reliable General Electric F110 and updated avionics, the thirty-eight-million-dollar fighter had power to spare.

When the movie came out in 1986, the Tomcat became a star. It would stand as the symbol of Topgun and naval aviation generally for decades. It would rival the Phantom as a favorite among fighter pilots and aviation enthusiasts alike. Plenty of squadrons continued operating the F-4 as the Tomcat made its way to the fleet. But the future was closing with us fast as I wound down my tour as air wing commander in the *Coral Sea*. At Miramar, Topgun continued its original mission of preparing to handle the threat of what lay ahead.

In 1975, the year Tomcats began deploying in larger numbers, Topgun went through a major evolution in the way it taught air combat maneuvering. This was made possible by new technology. The Cubic Corporation, based in San Diego, working with Navy engineers, devised a special telemetry pod that could be mounted on an aircraft's Sidewinder missile pylon. Dave Frost flew some of the first tests around 1972, exploring ways to capture a full, reviewable record of a dogfight within defined airspace over our combat training ranges. The so-called air combat maneuvering range (ACMR) would revolutionize how our fighter pilots were educated. It enabled us to push beyond a problem that hampered us in Topgun's early days. The problem looked like this.

The scene: Hangar One at Miramar. A student aircrew is slumped in their seats, exhausted after four or five dogfights in the mission just completed. Their faces are lined with the impressions of their oxygen masks cinched tight to stay in place under heavy G. Their flight suits are stained with sweat from the physical exertion of high-speed maneuvering. Before them stands their instructor, tall at the podium, resplendent in his tailored blue Topgun flight suit, his debrief polished by the murder boards, carefully consulting his notes of each student's moves. Topgun had long since embraced the good news/bad news approach to enlightenment. Sometimes, especially early in a class, it was difficult to find good news. But delivering and dissecting bad news was how people learned after taking a licking.

The instructor would say, "Cruiser, by offsetting on the third engagement you made a good initial turn after the Merge, and I had to go vertical to avoid an overshoot. At that point you seemed to lose sight of me—is that right? Rowdy, did you see me from the backseat?"

The instructor would turn to the chalkboard and diagram the fight as his notes from his knee board and memory permitted. But these data sources were fallible, especially when the mind that produced them was under strain of G forces, short on blood as all the aircraft changed speeds and altitudes. Multiply that complexity by the four or five engagements that typically took place in one flight, and the human senses can short-circuit trying to apprehend it all. A cassette tape recording of the radio calls could help, but only so much. The instructor had to do what he could to determine who did what to whom and derive the appropriate lessons. We used to say, "First man to the chalkboard wins the fight."

Captain Ault and his people anticipated this problem well in advance. His famous 1969 report had described the need for an electronic monitoring system to sort out the precise choreography of every ACM flight. Merle Gorder, the author of the report's recommendations, advised the major fighter commands on each coast to establish an ACMR, noting that cost estimates and plans were already available thanks to a report jointly filed in November 1968 by the Applied Physics Laboratory and Johns Hopkins University.

Less than a decade later, the potential of that system was realized at Topgun's range in Arizona, east of Marine Corps Air Station Yuma. Telemetry made it possible for the new system to record the myriad data of an air-to-air engagement in a given block of airspace, including the altitudes, speeds, headings, G forces, weapon status, everything. It gave our instructors a choice between a "God's-eye view" and switchable individual perspectives from any cockpit in the fight. Now that an unblinking electronic eye could show whether a pilot had fired his missile within its performance envelope, gone were the days of "I gotcha" versus "You did not." The ground stations would relay the hard data to a central station on the range and then via microwave data link to Miramar. With every squeeze of a trigger, the system would run numbers and function as an umpire, calling kill or no kill. It made possible a renaissance in fighter combat training.

With Mugs and Jack Ensch leading the way, Topgun's leadership in this new era was rock solid. Together, they fostered and perpetuated the elite atmosphere we started in the F-4 days, all while integrating new technology and concepts. Mugs and his always-useful political connections helped get the command a new fleet of aggressor aircraft, including a number of former South Vietnamese F-5 Freedom Fighters whose pilots had escaped with them to Thailand before the fall of Saigon. Finally Topgun had resources, access to almost whatever it needed, plus first-rate aircraft with which to teach. From those first days inside the condemned trailer back in 1969, we had come a long, long way.

When foreign aircrews came to the United States to train, they universally wanted to come to Topgun, something that left the Air Force and its Red Flag program feeling slighted. The staff at Miramar greeted everyone from Saudi princes to French Mirage pilots—and of course more hard-drinking Brits, whose antics on the ground matched their skill in the air.

The irrepressible Darrell Gary was right at the center of this evolution. Perhaps nobody else in the Navy was as connected to Topgun as Condor was through the 1970s. He first joined us as an RIO in 1969, the youngest of our nine. He served with skill and dedication as an instructor before going to flight school and becoming an F-4 pilot. He graduated from Topgun and returned to VF-51, then he and I crossed paths once again aboard the *Coral Sea* during the *Mayaguez* incident. After that cruise, he returned to Topgun for a third time. As an instructor pilot, and the project officer for the air combat maneuvering range at Yuma, Condor became a leading light in the technological revolution that took Topgun to a new level.

When Condor briefed the four-star in charge of USAF Tactical Air Command about the ACMR, the general said he didn't like the system. Darrell asked him why. The response was, "Because my guys know that everyone can see the mistakes as well as the good maneuvering. It will increase the accident rate. My guys would rather die than look bad." Darrell sensed he was only half joking.

It wasn't just Topgun instructors who needed to see the battle space in granular time-motion detail. Our fleet operators needed it, too, and thanks to new technology, they were getting it. The latest airborne early warning (AEW) aircraft were equipped with powerful radars that could detect the enemy at great ranges and target him. The state of the art was embodied by the E-2 Hawkeye's twenty-four-foot rotating dome, which covered hundreds of square miles of radar airspace. The five-man crew included three specialists—a combat information officer, an air control officer, and a radar operator—who were shoehorned in "the tunnel," a tight, confined workspace in the rear crammed with scopes, dials, and switches. The system for managing all that data required an enormous amount of expertise.

The full name of the Miramar command, as it happened, was Fighter and Airborne Early Warning Wing, Pacific Fleet (ComFit-AEWWingPac). The early warning aircraft community there had its own fleet readiness squadrons and a tactical school they called Top Dome. As fleet air defense required real-time information to be reliably exchanged, data link became increasingly important. Although Hawkeyes and fighters often worked together in exercises, they didn't have the type of hand-in-glove integration that Topgun fostered. In the years when Cobra Ruliffson and Hawk Smith were in charge, Topgun worked hard to change that.

Ruliffson conceived of a program to cultivate and sharpen the skill of our E-2 aircrews, the Maritime Air Superiority Threat (MAST) program, or "Topscope," and pitched it to the chief of naval operations in 1976. The new schoolhouse began in 1978. The following year, Topgun put ninety-four men through its five-week course, while next door, the four-week Topscope program graduated

109 aircrewmen and "air intercept controllers." In 1980, the two programs were formally consolidated and the curriculum expanded to six weeks.

These postwar developments came just in time to help save the supercarrier. The Russians, well aware of the threat our carrier battle groups represented, had spent decades devising ways to defeat them. Though they never were able to build their own supercarriers, they did come up with some weapons and aircraft that put our command of the sea at risk.

The Tu-22M Backfire bomber first flew in 1969. It joined operational squadrons in 1972 as a dedicated carrier killer. Armed with air-to-surface missiles with a three-hundred-mile range, the Tu-22M could race toward a carrier battle group at Mach 2 and fire a salvo of deadly missiles before our antiaircraft weapons could hit them. Each Backfire could carry four or more of these missiles. An attack by a full Backfire regiment—about forty planes—could throw almost two hundred missiles at our ships, overwhelming our defenses from stand-off distance. These long-range missiles could carry either conventional or nuclear warheads. In a worst-case scenario, one missile could destroy an entire battle group costing billions of dollars, manned by thousands of young Americans.

The discovery of the threat posed by Soviet Backfire bombers justified very serious concern in our senior command at the start of the 1970s. We had to counter that threat for the supercarrier to survive. The combination of the F-14, E-2, and the Phoenix missile system was our answer. The F-14's long legs allowed us to patrol greater distances from the carrier. The E-2 gave us radar coverage well away from the fleet. It also ensured we would have radar coverage when the battle group was running on "EMCON" control—with all of its electronic emissions shut down, to keep the Soviets from detecting our ships. The Phoenix gave us our own stand-off response to the

Tu-22 threat. Its hundred-mile-range enabled Tomcat aircrews to engage the Backfires far from the battle group.

It fell to Topgun to create these tactics. Through the late 1970s and early 1980s, Topgun sharpened our capability both in long-range interception and fighter-on-fighter dogfighting. When Monroe Smith was CO, he developed a tactic known as the "chainsaw." The idea was to keep Tomcats on patrol at their maximum range from the carriers. This required a constant cycle of E-2 Hawkeyes, Tomcats, and aerial refueling tankers. Together, they would create a defensive barrier two hundred miles from the battle group. It was easy to reinforce them with fighters on alert five status. The E-2 Hawkeyes would orbit nearby, providing radar coverage and control extending hundreds more miles out. When the Backfires appeared, the Tomcats could hit their burners, close the distance quickly, and fire their Phoenix missiles. Russian aircrews became painfully aware of the power of our argus-eyed orbiting radars. With in-flight refueling, Tomcats could chase Russians almost without limit, held back only by the constraints of our aircrews' endurance. We could only hope that the Phoenix would have been more reliable than the troubled Sparrow.

At Miramar, Topgun expanded its program to better prepare aircrews—fighter and early warning aircraft alike—for the challenge of fleet air defense. They got a broad-based understanding of how fighters could destroy other fighters while also protecting carriers from a Russian aerial swarm. We wanted to kill the archers rather than the arrows. The Miramar schoolhouse sent MAST teams to the East Coast to brief F-14 and E-2 squadrons on the latest Soviet anticarrier capability and how to counter it. At times, the Russians demonstrated their tactics against us. In the early 1980s, they actually launched a simulated attack on the *Enterprise* and *Midway*, closing to within 120 miles. As we monitored the exercise, we in turn learned a lot about how the Backfires planned to do business. We altered our tactics accordingly.

When Lonny "Eagle" McClung was the CO at Topgun in 1980 and 1981, he enlisted the Air Force to help him train his F-14 pilots to defeat the long-range Soviet cruise missile threat. It turned out the SR-71 Blackbird strategic reconnaissance aircraft was a superb imitator of a cruise missile. He would arrange for the boys from Beale Air Force Base to take off in their Blackbirds and track inbound toward the coast, starting far south of San Clemente Island. Topgun would station F-14s at ten-mile intervals along the radial of their approach, with their radars looking south. When the radars locked on a Blackbird, the Tomcat pilots would turn on their afterburners and climb, looking to gain a favorable position to shoot a Phoenix. With the stunning speed of the SR-71 faithfully matching an inbound antishipping missile, students learned how little time they had to set up a kill. The higher and faster they were, the more likely they were to achieve a good solution. According to Eagle, that meant climbing to forty thousand feet. There's no better way than to learn by doing, by experiencing those closure rates firsthand.

Thank God we never found out if any of these tactics worked. In a full-scale war with the Soviets, we would have faced not just hundreds of Backfire bombers, but older Tu-16 jet bombers and the venerable Tu-95 Bears as well. Well supported with electronic warfare aircraft and perhaps even fighter escort, the Soviet air armadas could have launched thousands of missiles at our battle groups. No tactic or weapon system is foolproof. Even if we were 99 percent successful in defeating their attacks, that 1 percent could have been enough to devastate the fleet.

As this threat took shape and Topgun responded through the postwar years, I was at sea more often than not. Commanding an air wing that included four F-4 Phantom squadrons, as well as attack aircraft, bombers, tankers, early warning planes, and helicopters, was one of the most challenging and fun jobs I ever had. In some ways, it is also a naval aviator's last hurrah with the fleet. Once you get promoted out of air wing command, your flying days are limited. Until that day comes, however, air wing commanders are expected to fly every type of plane in their inventory. It was a hair-on-fire experience. In the space of a few days, I might fly an F-4 Phantom, an A-6 Intruder, and a helicopter. In battle, I would have been leading strikes and coordinating the attacks of my individual squadrons.

The job is a culmination of everything learned earlier in a naval aviator's career. All the lessons, all the mentoring by other officers comes together in the way an air wing commander chooses to lead his men. Creating a culture of excellence, of openness and of self-evaluation so that your crews can improve and grow, is an essential element to success. Aboard the *Coral Sea*, I used the leadership techniques we developed at Topgun to set the framework, then I let my squadron commanders run their own shows without micromanaging them.

Our F-4 squadrons trained to tackle both the bomber threat and air-to-air combat with enemy fighters. The days of obsessively focusing on one mission set were over. We had learned the lessons of the 1960s, of Vietnam and the Topgun solutions. Now the new order of the day was to be a flexible force capable of responding to any threat.

It was an exciting time, and I cherished every moment. I knew that once it came to an end, I would have to let the younger guys do the flying. With the F-14 coming into the fleet in ever-increasing numbers, that was a bittersweet thing for me to accept. On one hand, with my career thriving, I could look forward to a staff job with Task Force 77, then my own carrier someday. On the other hand, I would have given almost anything to blast through the speed of sound in an F-14 heading for fifty thousand feet. I had come a long way from my days flying Fords from North Island.

One of the sweetest moments of my career took place at the officers' club at the Long Beach naval shipyard when my air wing was ashore. As CAG, I was invited to be the keynote speaker at the Daedalian Society, a wonderful aviation advocacy organization. I don't remember what I said to them. I do remember one man who lingered in his seat at the front table afterward. He was small and unassuming. He carried himself in an understated way. All the great ones do. It was General Jimmy Doolittle.

I am not easily overwhelmed, but when the general motioned me to his table and we fell into a conversation about aviation and everything related to it, I was overcome with gratitude—and awe. Imagine his courage, carrying out the famous Tokyo strike in April 1942 that bears his name. Leading a flight of sixteen Army bombers from an old straight-deck aircraft carrier when the war seemed nearly lost, he undertook a mission that was hard to tell from suicide. The general invited me to retire to the bar, where we drank a scotch and talked about what had been going on with my air wing on the *Coral Sea*. I took it as a high honor that he took the time with me. It suggested I might have done something right in my career. It was a most memorable drink with a great man.

In 1976 I stepped out of the cockpit for one last time as a full-time aviator and said farewell to my air wing. The Navy promoted me to captain, and now I was a senior officer at last. While I'd still get to fly from time to time, the truth was that my days as a combat aviator were over. I suppose it would have been harder to take had there been nothing but desk jobs on the horizon for me. Thank God, that was not the case. Ronald Wilson Reagan was my commander in chief. The prestige of naval aviation and the military generally was set for a resurgence, after many years in the doldrums following the withdrawal from Vietnam. It was a fine time for a newly minted captain to take command. I was going to sea as the skipper of my own ship.

CHAPTER EIGHTEEN

BLACK SHOES

Aboard USS *Wichita*
1978

Naval aviators are always considered a component of a total ship's company when serving aboard a carrier. This is true when we are acting either as a flying part of her air wing, or as a ship's officer. It should be understood that there are many nonflying jobs on board requiring seasoned naval aviator expertise. True, the aircraft and flight crews are the most visible and well known, the raison d'être of the vessel, but they are still only a component. It takes about five thousand sailors to get those ninety airplanes and their crews to where they need to go, but when you are part of the brown shoe, or aviation, set, much of that is invisible. We are focused on our squadrons, our air wing, and our flying. What the ship's company is doing represents almost a different universe to us, including engineering, navigation, supply, medical, dental, communication and, very importantly, the flight and hangar decks.

Decades ago, experience dictated that it was always best for a naval aviator to command our aircraft carriers due to the unique types of command decisions they made and the complexity of operating aircraft at sea. As a result, the career path for pilots and aircrew led through the traditional side of the Navy. Before they went to an aircraft carrier, they were designated a surface warfare officer or officer of the deck of an aircraft carrier. After I attended the Prospective Commanding Officers Course in Rhode Island, the Navy gave me command of my first ship, the replenishment oiler USS *Wichita* (AOR-1).

Talk about a wake-up call. From flying fighters at Mach 2, I found myself navigating the Pacific at twelve knots on the bridge of a forty-thousand-ton, 660-foot-long behemoth crewed by twenty-two officers and four hundred men. While we had two Boeing H-46 Sea Knight helicopters to help run "vertical replenishment" missions between our ship and those we serviced, for the first time in my career I had virtually no connection to flying fixed-wing aircraft. It was a big transition for me personally.

Why does the Navy send fighter pilots to command supply ships? Because prior to achieving the ultimate prize, aircraft carrier command, you must demonstrate your ability to command and operate a large ship at sea. You have to show you will never collide with another ship or run aground. More importantly, you need to learn the complex logistics of fleet operations. It is actually a stroke of institutional genius. During World War II, we needed to find ways to keep our carriers on station thousands of miles from port. This was no small challenge. A carrier crew consumes massive amounts of food and basic items like toothpaste, toilet paper, chewing gum, and cigarettes. The ship itself needs enormous amounts of fuel oil, aviation gas, and lubricants. To keep the carriers at sea functioning, we built an entire fleet of logistics ships that could transfer all those consumables at sea. It revolutionized the way the Navy projected power. Thirty years after the war, we had refined it to an art form.

When a big carrier came alongside us at sea, my crew would send across lines to the carrier, then run hoses linked with big connections and hose trolleys that move in and out on a steel cable to transport and replenish the carrier's supply of aviation fuel and bunker fuel. Our two helicopters, meanwhile, hauled sling loads of palletized supplies to the flight deck. In a few hours, the carrier was full up and ready to look for trouble.

Occasionally, we would replenish two ships at once, usually at night. I remember refueling a supercarrier and a foreign destroyer at the same time in open ocean, all three warships riding the swells together within a football field's length abreast. It took a lot of ship-handling skill for the receiving ships to do this, and even today few other navies have this kind of capacity. It is the secret behind our ability to operate anywhere in the world for as long as necessary.

Learning the logistical side of battle group operations was important to commanding a supercarrier. Thus, taking a supply ship to sea to work with the flattops was one of the stepping-stones to commanding a carrier of your own. Again, the keys to success were: "Don't hit anyone and never run her aground." If you were always on time and always filled out your customer's entire order, you would stay in the running for a supercarrier. Remember, there are always plenty of naval aviators, but only a few handfuls of ships like the *Wichita*, and even fewer supercarriers. Competition for command of one of those beautiful ships is understandably intense. It is well worth the study, time, and effort.

My great challenge came later in 1978 when the *Wichita* headed to the shipyard at Hunters Point, San Francisco, to undergo a refit and modernization. Aside from Candlestick Park, home of the 2–14 49ers that year, Hunters Point is a legendarily bad neighborhood, riddled with crime and drugs. We were slated to be at the shipyard for nine months. Our first problem: Where to billet the crew? I didn't want them to live aboard ship while it was being dry docked and overhauled, so I set off in search of suitable housing. A floating barracks ship was not available. We settled on an unused nice four-story building on the shipyard grounds, which the owner allowed us to convert into land-based crew quarters for the duration. We filled it with beds, televisions, and a keg of beer every afternoon at 5:30. The crew hung a sign out front reading "The *Wichita* Hilton." It made a nice hotel and my crew were out of the dirt and noise of a ship in overhaul.

In a weird, urban farm sort of twist, the shipyard owner allowed a number of barnyard animals to roam the place at random. I'd see pheasants, chickens, and even guinea hens scuttling about the vegetation along the bay in the shadow of the 49ers' stadium. Well, the crew saw them too, and we had a number of cooks who caught those little buggers and served them to our sailors. The shipyard owner only complained after one of his prize goats went missing the morning after the crew held a raucous barbecue. The goat, my boys swore, was last seen swimming the bay, heading toward Alameda.

It was here that I began to learn the biggest challenge every skipper faced in the Carter-era Navy: personnel issues. In the post-Vietnam years, with the draft ending and the birth of the all-volunteer military, we faced a lot of shortages in specialized areas, as I discovered when my new ship's doctor arrived at Hunters Point.

The fleet suffered a significant shortage of physicians back then. The *Wichita* wasn't supposed to be allotted a doctor, but I made a stink about that and was able to pry one loose. I think they gave me Dr. Jack Methner as punishment for shaking the tree.

He showed up in a new Porsche 911 convertible, which he drove right up to the gangway and parked in my slot. He jumped out, and we got our first look at his long, flowing white hair, chest full of ribbons, and a gaudy disco-era gold chain around his neck. He wore a tropical white uniform that looked out of place against our uniform of the day, khakis.

I found out later that the service was so short of doctors that he went straight to the fleet without any indoctrination training. This made his four rows of ribbons more than suspect. When asked, he shrugged, and with a Cheshire Cat smile said, "My recruiter told me to go get them."

He would be a project I never fully was able to tame. Jack was taken belowdecks by my executive officer and ordered to remove the ribbons and get a haircut. His first attempt at the latter turned out to be little more than a trim to his daring mane, so the XO sent him back to get a true high and tight. It never happened. Only a nice trim. I suppose they knew he was going to be the one giving them physicals.

Dr. Jack may have been a project, but he meant well and was a fine doctor and became a treasured friend when we left the service. He signed up with the Navy to see the world after becoming both a general practitioner and a psychiatrist. He had such an active mind (and libido) that I think he just got bored back in Texas and lit off for some high adventure in uniform.

The issues we faced as a Navy included racial tensions and a lot of drug use. It was a difficult time, stretching back to the Vietnam War, when a full-fledged race riot broke out aboard USS *Kitty Hawk*, resulting in dozens of injuries. Fortunately, as the Navy became more integrated, efforts were made to ensure better treatment for our African-American sailors. Gradually, such measures worked to overcome the most significant problems.

Drugs were another matter entirely. For many ships at sea, everything from angel dust to heroin, pot, and cocaine proved to be readily available. Some sailors took to making money on the side by dealing to their buddies. They received regular shipments through the U.S. Postal Service. We were not allowed to screen or censor incoming packages, so the flow from stateside drug dealers to those aboard ship could not be interdicted or shut off. The Navy's criminal investigation service was caught completely unprepared for the influx of narcotics into the fleet, and it would be years before they caught up. Our only hope was to catch the dealers actually making transactions, something that happened infrequently at best simply because we lacked the means to do it.

I saw only a few of these cases among the *Wichita*'s crew. The vast majority of my sailors were dedicated and hardworking professionals. In fact, we convinced our chain of command to let our ship's chiefs oversee and manage the overhaul. I figured nobody was more dedicated than our chiefs, and nobody knew the ship as well as they did. Why not let them take the lead? It turned out to be a great success. We completed the work two months early and came in two million dollars under budget, something that had never happened before.

One night, as we were getting ready to take the *Wichita* out to sea after the overhaul, I was working late. My ten-year-old son, Chris, got ahold of my ship-to-shore number and called my cabin. I picked up and heard him crying.

"Dad, you can't leave."

I thought about all the goodbyes since 1968. Time after time, he'd seen me fly out of his life at the controls of an F-4.

"I have to, Chris."

"Everyone else at school has a dad. I don't. You can't leave."

I thought of that barbecue in '73 when the phone call came telling me of Harley's disappearance and how my little guy clung to me as I said goodbye.

Navy life dictates an episodic family life. It is sometimes cruel and always hard. That night, all my accolades and promotions meant nothing. In that moment, I wasn't a ship's captain preparing to go to sea. I was just a dad who chose a career that would take me away from my son yet again. Nothing I could say could stem his tears. We sailed the next morning.

Given my own family experience, I always tried to be sensitive to my sailors. The best we could do was focus on the job at hand and look forward to mail calls and a few moments on the phone in port somewhere.

In April 1979, our sea trials went flawlessly, and we returned to the Far East to support our supercarriers out there. The *Wichita* received the Battle "E," the Pacific Fleet's award for most efficient ship in our type.

During the *Wichita*'s adventures in the Pacific, Doc Jack's inexperience with Navy tradition bubbled to the surface again. He was unused to the ocean, and being cooped up on our forty-thousand-ton floating home started to get to him. As we returned to Pearl Harbor from WestPac after about a month at sea, I could see the good doc's morale starting to suffer. I called him to my cabin and gave him a special mission. He would fly a helicopter to Honolulu, then on to Fort DeRussy to set up liberty accommodations at the Navy R&R center. And I asked him to plan a dinner reception for all the officers the night we got into Pearl.

When we docked at Ford Island a day later, I peered down from the bridge to see Doc Jack racing up to the berth in a convertible Mercedes-Benz, three gorgeous women in back and beside him. He waved to the crew lined up along the main deck. The crew stared in utter astonishment at the spectacle. Of course, right at that moment the base admiral rolled up in his sedan to make the traditional welcoming call. We'd been ready for him and extended our amidships officers' brow to bring him aboard.

Doc, clueless as ever to protocol, ignored the admiral completely, grabbed his three dates and scampered up the brow, and saluted the ensign ahead of our visiting dignitary. This sort of breach of naval propriety could cause havoc to careers and ships' companies if the admiral so wished. We saw it happen and dreaded the fallout. The admiral came aboard a few minutes later. As per custom, I hurried to go meet him in my cabin, where we would drink coffee and talk shop.

I rushed down to the cabin to discover not just the admiral waiting for me, but Doc Jack and the three gorgeous women he'd somehow met in one night ashore. For a split second, I saw my career flash before my eyes. Then the admiral gave me a sideways glance, a half-smile, and I realized he was thoroughly enjoying the company. Doc's party that night was a shot in the arm for our ship's officers. Weeks at sea can wear out any man no matter how much he loves the smell of salt air and the ocean spray on his face.

We had another kind of morale boost later on, one that affected the entire crew and remains one of the most meaningful moments in my own career.

One beautiful day, south of Baja, Mexico, after sailing from Hawaii, *Wichita* was awaiting a rendezvous with the USS *Constellation* battle group in four days. We were killing time, but my crew was tired and needed a break, so I requested a visit at Mazatlán for a night or two of R&R. There was a storm to the south, but it looked okay for a short visit.

We enjoyed the food and beverages at Señor Frog's. Then the storm started to move north, so we got underway early and headed for Cabo San Lucas. A couple of sailors missed the ship's movement, and I left instructions with our liaison in Mazatlán to send them via slow bus to Tijuana for the shore patrol. That evolved into a week-long trek, often stopping for food and water. Next time, those lads sailed with the rest of us.

I fell asleep on the bridge wing about daylight and slept for a couple of hours. When I woke I went in the bridge to listen to the radio. I caught an unusual change in the channel, and heard two men in two sailboats discussing their plight. One was a cardiologist and his wife whose boat was dead in the water. It was the *Infinity's* maiden voyage, and she had run with too much sail during the night, lost the mast, and fouled the running gear. The other boat contained a dentist and his family with five children. They were both lost, but the dentist could still sail.

Immediately we got our two helicopters searching even as I noticed two big cumulus cloud formations or thunderstorms over Baja. I took a bearing to each, which we triangulated, and asked both boats to do the same. They passed their bearings to us so we could chart them.

After confirming his position, the dentist departed for port in Magdalena Bay. Then I sent the helicopters to locate the *Infinity.* We found the boat just about dark and tried to pass a towline, but it washed overboard twice before we got a hookup. We took the *Infinity* in tow for about ten hours, brought it to the entrance to Magdalena Bay, and handed her off to the Mexican coast guard.

During the night I learned that the doctor was recovering from open-heart surgery, and his wife conned that beautiful sailboat in our wake. It was not the typical Navy service to the fleet, but it was the right thing to do. Plus, the impact it had on my crew was substantial. A typical American wants to help, wants to do right by Emerson's admonishment to leave the world a little better place than he found it. This was one of those moments for all of us. Late that night, as we churned north, running from the storm, I looked aft to see almost all my off-duty sailors lining the stern railing. They were keeping the couple aboard the *Infinity* company, reassuring them that the *Wichita* would take good care of them. They took turns talking to the surgeon's wife as she stood at the wheel, cracking jokes and keeping her relaxed. The heart on display that night is a memory I will always cherish.

We reached Magdalena Bay safely, said goodbye, and departed to join up with the *Constellation*. But after I reported the rescue, an admiral in San Diego wanted to see me. He threatened to court-martial me for endangering my ship. My master chief, who came with me to see him, spoke up right then. "Our actions were safe and in the proudest traditions of the naval service at sea, which includes helping and protecting those in danger," he told the admiral. He added that the press would not react well to the court-martialing of a ship's captain who had just saved American lives. The admiral dropped the matter.

The Navy is an up-or-out organization. If you do not continue to achieve at a high level, you don't make the next selection board list on the command ladder. In the fall of 1980, after two years with the *Wichita*, I received new orders. It was a major moment in my career. It would determine if I went to a staff post ashore, or was entrusted with a new command at sea.

I opened my orders, hopeful and confident. I thought we did a great job with the *Wichita*, but that admiral could make trouble.

I unfolded the orders and read them. Then read them again.

The Navy was giving me an aircraft carrier.

CHAPTER NINETEEN

THE BEST AND THE LAST

Somewhere in the Indian Ocean
November 1980

The tropical sun beat down on the flight-deck crew of USS *Ranger* as they choreographed the morning launch cycle. Tomcats first. Sidewinders and Sparrows mounted and armed, the big birds taxied one by one to the catapults, where the nose gear was attached to the piston. As the aircraft was put "in tension" with the catapult, the catapult officer signaled the pilot to push the throttles to full power and select afterburners. One last check of his instruments, and the pilot gave the salute for "All go" (or turned his lights on if it was at night). The cat officer snapped a salute to the pilot, then touched his wand to the deck, pointed toward the bow. This was the signal, "Launch 'em!" and the big piston hauled the Tomcat down the deck. Trailing two long tongues of flame, she took to the sky as another pair of Tomcats taxied to the catapults. Going from zero to 150 knots in two seconds was a real kick in the ass.

The *Ranger* was my ship now. Perched on the bridge, seated in a barber chair with "Skipper" stenciled on its back, I watched the bustle of the flight deck from the best seat in the house. I was forty-six, still wearing the Ray-Bans I bought in Pensacola and the Star of David chain around my neck. My little mouse from North Island was tucked away in the captain's cabin a few yards aft from this chair. My three talismans served every day as a reminder of who I was and where I came from since first climbing into a cockpit in Pensacola.

It was here that I learned why it is so important for an aviator to command a supercarrier. That ballet on the flight deck? We all had seen it from the cockpit of our Phantoms back in the day. But when we were coming aboard, it was just us and the landing signal officer working together to get our wheels back on the deck. There was another component to that which was largely invisible to the guys in the cockpit. The landing signal officer, the air boss, and the captain communicated constantly, asking for course and speed alterations depending on the velocity of the wind over the deck and how the seas were running. That coordination becomes crucial in bad weather or at night. The planes don't just line up on the carrier—the carrier lines up and maintains course perfectly for the planes.

Once I had six A-6 Intruders in the landing pattern with a thunderstorm bearing down on us. I was in constant contact with the air boss and landing signal officer, who confirmed what they needed. As the winds became more erratic, we altered course to keep the wind coming over the angled deck, where the planes landed. By the time we brought home all six birds, we had turned that big ship a full sixty degrees. Without the nuanced understanding of what the men in the cockpit were experiencing, there was no way a captain of a carrier could do his job to greatest effect in such moments.

I took command of the *Ranger* and its five thousand sailors at Subic Bay on October 20, 1980. I relieved former Topgun CO Roger Box, who had taken the ship the previous year after the *Ranger* collided at night with a tanker near the Straits of Malacca, one of the busiest sea lanes in the world. The tanker almost sank, and the carrier suffered heavy damage to its bow and two fuel tanks. After temporary repairs at Subic, the carrier steamed to Japan to complete the work. As a result of the incident, the skipper was relieved of command and Box given the ship.

Consecutive commanders of Topgun now took the *Ranger* to sea. After eleven years of classes, Topgun's graduates, instructors, and skippers had spread throughout the fleet, energizing it with our ethos and leadership style. We had never thought this far down the road about where our careers would take us into surface commands. Still, the values and leadership methods we used could be equally applied here on the *Ranger's* bridge, and I made a point of doing so.

I addressed my whole crew daily so that everyone felt a part of the team. Twice a day, my master chief and I toured different decks and compartments, getting to know the sailors. In some spaces far belowdecks, the men not only never saw sunlight while at sea, but they'd never seen a captain come through their compartments. The *Ranger* displaced more than eighty thousand tons. She was over a thousand feet long and divided into more than two thousand spaces. With our five thousand–plus sailors aboard, we were a small-sized, nautically mobile American city. Trying to get into every space and compartment was akin to trying to do the same in a comparable-sized town in the heartland. I visited as many as I could, usually with our master chief, Dave Hobbs.

On those twice-a-day trips belowdecks, I could get to know our sailors. The majority of these nineteen- and twenty-year-olds were aboard for the right reasons. They wanted to serve their country, learn a trade or skill, or go to college after their stint at sea. Others saw the Navy as their career, wanting to rise through the enlisted ranks like Master Chief Hobbs had. But a troublesome few, perhaps about 4 percent of the *Ranger's* crew, had fallen into the cycle of drugs and crime. A kid on angel dust was capable of anything. It was a hideous and totally unexpected problem. Until I held my first shipboard command, I hadn't had contact with drugs or drug users. Naval aviators were insulated from them. You can't drop acid and work on a carrier flight deck at night.

In the first months on the *Ranger*, we faced drug-related issues on a daily basis. When our investigators finally caught one of the most notorious dealers, we made sure he got a bad-conduct discharge. We tossed out another one not long after. It felt like throwing bricks into the Grand Canyon. Somebody else took their place and the flow of drugs remained a problem.

Sabotage was an issue as well. Draftees opposed to the war carried out more than two dozen acts of sabotage aboard the *Ranger* alone. Before I took command, one sailor caused millions of dollars of damage by dropping a paint scraper into some critical rotating machinery. It delayed the *Ranger*'s redeployment to WestPac for months. It was hard to track down the culprits. My predecessor, Roger Box, had to deal with a saboteur who crept into the hangar deck and activated the firefighting system. The chemical foam from pressured lines made a huge mess. When it happened to me, the whole hangar deck got doused while it was full of aircraft. The air wing was furious, but an investigation turned up no suspects.

Master Chief Dave Hobbs and I settled on a creative approach. The morning after the event, in my daily address over the intercom, I explained what had happened and the damage it had done. "Whoever did this, I'm offering you a deal. Today, and today only, I urge you to come forward to discuss this with us. We'll help you." I provided a secure phone number that our saboteur could call.

That night my bedside phone buzzed. Dave was on the line. "He's called in," he said. After a short negotiation, the culprit walked into the master chief's office. I hustled down to confront him and find out what the kid thought he was doing. As I entered, I saw our saboteur. He was a desperate-looking, emaciated kid of maybe twenty—hollowed eyes, the gaunt, skeletal face of a person in the grip of addiction. Looking at him, I couldn't be angry. Here was the embodiment of the cancer afflicting our navy, and our culture back home. What started out as a fun diversion for this kid had taken over his life.

He admitted he was addicted to angel dust—PCP. He couldn't explain his behavior, but was devastated by what he was doing. He pleaded for help.

We put him in protective custody. The damage and extra work he had caused everybody earned him considerable wrath from the crew. Had his identity become known, Dave and I feared he would be beaten by angry sailors or sent for a nighttime swim with the sharks. Later, we sent him to San Diego, where he underwent treatment for his drug addiction.

The obvious answer to the drug problem aboard our ships was to interdict the supply. All we needed to do was check the incoming packages sent from the States, and our long days at sea would have taken care of the situation. Whatever supplies had been smuggled aboard before our departure would have been quickly consumed, and our addicts would have been forced to go through withdrawal as a result.

We couldn't do that. The legal system ruled that our sailors had a right to privacy, and their packages could not be opened or searched. This changed later, and during the post-9/11 years, anything coming or going to or from a war zone was thoroughly searched. Contraband, including alcohol (often disguised as mouthwash), drugs, weapons, and weapon parts, was confiscated by the postal system. If only we could have done that in 1980, lives could have been saved.

Personnel issues occupied the majority of my time. Talk to any teacher, and they will tell you that the disciplinary cases in their classroom may include only two or three kids, but those two or three kids take up half their day trying to keep everything under control. It was the same aboard the *Ranger*.

Occasionally I glimpsed the stress and hardship the sailors endured as a result of their home lives back in the States. Dear John letters flowed into the ship with depressing frequency, and many of my men suffered serious heartbreak while we patrolled our nation's distant ramparts. Some dealt with it by focusing on their jobs and throwing themselves into their work with renewed intensity. Others tried everything they could to get home. This included jumping overboard. We had a number of cases like that until we broadcast on the ship's internal television system photos of the sharks in our area that fed on the garbage the Navy's ships released from our compactors. Once the men saw the teeth on those things, nobody willingly went overboard.

One evening while in port, I got a call telling me we had a sailor sitting on a flight-deck rail, bleeding from his arms. He was threatening to jump seventy feet to a concrete pier beneath him. I was attending a dinner reception at the time and was wearing my tropical white uniform. I dropped everything, sped back to the ship, and found the young sailor brokenhearted and sobbing. He held a pair of scissors in one hand, which he'd used to slash his wrists.

I talked to the young fellow, trying to coax his story out. Haltingly, he related to it me. It was a sad story, a mess of his own creation that now left him trapped. In his mental condition, death seemed to be the only way out. At length, I was able to coax him off the rail. He came over to me and grabbed me, hugging me desperately. We got him below to sick bay where the corpsmen treated his self-inflicted injuries. As I watched him depart, I realized my tropical whites were smeared with his blood. It turned out he had gotten both of his girlfriends pregnant.

Through it all, we showed the flag at ports of call from Thailand to Kenya and Sri Lanka while operating in the Persian Gulf on what we called Gonzo Station. This was near the end of the Iran hostage crisis, and we anxiously awaited word to attack. That word never came, but we were armed and ready.

The Iranians never tested us with their air force, which included a batch of F-14 Tomcats we had sold them just before the revolution deposed our ally, the shah. I sure wanted them to try. I had two squadrons of Tomcats—the two oldest and most storied units in the Navy (VF-1 and VF-2)—filled with hard-charging, type A fighter pilots who wanted a crack at Iranians as bad as anyone.

We didn't face the kind of threat from the Iranians that we did from the Soviet Backfire regiments, so we usually armed our F-14s with a mix of Sparrows, Sidewinders, and Guns, leaving the Phoenix missiles aboard ship. Whenever we went through the Strait of Hormuz into the Persian Gulf, we cycled our Tomcats off the deck and pushed them out between our ship and the edge of international waters within sight of the Iranian coast. Any low-flying Iranian bandits would have been caught the moment they were "in play" over neutral waters, and we would have torn them apart.

Instead of risking aircraft, they decided to harass us with fast-moving PT boats, something our battle group's destroyers and cruisers dealt with very effectively.

During intense operational cycles, a typical air wing usually loses five or six engines a month to "foreign object damage," or FOD. This can be any stray piece of metal like a screw, a bolt, or a nut that has fallen onto the flight deck that gets sucked into an intake and wrecks the engine's turbine blades. It is a constant problem, both at sea and on land, that is solved by frequent walkdowns by our sailors to find anything that could harm our aircraft. Of course, with the available crew, it was impossible to find every little nut or screw that fell into the tie-downs in the deck.

We computed that we needed three hundred to four hundred men for a thorough FOD search, but the flight-deck crew just couldn't provide that many bodies. I hit upon an idea from my visits to the ship's belowdecks spaces. I announced that at a specific time, called by the air boss who runs the flight deck, everyone not engaged in an essential job could report to the deck, breathe the sea air, get some exercise, and help eliminate FOD.

Sometimes I got on the 1MC circuit and encouraged the crew to come up and "smell the roses." While I got some laughs, it worked, and I often saw engineering "snipes" and mess cooks stretching themselves in search of the elusive FOD. Moreover, I offered three days' liberty to those who found a very small screw painted a particular color, usually black. That got the crew's attention. We even had cooks in aprons doing walkdowns.

Ranger's program was a huge success. We went 107 days without FOD damage, and the concept spread Navy-wide.

We stayed out on Gonzo Station keeping an eye on the Iranians and flying every day through the first weeks of 1981. In March, we headed back to Subic Bay and a much-needed break. As we reached the Strait of Malacca, the busiest shipping bottleneck in the world, my air wing commander asked if we could launch a few aircraft. I agreed. It made sense to get some eyes up there. It was a Friday morning, March 20, 1981, a day none of us ever forgot.

From my seat on the port side of the bridge, I watched the deck crew launch a couple of A-6 Intruder bombers. They fanned out ahead of us as we steamed east through the strait and into the South China Sea.

As our birds flew along, they caught sight of a tiny boat drifting on the swells. Circling back, they made a pass and reported it crowded with people. Apparently it was without power. It had no sails. They were just drifting with the tide. It was a humid, steamy day without even the benefit of a small breeze. The people on the boat were largely exposed to the sun's full strength.

We plotted the boat's position, and I ordered our ship to intercept it. Late that afternoon, we spotted it. The vessel was perhaps forty feet long with a tiny enclosed wheelhouse, and every square inch of it seemed to be covered by people. They were lying inert, one atop another, piled together in such terrible physical condition that some were said to be hallucinating. Most were too weak to even sit up and stare at the enormous supercarrier bearing down on them. A few had scraps of clothing. Most were bare from the waist up. Some had no clothes at all.

Our helicopters circled overhead, snapping photographs as we hove to and began rescuing these people. Some had to be taken aboard in stretchers lowered down to the boat. They had been at sea for two weeks after fleeing the violence continuing to plague Vietnam. Not long into their journey to freedom, the boat's engine failed. Food ran out first. Water soon followed. There were 138 people aboard a boat meant to hold, at most, 25. They grew weak. Several people died. The day we rescued them, we were told the survivors were considering cannibalism to survive.

We arrived just in time.

Our crew sprang into action, doting on the survivors with incredible tenderness. Our medical staff treated them for dehydration, heat exhaustion, and many other ailments, getting fluids in them with IV bags. Our tailors and parachute riggers sewed them clothing while our cooks prepared meals. It didn't take long for the crew and the refugees to bond. It was a beautiful sight, one of those unexpected moments in life where what you do plays a critical role in the well-being of others.

They were ordinary folks from Vietnam who had risked every-thing to escape an oppressive regime still killing or imprisoning its own people. Among those we rescued was a Vietnamese soldier who had deserted to seek a new life away from the fury and violence. It was impossible not to be affected by their ordeal, and by what they had risked everything for—the same things that drove generations to American shores.

We took them to Subic Bay with us, where the Philippine gov-ernment gave them sanctuary. We later found out their ordeal was far from over. The Filipinos treated them poorly. Food and clean water became scarce in their refugee camp. Ultimately, though, most of the 138 were able to immigrate to the United States, where they started new lives on the West Coast as American citizens.

As they waited for their chance to fly east to our nation, my ship's company suffered a terrible tragedy. A young airman named Paul Trerice collapsed and died while we were in Subic Bay about three weeks after we rescued the refugees.

Trerice was a sad story, a twenty-year-old from Michigan whose time in uniform was a case study of the devastation wrought by drugs in our Navy. Having served for three years, he had never been promoted. In fact, he was in frequent trouble and even tried to des-ert twice. His squadron commander disciplined him repeatedly, though he was no stranger to our correctional custody training unit [CCU]. (Some people mistakenly call it the brig, which was totally separate.) Nothing seemed to work. He remained an often belliger-ent hard case who frustrated his squadron commander. I never met this sailor, but his death changed my life forever.

The ship had just returned from a five-day visit to Hong Kong, where he was an unauthorized absentee. He was next in the CCU that April of 1981. My understanding from the Navy investigation that followed his death is that, combative as always, he fought with a couple of our senior petty officers, who then took him up on the flight deck and ordered him to start jogging. It was routine exercise in the sweltering Subic Bay heat. Trerice had previously been restricted to bread and water as a result of his combativeness. As he was running, he collapsed. Taken below, he began to have seizures. Thirty minutes later, medical personnel arrived to treat him, but sadly, he died soon after. The Navy determined he had gone into cardiac arrest as a result of heat exhaustion.

During the investigation, it came to light that he'd been smoking marijuana with several other sailors inside one of our S-3 Vikings in the hangar. Our chaplain came to see me months after Paul Trerice's death to tell me that he'd been treating him and his addiction for a year as part of the CREDO Program. It wasn't just pot; much more serious and dangerous drugs were in the picture. I asked, "Why didn't you tell me earlier?" The chaplain shook his head, saying, "That was between him and God."

The captain is ultimately responsible for everything that happens on his ship. Despite all the good things we accomplished and the high level at which the crew had performed, I knew this tragedy would have a reckoning. We commenced a Judge Advocate General investigation on the way home.

We arrived in San Diego in May, where I was summoned before the commander of Naval Air Forces, Pacific, Vice Admiral Robert "Dutch" Schoultz. Based on the way Trerice was treated while in the custody unit, the admiral issued me a nonpunitive letter of caution.

After he announced his decision in the matter, Schoultz said, "Dan, I'd like you to take *Ranger* on her next cruise."

Of course I said yes.

CHAPTER TWENTY

ONE MORE GOODBYE

Somewhere in the Pacific
Spring 1982

I sat in my captain's cabin, holding Mary Beth's letter like a precious gem. Two pages. I read and reread it until I had committed every sentence to memory. I still could not believe it had found its way to me, that she would be thinking of me all these decades after our parting outside the Whittier College cafeteria.

Dan, I want you to know that I know the kind of man you are and will always be. Your friends know it too, and they refuse to believe the things being said about you in the newspapers. The tragedy had been big news in the *Detroit Free Press*, the *Los Angeles Times*, and the *San Diego Union-Tribune*.

She reached out to me, knowing how devastating the media storm must have been. Then the *New York Times*, *Playboy* magazine, and the network nightly news all picked up the story. It became a national spectacle. Paul Trerice's death was without a doubt a terrible tragedy, but how it sparked a media frenzy shocked and mystified me. In 1981, 4,699 members of the U.S. military—all branches—died while in service to their country. It was a time of peace, and none of those deaths resulted from combat operations. Accidents, suicides, a scattering of murders, heart attacks, strokes—they happen.

Of all those, Trerice's was the only one that riveted the press for months. The death was a terrible tragedy that inflicted lifelong suffering on his family. For that, there was no excuse. Could it have been prevented? I asked that question every day for years. I just don't know. I think if we had known the extent of his apparent drug addiction, we might have been able to steer him to treatment instead of to the Correctional Custody Training Unit for his desertions and other acts. I thought about the saboteur we had sent to drug treatment, giving him another chance at a good life. I wish we had been able to do the same for Paul Trerice and his family. By the time his drug use came to light, it was too late to help him.

The West Coast press wasn't interested in my view of this. It tore into me with astonishing cruelty, relying on sources that included the two drug dealers we'd kicked out of the Navy to show me as a nautical tyrant, recklessly endangering the lives of my crew with sadistic punishments meted out on a whim. I became a Cold War version of Captain Bligh. Calls came from all over the country for my head.

My family received death threats almost daily for months. Hate mail poured in, especially from Michigan. The Trerice family filed several lawsuits against the Navy. One named me as a defendant. It was almost unheard of for an active-duty officer to be sued over something that happened in the line of duty.

In all the turmoil, this letter from Mary Beth arrived. We hadn't spoken since the Eisenhower years. I hadn't seen her since the football game where she gave me that cautious half-wave from the hip, tears in her eyes. It didn't matter. I thought about her very often.

I resolved to write her back and thank her, to tell her what her words of support meant to me. I had gone from being a respected naval aviator and ships captain whose peers had put my name on the admiral's list a year early, to the embodiment of every negative stereotype about the Navy and its officers.

I was putting my pen to the paper when I paused. *Don't do it. She made her choice. You have to honor it.*

Mary Beth was still married to her football player. I was married too. Given how I still felt for her, writing her back would be a betrayal. It would also open up that wound again. I'd be in touch with the person I'd always loved and could never share my life with. As bad as the media attacks had been, suffering that would be far worse.

I never wrote her back. Instead, I carried the letter with me aboard the *Ranger* for a month as the media firestorm continued. Each night, I reread it to remind myself that there were those I cared about who refused to believe what was being written about me and my style of leadership.

One day, I realized I was beginning to rely too heavily on it. I couldn't write her. I couldn't reestablish contact. In the moment, I needed to focus on my crew and my ship, and find the strength to ignore the publicity.

A federal court finally tossed the lawsuits, a decision that was upheld on appeal. But the blowback from Trerice's death affected a lot of good officers and petty officers aboard the *Ranger*. I did what I could to protect them, and by then my own career hung in the balance.

On June 11, 1982, I left the *Ranger* for a shoreside staff position. This was the classic career progression on the way to flag rank, and I was given a plum job serving as deputy chief of staff for current operations under the commander in chief, Pacific Fleet, at Pearl Harbor. It's probably the busiest I had ever been in the service, but the job historically had its rewards. It was known as an "admiral maker." About a year into this job, I got a summons to Washington from the chief of naval operations. In his office, with the door closed, we discussed what I faced going forward with the Navy. One of Michigan's senators had made Trerice's death a personal crusade. The CNO believed that this was motivated by the fact that Trerice's family members were substantial donors to the senator and the CNO saw the senator's attacks on the Navy as essentially political theater as he faced a difficult reelection campaign.

Whatever the motivation, when the lawsuits were dismissed by both of the federal courts that heard it, and the Navy inquiry concluded that the death was a tragic accident, the senator used his position on the Senate Armed Services Committee to block my promotion to admiral.

Our CNO fought for me. I'd had a good record from Topgun, with the two deployments with the *Ranger*, where we went two years without an aircraft accident, something no other carrier in the fleet had done during that period. But I was a political liability. Though the CNO urged me to stay the course, he was forced to pull my name off the admiral's list for 1983. I loved the Navy. What would I do without it? Yet I came to the conclusion that if I stayed, I wouldn't be able to win this fight. The senator would be reelected, and his opposition to my promotion would never waver. If the Navy resisted again, there could be fallout that would harm the service I loved. That's just how Washington worked. I resigned my staff position and retired two weeks later, on March 1, 1983, after twenty-nine years, one month, and one day in uniform.

As the Reagan administration continued boosting defense spending in the early '80s and I finished my tour as commanding officer of the *Ranger*, Topgun was in the hands of a terrific CO, Ernie Christensen. He had excellent access to Navy Secretary John F. Lehman, and constantly worked on him to elevate the Navy Fighter Weapons School position in the chain of command so that our rivals within the Pentagon bureaucracy would leave us alone.

The culture of Topgun and its larger Miramar tribe was always its own best critic. In 1982, in fact, the reviews were mixed. The fast pace of fleet operations, which were pushing our carriers to operate ever forward, close to Soviet territory, in line with President Reagan's aggressive new Maritime Strategy, had cut into training time and limited the availability of our very busy fleet pilots to go to Miramar. While proficiency in air combat maneuvering was high, it seemed that Topgun graduates were no longer having such a dramatic impact on squadron training. Part of the reason was all the new squadrons that were being created to field the F-18 Hornet, which was arriving in Navy inventories in large numbers. With twenty-four squadrons getting equipped with the Hornet from 1982 to 1985, the Navy didn't have enough graduates to go around.

And yet Topgun's influence within the Navy grew ever wider. The school sent detachments to the Philippines, Japan, and Saudi Arabia to work directly with forward-deployed air wings. We ran "road shows" for them, organizing lectures, booking simulator time, and conducting battle group defense exercises. Our Mobile Training Teams, meanwhile, visited our NATO allies. Norway and Germany were particularly receptive, and Topgun instructors relished assignments to help them get the most out of their F-5s, F-104s, and F-16s. Our Navy cousins in the surface warfare community, meanwhile, tried to use Topgun-style training to make commanders of frigates, destroyers, and cruisers into better warriors. As I heard it, though, our way of giving a lot of voice to junior officers was a problem for the more tradition-bound parts of the Navy.

With all of this going on, it was only a matter of time before the larger public began to get wind of Topgun. In 1983, *California* magazine published an article about Topgun, focusing on a single F-14 Tomcat crew. When movie producers Jerry Bruckheimer and Don Simpson read it, they saw the potential for a movie set in the world of Fightertown USA. The XO of Topgun at the time, Mike "Wizzard" McCabe, hosted the moviemakers at Miramar to explore the idea. After the producers hired screenwriters Jim Cash and Jack Epps to create the script, they approached the Navy about supporting the project.

The CNO, Admiral James Holloway, ended up granting them full cooperation on the condition that the Navy have the right to approve the script. With that agreement in place, two aircraft carriers were made available to the filmmakers, as well as several F-14 Tomcats modified to carry cameras. With the Navy billing the Paramount production team $7,800 per flying hour, Tony Scott began shooting in June 1985.

Though Scott said he wanted originally to make "Apocalypse Now on an aircraft carrier," the producers thought better of that dark idea. Bruckheimer and Simpson wanted to make "a rock-and-roll movie about fighter pilots." And that was Top Gun,* released to much fanfare in May 1986.

The plot was built around the rivalry of two Topgun student pilots, Lieutenants Pete "Maverick" Mitchell, played by Tom Cruise, and Tom "Iceman" Kazansky, played by Val Kilmer. Tom Skerritt pretty well nailed the role of their skipper, Mike "Viper" Metcalf, conveying the character of Topgun leadership and the rigor of the training in a way that reflected reality far better than the conflict between the youngsters did. The one character in the film who might have seemed to be a Hollywood fabrication, Charlie

---

* Although the Navy always uses the term "Topgun" in one-word form, the filmmakers insisted upon using two words. I guess it looks better that way on movie posters—or on the cover of a book, like this one.

Blackwood—the female lead played by Kelly McGillis—was actually inspired by a real person. This was Christine H. Fox, a mathematician who went to Miramar as a field analyst to advise the commander of the Airborne Early Warning Wing. Though she had little direct contact with Topgun, her boss, Rear Admiral Thomas J. Cassidy—who happened to be the Navy's liaison to the film producers—was so impressed with her that he persuaded the filmmakers to change Tom Cruise's love interest from an aerobics instructor to a brainy tactical consultant. Christine Fox went on to serve as a deputy secretary of defense, making her the highest-ranking woman in the history of the Pentagon.

Who would have expected such a film to be a boon to feminism? Because as we all know, the testosterone in that movie ran hot. It portrayed Topgun more as a glorified intramural tournament than as the academically rigorous graduate schoolhouse it really is. But hand it to Tony Scott and his team: The aerial photography was among the finest ever shot. Among the technical advisers was Captain (later Rear Admiral) Pete Pettigrew, a Vietnam MiG killer and Topgun instructor, who also appeared onscreen. Some nitpicking aside, they did very fine work demonstrating the F-14's capabilities in great shots set up by Mr. Scott and his cinematographer, Jeffrey L. Kimball, with a soundtrack that seemed to pull you into the cockpit for the ride. The film topped the U.S. box office that year, narrowly beating *Crocodile Dundee*. It eventually earned more than $350 million worldwide and won an Oscar for best original song ("Take My Breath Away" by Giorgio Moroder and Tom Whitlock, performed by Berlin).

Having watched some of the filming, Pete Pettigrew was impressed with Meg Ryan, in the role of the wife of Goose, Maverick's RIO. He says she cried on cue for twenty-two straight takes. I think Anthony Edwards stole the show as Goose. His son's experience as a Topgun pilot is the focus of the sequel, *Top Gun: Maverick* (coming in 2020), which I consider a deserved tribute to the importance of a pilot's eyes and ears in the rear seat.

Several Topgun instructors got camera time in the publicity campaign. Asked about Maverick's cocky character, one of them said, "Well, he has the right stuff, but with that attitude we wouldn't let him in the back door." That's how we felt about egos in my day. It makes for good entertainment but isn't what you want in your ready room. The loner glory seeker—the maverick—doesn't last. He kills himself trying to impress people. Topgun wants solid, mature professionals, maybe touched by a divine spark of inspiration, but intelligent warriors who fight with the head, heart, and hands.

However, Navy Secretary Lehman wrote just recently that the bravado was meant with a particular audience in mind: the Russians. "The swashbuckling, confidently professional naval aviators kicking their ass was exactly the message we had intended to project, but it was not quite the nuanced approach conducive to diplomacy." No, it wasn't. But who knows? The movie as a psychological warfare operation might have helped push the Soviet Union to collapse just five years later.

It's easy to take shots at a film, because realism is seldom its primary goal. No Topgun pilot would ever invert himself and fly upside down, canopy to canopy, with an enemy pilot. And the maneuver where Maverick bagged his instructor by pulling up and reducing power to idle, causing the instructor to overshoot, is nothing more than what Jerry Beaulier has called a "kill self" maneuver. But there was no disputing the movie's value to naval aviation. It attracted hordes of new potential aviators and sailors to recruiting offices, which was definitely the Navy's goal. Admiral Holloway said that when applications from qualified candidates to go to Pensacola surged past the training quotas by 300 percent, he got Secretary of

Defense Caspar Weinberger to approve "banking" the applications, spreading them over the next three years to assure the supply of candidates. The Air Force tried to keep pace. Reports circulated of their recruiters setting up in lobbies of theaters showing the film.

Few people outside the aviation community remember that a real tragedy marred the shooting of the film. In September 1985, the famed aerobatics champion and air-show favorite Art Scholl was killed while filming an aerial sequence in a camera-equipped biplane. Unable to recover from an inverted spin, he went into the water with his two-seater Pitts Special about five miles off Encinitas. The film was dedicated to his memory.

While the movie provided a shot in the arm for the Reagan-era Navy and its recruitment goals, there were unintended consequences within naval aviation that affected Topgun for years to come. The other communities, especially our attack crews, felt slighted by the movie. It stirred old resentments, and as the 1980s came to a close, the school faced another series of bureaucratic assaults that I believe were designed to cripple it.

Of course, I was a civilian by then, for the first time since I was selling shoes in downtown Whittier. I had challenges of my own. I went from commanding a supercarrier off the Persian Gulf to being another casually dressed California businessman. My entire social circle was gone. When I returned to California that spring, I felt like a refugee in my own hometown. I was almost fifty years old, starting over from scratch. I needed to find a new sense of normal.

For me, normal was waking up in my cabin to the smell of salt air coming through a brass porthole. It was the heavy jolt of a cat- apult launch, and the euphoria of breaking Mach 1 in a vertical climb. It was long, beautiful night flights across our country, and the sense of purpose I felt when we saved lives at sea. It was the fear of flying strikes into North Vietnam, and the honor of leading Topgun, alongside some of the finest young men America ever produced. It was welcoming old friends back from the Hanoi Hilton, and holding membership in a brotherhood that defined my entire adult life. In civilian life, there was no normal for me.

I struggled. My first marriage did not survive the many deployments of the 1970s. Being gone so much finally drove a wedge between us that could not be removed. I married a second time while serving in surface ships. Ever the optimist, I guess. It wasn't meant to be. The best part of our time together was the birth of my third child, a daughter. For beautiful Candice, I will always be grateful.

I could have gone into the defense industry like so many other retired military officers do—great salaries, great benefits. I refused to do that. I'd long since concluded that many of the problems we faced originated in the procurement system and the defense industry's influence in Washington and the Pentagon. I didn't want to use the military-corporate revolving door that makes the influence possible.

Instead, I went into business for myself in Southern California. The leadership principles I learned in the Navy played a large role in my success. So did a great businessman named Joe Sinay, who took me under his wing and mentored me. We became close friends over the years, and I owed him a tremendous debt of gratitude.

My folks passed, Dad first, then Mom a few years later. Even so, whenever I had business in the Los Angeles area, I'd make a point of getting back to Whittier to see my mom's oldest and closest friend, Louise Seacrest. She was ninety-four, sharp as ever, and the only family I had left there.

One night, after I'd taken her to dinner, she turned to me and said, "Dan, I've known you almost all your life. I have never seen you so miserable."

I thought I'd been doing a good job hiding it.

"Yeah, I'm pretty unhappy."

"I have the answer for you."

She pulled out a notepad and pen, scrawled on it, then tore the sheet off and handed it to me. I looked down at a phone number.

"Call it. Do it now. You should have done it thirty years ago."

I had no idea what she was talking about.

"Dan, Mary Beth is single. Call the number."

I was speechless. I'd lost touch with our mutual friends long ago. With my mom gone, I had no conduit to information about Mary Beth. I had no idea her marriage had ended too.

I had a car phone that I used for work, and after I saw my mom's friend to her door, I returned to my sedan and called the number. Mary Beth's mom answered the phone. I introduced myself, unsure if she would remember me. She was happy to hear from me, and we talked for several minutes, catching up. Then she gave me Mary Beth's number. I made the call.

Her voice sounded exactly the same, and for an instant I was back under the nose of that T-33 at El Toro, home for Christmas with her rushing into my arms.

"Beth, this is Dan Pedersen."

Dead silence on the phone.

I said my name again.

Thinking this was a prank call from her brother, pretending to be me, she scolded me. This was not how I expected it to go.

I promised her I was not her brother. We started laughing with an effortlessness I hadn't felt in years.

"Are you in town? Where are you?" she asked.

"Put a pot of coffee on, I'll be right over."

She gave me her address and I began breaking speed limits.

I stepped out of the car in front of a well-kept condominium, dressed in a polo shirt, slacks, and good loafers. (Always wear a good pair of shoes, just in case you have the luck to run into the love of your life.)

The front door opened, and there she was, Mary Beth, looking as breathtakingly beautiful thirty years later as she'd been in every thought and memory that I had carried across the oceans. It seemed almost surreal. Thirty years. I never thought I would see her again. I realized I had felt her absence every day. It lessened with time, but never left me.

Who was I really thinking about on the day I ejected from my crippled F-4, chute opening late, swinging once, twice, before slamming into the water off La Jolla? It was the woman in front of me, dressed fabulously as always, looking at me with so much happiness and excitement.

I stepped toward her as she smiled and opened her arms. I reached her and went in for a hug. She had something more in mind. A gentle kiss, warm and open. Connecting. Not the kind you give an old friend; the kind you give your long-lost love.

I felt a strange sensation right then. The hole inside me disappeared. Time and distance held no meaning in the moment. When our lips parted, all I could see were her brown eyes looking into mine.

In them, I saw at last I was home.

CHAPTER TWENTY-ONE

SAVING TOPGUN

As I write this, I'm eighty-three years old. I still look up whenever a plane passes overhead. Now you know why. Flying was one great love of my life. For thirty years, it consumed everything, gave me everything I ever felt was valuable and valued. It gave me a home, both in the air and on sea or land. In the end, though, Mary Beth came along and showed me what I had been missing. More and better family moments. Love and connection between my kids that I never got to share while searching for targets south of Haiphong.

It is past midnight now. The moon is rising, and the airliners are still passing by as we sit beside the pool here. Truth is, I have only one regret: I should have found a way to spend more time with Dana, Chris, and Candice, who was born in 1980. In retrospect, there was no way either of my first marriages was going to survive the constant deployments, the politics, and the press coverage. They were fine women; I will always care about them, and I hope they will forgive me for my priorities and pursuits when we were together.

In time of war, our country needed us. I couldn't walk away when my friends were fighting for their lives against those flaming telephone poles and MiG-17s. When you take the oath and don the uniform, it changes you. It changes your priorities.

Take a look right there. See that light moving in the sky? I bet she's a 737 outbound from LAX. I see her every night around this time. Right on schedule; no delays at the gate or surly passengers, I guess.

God, how I loved flying. On a night like this, you could see for hundreds of miles at forty thousand feet. Crystal black sky overhead, lit with an infinite number of galaxies and their stars, the glittering cities below, like diamonds reflecting sunlight. Earth and life in all their beauty. Until you see it for yourself and feel how it opens you up and then hooks you like an addict, you'll never know what a transformative experience flying can be.

There aren't many military aircraft in this part of the sky at night anymore. With the budget cuts and the spare parts crisis, the crews just don't get much flight time. If I dwell on it, I worry about where we're going and what will happen to Topgun.

In 1993, the end of our rivalry with the Soviet Union triggered massive budget cuts and base closures. The peace dividend forced the Marines to move from El Toro to Miramar, which crowded Topgun out of the picture. Those running the show decided to move us to Fallon, Nevada, where it would fall under the Naval Strike Air Warfare Center, or "Strike U." Just like that, the plot of land with the dubious "view of the sea" where we had first parked our stolen trailer was no longer home. The attack aviators in the chain of command scored a decisive victory by forcing this move, one that ultimately imperiled our legacy.

Resentment against the fighter community and Topgun ran high in the mid-1990s. Not all of that was a result of the rock-star status the movie seemed to give us within the public. The controversy over the alleged sexual assaults at the Tailhook Convention in 1991 left a stain on naval aviation. As Rolland G. "Dawg" Thompson, then Topgun's CO, put it, "Topgun represented, to many, the last bastion of fighter aviation—the hallmark of what many on the outside of our culture despised at the time."

From the beauty, beaches, and pulse of Southern California, Topgun decamped for a place that seemed at times like the edge of civilization. The press paid a lot of attention to this, and as our trucks moved out, people lined the freeway holding signs, saying goodbye and wishing us well. More than one Topgun wife cried as they drove into Fallon, seeing the valley's desolation, feeling the high desert heat on their faces, and thinking of what they had left behind in San Diego. Their beautiful homes and fine schools—gone.

The chief of naval operations at the time, Admiral Jeremy Michael Boorda, protected us quite well, mandating that while the graduate school would come under the umbrella of Strike U, it would remain its own command. Based on Topgun principles of training, Strike U had once set high standards for the attack aviators that it trained. But by the time Dawg's boys began arriving, along with their eighteen Hornets and four Tomcats, the strike aircraft instructors were no longer even murder-boarding their lectures during instructor qualification. They didn't even have their own aircraft to fly and teach with.

Nineteen ninety-six was a year of tragedy for the Navy. The CNO, Admiral Boorda, took his life, leaving a note that explained his shame over wearing an unearned valor award on his uniform. After his death, Topgun apparently lost the last flag officer in a position to protect the school. With his passing, Topgun was demoted from an independent command to just a department of Strike U, under a two-star, a rear admiral.

I tell you, it broke my heart when we lost that fight. It broke the heart of all of us who'd devoted so much of our lives to create and foster Topgun, who had risked their careers to keep it going in the face of increasing hostility. Our success was living testimony to the ability of dynamic, creative, motivated junior officers to do great things. Was this message considered dangerous or something? I don't know.

I do know they even tried to take the name Topgun away from us. When Dawg showed up at Fallon one day after Admiral Boorda's death, he found that the Strike U headquarters building no longer had a sign reading "Topgun." It had been replaced with "N7," an obscure bureaucratic designator for the Navy Fighter Weapons School.

Boorda was replaced by Admiral Jay Johnson (who to this day remains the last aviator to become CNO). Dawg took this as a bad sign at first, as Johnson was a friend of the incoming Strike U commander, Rear Admiral Bernie Smith. Merging the attack and fighter communities into a single entity threatened to dilute our culture. But give Admiral Smith credit. Seeing what was at risk, he put Thompson in charge of all training. At the decommissioning change-of-command ceremony, Dawg invited his boss as guest speaker, just to make sure he was in attendance. That's where the Topgun skipper made a dramatic declaration: "I will compromise my career before I compromise the standards of this organization." He would make good on the promise.

The Strike U establishment at Fallon ended up leaving the Topgun Bros alone, though their wives were very unhappy with the way they were treated by the established social clique at Fallon. It mattered. The divisive atmosphere hurt morale badly, which was part of why more than a few well-qualified people turned down orders to go to Topgun. Its prestige had been badly diminished by making it just a department in the "Strike U" with command leadership going from a junior officer to a rear admiral.

Dawg realized he had to change things. Leveraging his position as director of training, he required Topgun's instructors to become involved with the strike curriculum too. "The game plan was that they were not going to absorb us; we were going to absorb them," he said. That was easier said than done. The schism persisted.

But so did Topgun. With Dawg flying top cover to preserve the integrity of the program, his junior officers did what they've always done—they continued the mission. This is how bureaucratic warfare is waged in the military. Organizations come and organizations go, but they can often be saved by someone who is willing to swallow his pride and pursue a matter of principle with calm conviction. I credit Rolland Thompson for saving the program in a very difficult time. When one of his instructors, Richard W. "Rhett" Butler, returned as CO of the Topgun department six years later, he was gratified to notice that the "N7" label on the wall was gone. It had been changed to "Topgun Training Department."

It's not well realized even in our community how precarious our existence was during the move from Miramar to Nevada. Reportedly about 80 percent of the junior instructor pilots were prepared to leave the Navy. But with Dawg's leadership guiding the success of the combined strike fighter training program, most all of them stayed for a full tour. If not for our resilient group of JOs, who were given strong direction by their devoted leader, Topgun might well have ceased to exist.

I try not to think about all this needless bureaucratic infighting, especially on gorgeous nights like this one. I come out here by the pool for peace. Sometimes I relive the best moments of my career and feel that old sense of pride return. You know, though? As much as I loved the flying, the best moments to me now were those where we saved lives. The couple stranded off Baja, the boat full of dying refugees we rescued in the South China Sea. Those were the best moments.

*   *   *

It is one of life's great beauties—and mysteries—how things put in motion years before can well up from the past to alter your present. The boat full of refugees turned out to be one of those pivotal episodes in my life. Many years later, in 1998, I received a call from the Navy's chief of information in Washington. He told me that one of the survivors we rescued in the South China Sea back in 1981 wanted to meet with me. He had been thirteen years old when his mother, brother, and two sisters paid for passage aboard that decrepit boat. He never forgot the sight of our carrier pulling alongside, the big number "61" painted on the side of the island superstructure. Now he wanted to thank me in person for stopping and saving 138 strangers.

I readily agreed, thinking we would just talk on the phone. Instead, the Navy asked if we could meet on the set of *Good Morning America*. I'll tell you what, I never thought that a moment on a soundstage would lead to so many great things in my life. Lan Dalat came on camera next to me, and from that first greeting, I knew we were destined to be close.

His family stayed for several months in the refugee camp on Luzon before emigrating to Washington State. Later, they moved to Southern California in search of a warmer climate that was a bit more like home for them. Lan and his siblings suffered bullying in the public school system. They were called names, derided for being "boat people." It was a tough and sometimes cruel end to childhood as he came of age in his adopted country, but the opportunities America offered were seized upon by his family.

All four kids graduated from college and embarked on highly successful careers, starting families along the way. Lan asked me to come speak at his college graduation, and later at his commissioning ceremony in the U.S. Army. I did the same with his brother Tony, who served in the Army's Special Operations Command during the war in Afghanistan.

More than just about anyone I've ever known, Lan Dalat and his family understand the real heart and real power of America, and they devoted their lives to defending those things.

Want to know the best part of their story? At least to me, anyway, but I'm biased of course. When Lan got married and had a baby boy, they named him Dan, after me. I think about that and get emotional. I almost lost my tribe, my brotherhood, when I left the Navy in 1983. In my worst and most isolated moments, I made plans to refit a 110-foot oceangoing tug so I could once again sail away to sea. I was going to ride the Pacific waves to Japan, the Philippines, or wherever else the wind and stars took me. It sounded romantic. It would have been desperately lonely.

I went from that low point to reconnecting with Mary Beth. Then Lan Dalat and his family entered my life. Old friends retired from the Navy, and almost all the Original Bros settled down close by in Southern California.

On March 1, 1983, I started my new life as an alienated civilian, unsure what my path might be in a country I had defended all my life but no longer knew. In the end, my new normal became a full and happy life, filled with love and friendships and family—my kids, Beth's kids (we have a Brady Bunch–sized clan these days), and the men I went to war with back in our youth.

Topgun's Original Bros get together for dinner periodically, though there are only seven left of the original nine as I write this. Beth and I waited over a year after our doorway moment, then I flew her to Denmark and married her in the church my dad had been baptized in as a child before his family, just like Lan's, made the journey to America's shores.

Beth and I made up for lost time in the 1990s and after the turn of the millennium. We worked together, built things together, explored and traveled and celebrated life. She was my missing part, and when she fit into my heart again, there were no more bad days.

I do worry, though, that those who took our place in the cockpit will face bad days in the years to come.

CHAPTER TWENTY-TWO

WILL WE HAVE TO LOSE A WAR AGAIN?

(or, Back to the Future in an F-35)

Just like the old F-4 Phantom, the F-14 Tomcat will live long in the memories of fighter pilots. The famous plane met its end in 2006. Focused on acquiring the Tomcat's replacement, the F-18 Hornet, and the A-12 Avenger II stealth bomber, an upgrade for the A-6 Intruder, the Navy decided there wasn't enough money to keep the Tomcats flying. It didn't help the old bird's cause that the secretary of defense, Dick Cheney, seemed to have it in for New York's congressional delegation. Grumman Aircraft was located on Long Island. As the Pentagon's axe fell, it was a sad case of the new and the expensive driving out the affordable and the reliable. When Secretary Cheney ended the lives of those two iconic Grumman carrier planes, the Intruder and the Tomcat, the future got a whole lot more costly.

The Navy's $4.8 billion contract with McDonnell Douglas and General Dynamics to build the A-12 became a fiasco of lawsuits. It never produced a single aircraft. The litigation lasted twenty-three years, ending with the contractors repaying some $400 million to the government. Stealth technology was at the heart of the dispute.

The contractors said that they could not deliver on schedule with the government withholding classified data on its requirements for radar-evading features. They had a point. According to former Top-gun skipper Lonny "Eagle" McClung, "The A-12 was in the black world"—highly classified. "You could not take the material to your desk. You had to read it in a vault." But the Pentagon seemed to be putting a great deal of faith in stealth.

"We were selling our soul for stealth," Eagle said. "The attitude in the Pentagon was that if we did not come up with stealth, the USAF would own the strike mission. I kept saying that somewhere in some dark basement in Eastern Europe was a group of guys wearing glasses about as thick as Coke bottles who were figuring out how to defeat stealth. . . . The airplane had a lot of problems. Cancelling the thing saved the Navy from itself."*

In the end, the F-18 was reengineered to handle the A-12's mission. Today the Super Hornet, as the F/A-18's E and F models are known, is performing that role well enough, though with a combat range that doesn't come close to the old Tomcat's.

How sad that the only F-14s that you'll find in service today are flying for the government of Iran, which began acquiring them in 1976, when Tehran's leaders were friendly to the United States and we were happy to help them counter the Soviet Union's vaunted MiG-25 Foxbat. Decades after America lost Iran, following the rise of the ayatollah, Secretary Cheney killed the F-14 in part to shut down the availability of spare parts for the Persian Tomcat squadrons. But somehow, to this day, Iran is proving up the F-14's reliability and maintainability by flying it alongside Russian bombers on strikes into Syria. (I can remember that some Iranian pilots were

* McClung is quoted here from Barrett Tillman's fine book *On Wave and Wing: The 100-Year Quest to Perfect the Aircraft Carrier* (Washington, DC: Regnery History, 2017), p. 272.

posted at VF-121 at Miramar on foreign exchange, back in the day. All they did, I remember, was chase American women and spend money on fancy new cars. They were lousy students.)

When I poke around the Internet today, catching up with the posts on my naval aviation mail lists, I find a lot of comments from chief petty officers who maintained the F-14 when it was in its prime. Their constant refrain, in essence, is "OMG, if only we had that airplane again." Most of these guys are really sharp. They want the Navy to retool and resume building Tomcats, upgraded a bit but mostly just like they were. I feel as they do. The evolution toward high technology has pushed us backward in many ways. And the Iranians are having a laugh, I'm sure, still flying one of the best fighter aircraft ever built to serve the U.S. Navy.

There's nothing new about an old guy with all the answers. So, at the risk of playing to type, please allow this former aircraft engine mechanic to complain that our country has been put at risk by the Pentagon's fascination with stealth technology. We've lost the lessons we learned painfully in the 1960s. We worship at high technology's altar and are on the verge of selling our souls. Stealth is like a zombie—a very expensive zombie. It's coming back to life to haunt us.

The new aircraft that is supposed to replace the F/A-18 someday is Lockheed Martin's F-35 Lightning II. The stealth-equipped "multi-purpose aircraft" is designed to do all things. Three different models of this "fifth-generation" plane are in development to meet the needs of the Navy, Marine Corps, and Air Force. We ought to have learned a lesson from the failure of Robert McNamara's F-111 "Flying Edsel," which was supposed to serve both the Air Force and Navy. But we did not. So now comes the F-35 in three flavors: the Air Force A model, the Marine Corps B model (a short takeoff/ vertical landing model that will replace the AV-8 Harrier jump jet), and the Navy F-35C.

With total program costs figuring to exceed a trillion dollars, the F-35 is the most expensive weapons system in history.* The unit production cost of the Navy variant (not counting development and testing costs) has been pegged north of $330 million and growing.†

The late, great John Nash used to say that modern aircraft components are designed to fail. Defense contractors have done a good job ensuring the profit margin in "line-replaceable units," as they call spare parts today. In total, over the life of the program, the parts will cost more than the aircraft do. Think of the inkjet printer you bought at the office warehouse for $75. The ink cartridges will set you back half again that amount every six months. That's basically true in the high-performance aircraft business, too.

The F-35 is so expensive I fear we'll end up with a fleet full of beautiful new nuclear-powered supercarriers with partially empty flight decks. There's simply no way the U.S. Treasury can afford to buy the numbers we'll need to fill out the air wings.

The F-35's problems are many, from the tail hook, which basically just didn't work, to the oxygen system for the pilot, to the super-sophisticated helmet, built with advanced sensors, an information-packed visor display, and the ability to aim weapons by line of sight, based on the pilot's head movements. The unit price for that fancy dome was $400,000, but who knows what it really costs? The total program cost of this aircraft continues to rocket skyward like an F-4 Phantom heading to the top of the Egg. Meanwhile, the

---

* Valerie Insinna, "4 Ways Lockheed's New F-35 Head Wants to Fix the Fighter Jet Program," *Defense News*, July 14, 2018, www.defensenews.com/digital-show-dailies/farnborough/2018/07/10/4-ways-lockheeds-new-f-35-head-wants-to-fix-the-fighter-jet-program/. Accessed by the author on August 23, 2018.

† Winslow Wheeler, "How Much Does an F-35 Actually Cost?," *War Is Boring*, Medium, July 27, 2014, https://medium.com/war-is-boring/how-much-does-an-f-35-actually-cost-21f95d239398. Accessed by the author on August 23, 2018.

nickname for the F-35 among pilots who have lost confidence in it is "the penguin." It flies like one.

No one agency can fix this problem. Not the Navy or the other services, not the defense contractors, and not Congress. Each of these has powerful incentives to avoid doing the right thing. The lucrative subcontracts associated with the F-35 are spread strategically across most every congressional district in America. With so many House members having a stake in the program, it is assured to have broad-based political support, regardless of its actual capabilities or costs. So when a defense contractor proposes a new feature for the new aircraft, even if it's not one that the Navy's frontline squadrons want or need, there's nobody on hand to say no. Why would some rear admiral at the Pentagon stand in the way of a "yes" vote for the Navy's appropriations in the House of Representatives by turning down the unwanted bells and whistles? A lot of those admirals, you know, have golden parachutes waiting for them after they retire—a well-paying job as an executive vice president at that one-and-the-same company. Should he risk the windfall by asking questions?

One question deserves to be whether we even need such expensive capabilities as stealth in our planes. I'm not so sure. New sensors that are within the current capability of Russia and China to field don't even use radar waves. These infrared search-and-track devices can detect the friction heat of an aircraft's skin moving through the atmosphere, as well as disturbances in airflow.

Yet the defense contractors' marketing brochures, and a few pilots too, assure us that the F-35 is "transformational." According to the Lockheed Martin website, "With stealth technology, advanced sensors, weapons capacity and range, the F-35 is the most lethal, survivable and connected fighter aircraft ever built. More than a fighter jet, the F-35's ability to collect, analyze and share data is a powerful force multiplier enhancing all airborne, surface and ground-based assets in the battlespace and enabling men and women in uniform to execute their mission and come home safe."

That pitch makes the F-35 sound like an early warning aircraft—transformational indeed. It doesn't say anything about winning a dogfight. Maybe that's the point, because the pilots who have a lot of experience flying the "penguin" say it's no dogfighter. My ears are ringing from the echo of the nonsense we heard in the '60s about the F-4 Phantom transforming the fighter pilot's traditional mission.

At Topgun in my day, a pilot had to log a minimum of thirty-five to forty flight hours every month to be considered combat-ready. This is no longer possible. As the F-35 continues to swallow up the money available to naval aviation, the low rate of production all but ensures that our pilots will not soon gain the flight hours that they need to get good. For the past few years Super Hornet pilots have been getting just ten to twelve hours per month between deployments—barely enough to learn to fly the jet safely. The F-35 has far less availability. Its pilots have to rely on simulators to make up the deficit. Its cost per flight hour is exorbitant.

But the magnitude of the problem of the F-35 is probably best understood in terms of time rather than money. And here it is in a nutshell: We are twenty-seven years into the development cycle of that plane.

After twenty-seven years and untold billions spent, no fully operational version of the F-35 has reached a U.S. squadron. That's right. Development started in 1992, yet it has not achieved operational status in any of the services that have ordered it.* The photos we see of the aircraft flying are misleading. Not one of these planes is

---

* In 2015, the Marine Corps prematurely declared its version, the F-35B, operational, although its systems, including its eight million lines of software code, remain plagued with problems.

ready for combat. The Israelis claim to have used the export model of the F-35 in an engagement. I don't know if that's true, but it's possible the lucrative foreign market for the plane helps explain its undeserved longevity after nearly three decades of delays and cost overruns. Israel, Japan, and South Korea are supposedly on board to buy it, as are the eight other "partner nations" who are helping to develop it. Unfortunately, the program has run so long that one of those partners, Turkey, is on the verge of no longer being a U.S. ally. (Maybe they'll still fulfill their contract with Lockheed to keep supplying important parts for the F-35 as they cozy up to the Russians.)

Twenty-seven years. That's more than a generation. Compare that to the development timeline of the F-14 Tomcat. The elapsed time from the Navy's first request for proposals to the deployment of the F-14 in the fleet was four years. Yes, four years. With the F-18 Hornet, it was nine years.

Now twenty-seven?

Something is rotten in Washington, and one day, sadly, we will lose a war because of it. Maybe that tragic result will serve to wake up our political and defense establishments and give them the courage to begin removing the rot.

Meanwhile, the state of the art in air-to-air combat as it's actually practiced over the battlefields of the world doesn't seem to have advanced very much. The future looks a lot like the past. Let me tell you a very recent story.

On June 18, 2017, Lieutenant Commander Michael "Mob" Tremel, a Topgun graduate and former instructor, took off from USS *George H. W. Bush* in an F/A-18E Super Hornet. Flying a close air support mission near Raqqa, Syria, he led four Super Hornets inland to join a "stack" of jets waiting their turn to bomb Islamic State positions. That was when he and his cohorts detected the Syrian aircraft. The approaching pilot ignored numerous warnings to turn away. After a Sukhoi Su-22 Fitter made a bombing run on allied troops, Commander Tremel engaged.

Adhering to the rules of engagement, he made visual identification and fired an AIM-9X Sidewinder. The enemy pilot detected the launch and dropped flares. The missile, "spoofed" in spite of all its advanced features, missed. Tremel switched to a radar-guided AMRAAM—the Sparrow's replacement—and fired. The eight-minute affair ended with the Syrian plane exploding, leaving Tremel to dodge a cloud of debris. The pilot, Captain Ali Fahd, ejected and floated to earth below his chute. It was the first victory by an American fighter pilot since the spring of 1999, when Air Force pilots bagged three Yugoslav MiG-29s in the Kosovo War.

In the 2017 action, three of the four Hornet pilots were Topgun grads, so they would be well qualified to teach us the lessons here, which are familiar. First, high technology can still be foiled by simple countermeasures. Missiles are never a sure thing. But the real lesson was that, against the fashionably futuristic expectations, Tremel was forced to fight in close visual range because the rules of engagement required it. Why spend fortunes on technology that our own rules of engagement make useless?

Even if its many problems are solved and it's fielded in numbers that matter, the F-35 and its beyond-visual-range capability will mean nothing if the pilot has to see and identify his target before shooting it. That has been true now for more than forty years. As Condor says, "If you can see him, he can see you, and you're in a dogfight." This is not where the "penguin" is at its best. At least it will, apparently, have a gun. That's one thing they might be getting right.

I was a pretty good fighter pilot, but I might be old-fashioned. I devoutly believe that simpler is better. I've learned that lesson repeatedly in my career. After thirty years in naval aviation, I can tell you what a plane can do in the air by looking at its engine specs and the sweep of its wings and its tail. Few planes I've seen are better dog-fighters than the tried-and-true F-5, the old Northrop birds we used at Topgun as aggressors. Some are still in service today.

At night, sometimes while I lay beside the pool watching the jets and satellites ease by overhead, I use my imagination to design my ultimate fighter aircraft. I'd make it a basic hot rod, a single-seater akin to the old F-5. Light, maneuverable, and compact—hard to see in a fight. I'd want it cheap, easy to mass-produce and replace should we start taking losses in combat over time.

The cockpit systems will be engineered to avoid overwhelming the pilot's senses with data. My pilots will not be emotionally and mentally overloaded by the bells and whistles that characterize the fifth-generation cockpit. The Navy busts its budgets by installing integrated command and control electronics, but most pilots I know don't touch them. So we'll get rid of them. My guys won't need a non-combatant staffer or distant admiral somewhere hearing all their comms and butting in to micromanage. The only conversa-tions they'll need are with a good radar controller somewhere, their mother carrier, and their squadron mates.

That little hot rod will cost less than ten million dollars apiece, and so we'll never have to sell it to a foreign country. Except to the Brits and the Israelis, of course. With the money we save, the enlisted men in the maintenance hangar will have everything they need. The defense contractors can golf on their own dime.

Give me a few hundred planes like the F-5N, with a reliable gun, a lead-computing gunsight, four Sidewinders, electronic countermea-sures support, and pilots who get forty or fifty flight hours a month, and we'll beat any air force that's bankrupting its nation with fifth-generation stealthy penguins. Pilot retention problems will go away.

Because the basic truth of fighter combat remains the same: It is not the aircraft that wins a fight, it's the man in the cockpit. Flying is a perishable skill. It has to be practiced constantly and maintained on a consistent basis. That isn't happening anymore, thanks to the year-to-year budgeting process called for by "the sequester" and its defense cuts. And on that count, looking back, I can see that as bad as things looked to us over Vietnam, my comrades and I may well have flown in the best of times.

Darrell "Condor" Gary's logbook for June 1976 shows that he flew forty-six flights that month for a total or 65.5 hours, including five in the F-4N Phantom, seventeen in the A-4E Skyhawk, and twenty-four in the F-5E Tiger. All of these were real air combat maneuvering flights, not cross-country transits. With that much time in the air, Condor says, you couldn't avoid becoming proficient as a warrior.

My boys will all be dogfighters. With enough planes in inventory, we can return to the days when any pilot who's in good with the senior chief in maintenance control can check out a bird and go find a "fight club" somewhere off the coast. That's how we'll sharpen our edge in dogfighting again. Give those boys lots of flight hours under heavy-caliber leadership and they'll win almost every time. I feel so strongly about the need for more pilot training that I'd propose this: We should consider tapping our federal petroleum reserve for jet fuel production, so that our aviation training commands can keep new pilots flying every day. If we wait until we're at the threshold of a war before doing it, it will be too late.

I run through this mental exercise often. Always I come back to our Topgun axiom: What matters is the man, not the machine. So let's talk about what a good fighter pilot candidate looks like. Over the years and thousands of aviators I've known, I noticed the best shared some common traits.

A good pilot should have a strong family background with a patriotic mindset and a self-starting work ethic. He should believe in something greater than himself while remaining self-reliant and confident without being overbearing. (Some ego is necessary—I wouldn't want a soul filled with doubt flying my wing.) An athletic background helps, because when properly coached at the right age, youngsters learn trust, teamwork, and goal setting. They'll need all those things in the air. I'll pass on anybody who displays his participation trophies. Self-esteem without real accomplishment will make anyone crash and burn. Give me a committed B student with a boiling will to win over an A-plus scholar with a careerist agenda, and we'll be on our way.

Finally, it's important to have a sincere interest in the history and lore of your calling. Good pilots strive constantly for self-improvement. In my first years in the Navy, I had the opportunity to meet the World War II generation and hear their stories and lessons. I read every air combat memoir I could and gleaned a lot of little things from them that helped me in my journey. We lived on the edge of life and death, and the margin between them was narrow. I think Jimmy Doolittle bought me a scotch because he saw that we had shared residency there. History is a wellspring of lifesaving lessons. No one really invents anything.

Successful leaders recognize those traits and encourage them, even at the risk of bending a rule—or a jet—once in a while. Just like we did in Miramar every day, and much as you saw in that thirty-three-year-old movie, long may it stream. In between its scenes of beach volleyball, romantic sunset motorcycle rides along the runway, and crazy, dangerous moves in the air, the movie has some important messages. It reminds me of better days. And I think that reminder can help us today, if we let it.

Well, that's what naval aviation would look like if I were King of Everything. Since I'm not, I think I ought to call it a night. Come on inside; I have one last thing to show you.

I kept my 1950s Ray-Bans until just a few years ago, when I replaced the lenses and gave them to my granddaughter, at her request, as a Christmas gift. After fifty years, I figured it was time for a new pair. My youngest daughter, Candice, ended up with my Star of David and gold chain. But I still have my little mouse. After all the sea duty he endured, he enjoys a cushy retirement on my bookshelf. From time to time I look at him and say, *It was a hell of a ride, wasn't it, little fella?*

He is surrounded by books and other treasured items from my career. But what I value most was my time at Miramar with the Bros. Their enduring friendships are my real treasures, not any physical things in my library. Topgun will always be the centerpiece of my career and my life's most important accomplishment. None of it would have happened without the Bros, or the ever-present hands of God.

ACKNOWLEDGMENTS

This book has been in the works for about eighteen months. It all started when Jim Hornfischer, president of Hornfischer Literary Management, contacted one of Topgun's Original Bros, Darrell Gary in San Diego, to discuss a legacy book to be written and published in time for the fiftieth anniversary of Topgun. As I had been the original Topgun leader during the formation of the Navy Fighter Weapons School in 1968 and 1969, Jim felt I should tell Topgun's story by way of a personal memoir. Jim helped us develop the idea, brought our proposal to New York, and set us up with Hachette Books, my estimable publisher.

For the first year of this effort, I had the honor of working closely with naval aviation's premier historian, Barrett Tillman. Barrett's work is the gold standard of naval aviation history, based on his dozens of books and hundreds of articles in his award-winning career. Working under an extremely short deadline, we thoroughly researched and co-wrote the original draft, providing accuracy and authentication while we recounted most of the story. It was the experience of a lifetime to share my naval aviation career and Vietnam experience with this fine man. He is a walking encyclopedia of naval aviation. Our relationship has grown.

When the original manuscript was delivered, it was decided that more could be added to the story. In the final two months in which the book was finalized, John R. Bruning Jr. helped me to transform it into what it is today. John and I became fast friends as we worked daily to adapt the original manuscript on a tough schedule. It was a true pleasure to work with and learn from him. He has authored or co-authored twenty-one military books, including *House to House, Outlaw Platoon, Level Zero Heroes, The Trident,* and *Indestructible,* and has embedded with our combat ground forces in the Afghanistan war. He is one special American.

As my literary agent, Jim Hornfischer navigated the project from beginning to completion and helped shape the final manuscript. An author in his own right (recipient of the Samuel Eliot Morison Award for his work, which includes *The Fleet at Flood Tide, Neptune's Inferno, Ship of Ghosts,* and *The Last Stand of the Tin Can Sailors*), he is a skilled literary guide who worked tirelessly to help me tell this story the right way.

It truly was a once-in-a-lifetime experience to recall and relive my life and Navy career with the assistance of these gifted professional gentlemen. The true legacy of the Navy Fighter Weapons School would not have been told without their devotion and close involvement. They can fly my wing anytime.

My publisher at Hachette Books, Mauro DiPreta, has been a great advocate for this book and a skilled editor of the manuscript. Thanks also to his very capable assistant, David Lamb, and to the rest of the Hachette Books publishing team, including associate publisher Michelle Aielli, marketing director Michael Barrs, and senior publicist Sarah Falter. All of them play key roles in the work of bringing a new book to the public.

The founding instructors of Topgun, the Original Bros as we call each other, gave life to the new organization and have been friends of mine since we began our association more than fifty years ago. My thanks to these great patriots: Darrell Gary, Mel Holmes, Jim Ruliffson, John Nash, Jerry Sawatzky, Steve Smith, J. C. Smith,

Jim Laing, and Chuck Hildebrand. With the outstanding leadership of succeeding generations, including forty-two skippers, numerous young instructors, and the always-hard-working enlisted maintenance crews and staff, the Navy Fighter Weapons School grew to international fame. I thank you all for the risks you took, your sacrifices and those of your families, and your superb performance over many decades. This story, our story, is one that I've longed to tell. I hope I've done it right, because we all did it right, back when our country needed us. You were then, and you are today, the best of the best.

Special thanks to the Navy's greatest sailors. Master Chief David M. Hobbs, a great friend with whom I served in USS *Ranger,* is at the very top of that list.

It was my family who made everything possible. My grandfather, Arthur Lamp, was my guiding light. My folks, Orla and Henrietta Pedersen, always encouraged me.

Lastly, my wonderful Mary Beth: This book is dedicated to you for your sustained and sustaining support and love for all these many years. You made it all complete.

GLOSSARY OF ACRONYMS AND TERMS

AAA: Antiaircraft artillery

AAW: Antiair warfare

ACM: Air combat maneuvering

ACMI: Air combat maneuvering instrumentation

ACMR: Air combat maneuvering range

AIM: Air intercept missile

AOR: Underway replenishment ship

Bandit: Hostile aircraft

BarCAP: Barrier combat air patrol

Bogey: Unidentified aircraft

BOQ: Bachelor officers' quarters

CAG: Air wing commander

CAP: Combat air patrol

CCA: Carrier controlled approach

CNO: Chief of naval operations

CO: Commanding officer

ComFit: Commander, Fighter and Airborne Early Warning Wing

ComNavAirPac: Naval Air Force, U.S. Pacific Fleet

CV: Aircraft carrier

CVN: Nuclear-powered aircraft carrier

CVW: Carrier air wing

DCNO:	Deputy chief of naval operations
ECM:	Electronic countermeasures
FAGU:	Fleet Air Gunnery Unit
FAST:	Fleet air superiority training
FRS:	Fleet replacement squadron (RAG)
GCA:	Ground-controlled approach
IFF:	Identification friend or foe transponder
IP:	Instructor pilot
J.G.:	Junior grade
JO:	Junior officer
LSO:	Landing signal officer
MCAS:	Marine Corps Air Station
MiGCAP:	MiG combat air patrol
NAS:	Naval air station
NFWS:	Navy Fighter Weapons School (Topgun)
NAWDC:	Naval Air Warfare Development Center (previously NSAWC)
NSAWC:	Naval Strike and Air Warfare Center
OP-05:	Office of the CNO, deputy chief of naval operations for air
RAG:	Replacement air group (FRS)
RIO:	Radar intercept officer
ROE:	Rules of engagement
SAM:	Surface-to-air missile
TarCAP:	Target combat air patrol
VA:	Attack squadron
VAW:	Airborne early warning squadron
VF:	Fighter squadron

VF(AW): All-weather fighter squadron

VFA: Strike fighter squadron

VS: Antisubmarine squadron

VX: Air test and evaluation squadron

WestPac: Western Pacific

XO: Executive officer

TOPGUN OFFICERS IN CHARGE AND COMMANDING OFFICERS

Officers in Charge

1969   Dan A. "Yankee" Pedersen

1969–71   John C. "J. C." Smith

Commanding Officers

1971–72   Roger E. "Buckshot" Box

1972–73   David E. "Frosty" Frost

1973–75   Ronald E. "Mugs" McKeown

1975   John K. "Sunshine" Ready

1975–76   James H. "Cobra" Ruliffson

1976–78   Monroe "Hawk" Smith

1978–79   Jerry L. "Thunder" Unruh

1979–81   Lonny K. "Eagle" McClung

1981   Roy "Outlaw" Cash Jr.

1982–83   Ernest "Ratchet" Christensen

1983–84   Christopher T. "Boomer" Wilson

1984   Joseph "Joedog" Daughtry Jr.

1984–85   Thomas G. "Otter" Otterbein

1985–86   Daniel L. "Dirty" Shewell

1986–88   Frederic G. "Wigs" Ludwig Jr.

1988–89   Jay B. "Spook" Yakeley III

1989–90   Russell M. "Bud" Taylor II

1990–92   James A. "Rookie" Robb

1992–93   Robert L. "Puke" McLane

1993–94   Richard "Weasel" Gallagher

1994–96   Thomas "Trotts" Trotter

1996–97   Rolland G. "Dawg" Thompson

1997–99   Gerald S. "Spud" Gallop

1999–2001   William "Size" Sizemore

2001–03   Daniel "Dix" Dixon

2003–04   Richard W. "Rhett" Butler

2004–05   Thomas M. "Trim" Downing

2005–06   Mike R. "Trigger" Saunders

2006–07   Keith T. "Opie" Taylor

2007–08   Michael D. "Dice" Neumann

2008–09   Daniel L. "Undra" Cheever

2009–10   Paul S. "Dorf" Olin

2010–11   Matthew L. "Yodel" Leahey

2011–12   Steven T. "Sonic" Hejmanowski

2012–13   Kevin M. "Proton" McLaughlin

2013–14   James D. "Cruiser" Christie

2014–15   Edward S. "Stevie" Smith

2015–16   Michael A. "Chopper" Rovenolt

2016–18   Andrew "Grand" Mariner

2018–   Christopher "Pops" Papaioanu

INDEX

PHOTO CREDITS